Praise fo...

The Trouble with Europe

I recommend our diplomats and ministers read this book: it will provide them with an intellectual backbone.

On the big calls [Bootle] has a spectacularly good record. He warned about the bubble in US real estate which led to the credit crunch. Earlier, he forecast the collapse of the dot com boom. Most creditably of all, back in 1992 he identified the pound would be forced out of the ERM – and that this would be a good thing for the British economy.

—Dominic Lawson, *The Sunday Times*

Bootle is right on every count.

—Larry Elliott, *The Guardian*

Bootle writes with energetic prose and makes some good points. He is an accomplished economist whose The Trouble with Markets *provided a penetrating analysis of the origins of the financial crisis. In this book he maps out a fresh start for UK–EU relations.* —*Financial Times*

An outstanding, grown-up account of the failures of the European Union. Bootle is certainly no little Englander, but his argument is calm, conversational, rigorous and – quite remarkably for an economist – entirely free of bafflegab. Engaging and absorbing, here is an eye-opening book that will inspire you to think through the issues clearly – without starting a saloon-bar brawl. —*The Daily Telegraph*

Roger Bootle perceptively analyses how we can most sensibly conduct ourselves outside the EU. It is essential background reading. —Rt. Hon. Nigel Lawson, former Chancellor of the Exchequer

As I have come to expect from Roger Bootle, he gets to the heart of the matter with crystal-clear analysis and punchy comment. —Jeff Randall, Sky News business presenter

Brilliant, albeit radical solutions. One of the most thoughtful accounts that I have yet read about the European question. —Independent on Sunday

Here it is – a book for every faint-heart who thinks this country could never prosper outside the European Union. A timely and balanced analysis.
—Boris Johnson, former Mayor of London

Roger Bootle's well-informed and rigorously-argued book brutally exposes the problems besetting Europe and Britain's position. —David Marsh, Co-chairman of OMFIF, and author of *Europe's Deadlock*

Roger Bootle manages to weave the economic, political and diplomatic aspects into a compulsively readable analysis which should be of engrossing interest to europhiles and eurosceptics alike.
—William Keegan, Senior Economics Editor, *The Observer*, and author of *The Prudence of Mr. Gordon Brown*

Making a Success of Brexit and Reforming the EU

The Brexit Edition of
The Trouble with Europe

Fourth Edition

Roger Bootle

NICHOLAS BREALEY
PUBLISHING

London • Boston

First published in Great Britain in 2014 by Nicholas Brealey Publishing
An imprint of John Murray Press
An Hachette UK Company

Fourth edition first published in 2017

1

A CIP catalogue record for this title is available from the British Library

ISBN 978-1-47366-847-8
Ebook ISBN UK 978-1-85788-967-3
Ebook ISBN US 978-1-47364-512-7

Typeset in Celeste by Palimpsest Book Production Ltd, Falkirk, Stirlingshire

Printed and bound in Great Britain by Clays Ltd, St Ives plc

John Murray Press policy is to use papers that are natural, renewable
and recyclable products and made from wood grown in sustainable forests.
The logging and manufacturing processes are expected to conform to the
environmental regulations of the country of origin.

Nicholas Brealey Publishing
John Murray Press
Carmelite House
50 Victoria Embankment
London EC4Y 0DZ
Tel: 020 3122 6000

Nicholas Brealey Publishing
Hachette Book Group
Market Place Center, 53 State Street
Boston, MA 02109, USA
Tel: (617) 263 1834

www.nicholasbrealey.com
www.capitaleconomics.com

Contents

Acknowledgements

Inevitably, I owe many people debts of gratitude. The book was inspired by David Green of the think tank Civitas, which generously provided a research grant. For both David's inspiration and encouragement and Civitas' grant, I am extremely grateful. It was David who galvanized me into writing the book. Meanwhile, Civitas' grant enabled me to employ research assistants Melanie DeBono, Sam Dickens and Konrad Malinowski, who greatly increased my productivity and allowed me to finish the book that much more quickly.

I also owe a debt to *The Daily Telegraph*, for which I write a weekly column, published on Mondays, for permission to draw on some of the material that first appeared in those columns and for continuing to give me a platform from which to air my developing views on Europe and other subjects. In many ways this book is the culmination of the 'conversations' I have been having with *Telegraph* readers over a number of years.

My good friend Leonard Lipman provided much-needed encouragement and solace when my general confidence and belief in the book flagged. Without him, I don't think the book would have been completed. Thanks are also due to Joaly Smith, Faith Elliott, Hayley Charlick and Suhayla Egan for organizing the various versions of the typescript and to Oliver Allen, Ben Blanchard, Alexander Burgess, Isabel Cairns, Rebecca Heywood, Jessica Hinds, Nina Loncar, Alice Major and Helena Patterson for help with the data and maps included in the book. Special thanks are due to my PAs, Sam Howard-Carr and, more latterly, Holly Jackson, not only for help with the typescript but also for organizing me and helping to keep Capital

Economics going while I was writing the book. Their support has been invaluable.

As with my last three books, I received helpful comments, guidance and criticism from the editorial team at Nicholas Brealey. Several other people helped me by reading early drafts and making critical, but helpful, suggestions. I should especially mention David Barchard, Tony Courakis, David Green, Jonathan Lindsell, John Llewellyn, George de Nemeskeri-Kiss, Robert Rowthorn, Christopher Smallwood and Richard Thoburn.

Several colleagues at Capital Economics also read and commented on early drafts: Paul Dales, Mark Harris, Julian Jessop, Andrew Kenningham, Jonathan Loynes, Ben May and Mark Pragnell. Sam Tombs was also very helpful in digging out data. I am grateful to them all, not only for their help with the book but also for their hard work at Capital Economics – especially while I was preoccupied with *The Trouble with Europe*.

Several fellow members of a group called 'Economists for Brexit', subsequently rebranded 'Economists for Free Trade', also provided very helpful comments. I would particularly single out Martin Howe QC, Edgar Miller and Professor Patrick Minford.

Last but not least, I must thank my family, who have had to put up with another period of my absorption in writing a book.

As always, none of the above is responsible for any errors of omission or commission. These remain the responsibility of the author alone.

Roger Bootle
London, August 2017

Preface to the Fourth Edition

Since the third edition of this book was published in 2016, several important aspects of the subject have taken a new turn – although nothing has happened to undermine the book's main thrust. Most importantly, the UK voted to leave the European Union and up to two years of negotiations lie ahead. Those negotiations could be made all the more difficult by Mrs May's failure to secure an overall majority in the General Election of June 2017.

Added to this, many observers reckon that because a majority of Scottish voters opted to remain in the EU, even after the Scottish Nationalists' weakened performance in the 2017 General Election, at some point there will be a second referendum on Scottish independence. Similarly in Northern Ireland, where a referendum on leaving the UK and forming a united Ireland seems a distinct possibility. So after the Brexit vote, the UK could soon be losing Scotland, or Northern Ireland, or both. In that case, British voters would have brought about the severing of not one union but two.

Yet that is not all. Europe was in turmoil before the UK's referendum on 23 June 2016. The Brexit vote merely intensified the crisis. The UK's exit brings to an end over sixty years of one-directional travel in which the EU became bigger and more powerful, while the role and importance of nation states receded. With the Brexit vote, nationalism has come roaring back, like an incoming tide.

Until fairly recently it was widely assumed that euroscepticism – at least the red-meat variety – was largely a British phenomenon. But that is clearly no longer true. Eurosceptic parties have substantially increased their popularity in France, Italy, the Netherlands, Austria, Spain, Portugal and

Greece. Even in Germany, the anti-euro party, the Alternative für Deutschland (AFD), has risen from nowhere to be on the brink of gaining some seats in the Bundestag.

Over and above the litany of stories about EU incompetence, corruption and bossiness that have been bubbling up for years now, as envisaged by earlier editions of this book, there have been two main factors that have given euroscepticism a strong boost: the evident failure of the euro and intensified concern about inward migration and the free movement of labour within the Union.

The euro did not follow the path to self-destruction that seemed scripted for it in 2012, when Greece was very nearly forced out. But thereafter the eurozone, if not dead, was in the category of the walking wounded. An economic upturn in 2016/17 brought some respite but there was no real recovery in Italy or Greece, with the result that their financial problems continued to grow.

Meanwhile, France continued to lose ground relative to Germany and other core countries. Increasingly, the markets came to wonder whether France should be regarded as part of the soft, Latin underbelly of the euro, rather than part of the Teutonic, northern, hard core. And in that core – in the Netherlands, Germany, Austria and Finland – there was growing anxiety that they were severely at risk from the southern countries' weakness, as their financial exposure to them continued to build.

To survive, the euro needs more integration and the further pooling of risk and financial resources. This is perfectly understood by the new French President, Emmanuel Macron. But whether the electorates of Northern Europe are prepared to accept further integration is a different matter. Germany is the main stumbling block.

Heightened anxiety about freedom of movement for citizens of the EU is a fairly recent phenomenon. That freedom is deeply embedded in the EU and goes back to the Treaty of Rome. For the first few decades electorates did not turn a hair about free movement.

Two things changed this – one self-inflicted and the other deriving from powerful forces outside the Union. The self-inflicted change was the extension of the Union to the east to include former members of the Soviet bloc, in two main waves in 2004 and 2007, with Croatia also joining in 2013. Because these countries were much poorer than the existing members of the Union, it was likely than there would be a large one-way flow of people from east to west. This is indeed what happened.

The powerful force from outside was the collapse of several states in the Middle East that led to tragic waves of refugees trying to enter the EU. Many entered the Union illegally but the German Chancellor, Angela Merkel, welcomed 1 million refugees. Meanwhile, a series of terrorist outrages across Europe prompted an upsurge of anti-Islamic sentiment that grew to encompass all immigrants of whatever religion or ethnic background.

These two problems go right to the heart of the EU's identity crisis. Is the EU on course to become a United States of Europe? And what *is* Europe anyway? Given its Judaeo-Christian heritage, can Europe be Europe if it includes a large number of Muslims? Already the resulting strains have been so great that the Schengen Agreement on passport-free travel across much of Europe has come close to collapse. This is potentially the second major reverse for the European project.

So you could say that the EU now faces its most serious crisis ever as four challenges come together at the same time: the prospective exit of one of its largest members, the breakdown of the Schengen Agreement, the continued fragility of the euro and the gathering unpopularity of the

Union among European electorates. Furthermore, these threats are related; a shock emanating in any of these four spheres risks setting off a chain reaction involving the other three. Truly, we are living through *The Trouble with Europe.*

In this fourth edition, I have not only updated facts and figures where necessary but also brought in a large amount of new material in six new chapters in two new Parts, III and IV. Part III is devoted to Brexit. Part IV is about the future of the EU.

I was fortunate to receive a good deal of praise for earlier editions – as well as a few well-argued, and well-deserved, critiques, from which I have tried to learn. But three criticisms have riled me. One is that I am wishy-washy in my conclusions. Apparently, I seem to think that there are both advantages and disadvantages to leaving the EU. Not only that, but when it comes to quantifying various costs and benefits, although I quote a lot of numbers, I am reluctant to come down on a hard-and-fast figure for the net result. Indeed, I stress that so many of the factors that bear on these issues are uncertain. Heaven forfend. And to think I considered my balanced approach a virtue!

At the polar opposite, another critic complained that although I acknowledge these uncertainties, I nevertheless conclude that the UK can make a success of life outside the EU. Without certainty and precision, they say, this is a leap in the dark and they are aghast that I could possibly endorse such a thing. Well I never! As though uncertainty does not bedevil our choices and actions if we decide to stay in. I never cease to be amazed by the difficulties people get into over uncertainty. I wonder how they cope with everyday life. I make no apologies for my attempt to be even-handed and to acknowledge the difficulties, dangers and uncertainties – nor for my decided position, despite the impression about key magnitudes, on what is the best way forward.

The third strand of criticism I could find hurtful if it were not so ridiculous – and also so revealing. In debates and discussions about the EU, many times I have been opposed by people who begin by asserting their difference from me by saying they are 'pro-European'. By extension, I suppose, I am 'anti-European'. That is news to me. On one occasion when I was extolling the virtues of British political institutions and criticizing the EU's equivalents as being essentially undemocratic and brittle, I was even accused of being a racist!

It is extraordinary that people have become so brainwashed by the current pro-EU consensus that they cannot distinguish between an identity, culture and civilization on the one hand, and a particular set of political arrangements and institutions on the other. If I needed something to goad me into renewing my critical assessment of the EU and all its works, this has provided it.

As it happens, I didn't need it. The issues that form the subject matter of this book are, if anything, more alive than when I wrote the first edition. In short, Europe is in turmoil and its future lies in the balance. What is more, you, the reader, in whatever country you reside, may have a key role to play in shaping that future. My purpose in writing this is to help you play that part to the fullest extent – as someone who is well informed on key issues and aware of the consequences of the EU's future going one way or the other. An author could not wish for a better incentive.

Roger Bootle
London, August 2017

Introduction: The Trouble with Europe

The European Union is at a decision point. The objectives with which it was launched and the logic of existing relationships are pushing it towards full political union – some sort of United States of Europe, or at least of the eurozone. In other words more Europe; deeper integration. This is in tune with the thrust of the EU's historical development and with the EU's past success.

But the EU is a malfunctioning construct for today's world – and even more so for tomorrow's. It needs either to undergo fundamental reform or to break up. It was conceived in a world of large blocs, dominated by the Cold War rivalry between the United States and the Soviet Union and before globalization and the rise of the emerging markets. Its agenda of harmonization and integration inevitably leads to excessive regulation and the smothering of competition. This is largely why, in contrast to the prevailing view that the EU has been an economic success, its economic performance has in fact been relatively poor.

What is more, if nothing changes, the EU's share of world GDP is set to fall sharply and with it Europe's influence in the world. Yet to the European establishment that is exactly what integration is supposed to prevent. Meanwhile, the EU is becoming more unpopular; most people do not want to press on to a full political union; and increasing numbers of its citizens want to leave the EU altogether. One way or another, Europe faces some extraordinary challenges. It seems clear to me that European integration is the great issue of our day and that so many other issues hang on its outcome. That is why I felt I had to write this book.

My perspective is that of an economist, and a British one

at that. As such, I could be criticized for under-emphasizing political aspects. Yet I recognize that in this instance politics and economics are closely related, as they often are. In this book I put politics at the forefront. My argument is that the EU's tortured politics produce poor economic performance. The best example is the formation of the euro, which was undertaken for political reasons intrinsic to the European project. It has turned out to be an economic disaster.

As a British citizen, I am bound to be attacked in Europe as being yet another little Englander, harking back to the past and railing against developments on the continent, congenitally predisposed against them – while failing to understand them properly. However, this book is not motivated by any sort of animus against Europe; quite the opposite. Like many British people, I feel both British and European. Indeed, despite the close links between Britain and America, whenever I go to the US I feel more European. The culture I love is European – its food and its wine, its history and its buildings, its literature and its art and, for me, especially its music. It is precisely because I am so much of a European, and because I desperately want Europe to succeed in the world, that I take issue with the EU as it is currently constituted. For me, the EU is the most important thing that stands between Europe and success.

Naturally, I have written this book hoping that many of my fellow citizens will read it. Nevertheless, it is not written especially for British readers. It tries to take a European perspective and in the process reveals some of the mistakes and foibles of the typical British eurosceptic position.

Different audiences may be shocked by some of what I have to say: eurosceptics in Britain and elsewhere may be appalled by my sympathy and admiration for some of what the EU has achieved; continentals of all persuasions may be surprised and appalled to learn of the EU's relatively poor economic performance and disappointing prospects; continental readers especially may also be intrigued by my verdict that the EU's prospects would be better if the euro were disbanded; and readers everywhere should be surprised by the emphasis I place on the importance of competition between governments in generating successful political and economic outcomes.

Although, as an economist, I give economic factors full weight, I do not write for professional economists but rather for the general reader. To this end, I have tried to keep the use of technical terms to a minimum. For the reader's convenience, I have included a glossary of terms and acronyms at the back of the book. I have also kept notes on the text to a minimum and confined these to the back.

The aim of the book is to inform all those who may be called on to contribute to a decision about Europe's future, or their country's part in it, about how Europe stands in the world, how the EU's institutions contribute to that standing and what Europe's prospects are, with or without the EU. When looking for material to help them come to a view, many people find only the ravings of extremists on both sides of the debate, wads of incomprehensible statistics, or oodles of impenetrable euro-speak.

In contrast, my aim is to give a balanced and comprehensible account of the EU's development and of the issues now facing it. So this is not a polemic.

Readers may be interested to know that in the 1975 referendum I voted to Remain. Moreover, I continued to support EU membership until comparatively recently. Indeed, when I started work on the first edition of this book in 2013, I was still in favour. During the course of my research, however, I became steadily more eurosceptic. And in the 2016 referendum I campaigned for 'Leave'. This book traces the intellectual journey that I made over these years.

Perhaps many of my readers will find themselves taking a similar journey as they move through the chapters towards my conclusion in Chapter 11.

Part I of the book is about political, institutional and ideological issues. Chapter 1 explains how the EU came to be what it is, the guiding beliefs of those who forged it and the motives of countries that have wanted, or still want, to join it. Chapter 2 explains, however, that what the EU has become makes it ill-suited to current economic and political realities and shows how this tends to lead to bad decisions, which produce poor economic performance.

Part II is devoted to economics. Chapter 3 analyses the EU's economic record and shows how and why it has been disappointing, while Chapter 4 analyses one of the EU's worst decisions, namely to launch the euro, and discusses what policies could relieve the EU's economic predicament. In contrasting vein, Chapter 5 looks at the EU's economic prospects if nothing changes and argues that the outlook is for continued relative European decline.

Part III is devoted to Brexit. Chapter 6 discusses the principles governing the negotiations; Chapter 7 analyses the Single Market, the Customs Union and Free Trade Agreements (FTAs); Chapter 8 examines the effect on particular industries and assesses the overall impact on the UK economy.

Part IV is devoted to the political future of the EU. Chapter 9 asks whether the EU could successfully reform itself, whereas Chapter 10 discusses whether 'more Europe' is the answer to its problems. Chapter 11 discusses the consequences for Europe and the world if the EU were to break up.

But the place to start is surely with the origins of the EU – and the ideas that underpinned its development.

Part I

Past History and Present Purpose

1

How the EU Came into Being and Why

We must build a United States of Europe ... The first step in the re-creation of the European family must be a partnership between France and Germany.
—Winston Churchill, 1946

For Germany, Europe is not only indispensable, it is part and parcel of our identity. We've always said German unity, European unity and integration, that's two parts of one and the same coin.
—Angela Merkel, German Chancellor, June 2011

The history of the EU is a story of remarkable development. In this chapter I trace its beginnings in war, before going on to discuss how the EU has changed as regards both its relationship with member states and its geographical reach. I then discuss what has driven the urge towards integration and why countries have wanted to join the Union – and still do.

War and peace

What we now call the European Union was born out of the carnage of the Second World War – and what carnage. It is well known that about 6 million Jews perished at the hands of the Nazis in brutal acts of ethnic cleansing and racial hatred, an astonishing 60% or so of European Jewry. In respect of proportions of a population, or the sheer horror of what took place, nothing can bear comparison with this.

However, umpteen million other people died as well,

largely as a consequence of more conventional ways of war. Estimates of Russian dead are particularly unreliable, but it is probably a reasonable approximation that about 20 million Russians (or, more accurately, Soviets) perished during and because of the war – about 10% of the population. Roughly a third of these were civilians.

Less widely known, and still less widely acknowledged, is that about 7 million Germans died in and because of the war, also representing about 10% of the population, rather more than half of them civilians, killed in bombing raids or attacks by the Allied armies or wasted by cold and hunger.

Different people have different views on which episodes were the most traumatic for ordinary German people. Many cite the firestorms unleashed by the bombing of Dresden or Hamburg; and with good reason. But the image that has touched me most deeply is of the wretched rabbles of people, including old men, women and children, trying to flee from the advancing Red Army in the expanses of East Prussia. Taking to the frozen coastal lagoons of the region, in desperation trying to head west, away from the advancing Soviets, the words they most dreaded to hear from their fellow refugees were, 'The ice is cracking.'

German people understandably find it difficult to utter this sentiment in polite company but, as a proud and patriotic citizen of the United Kingdom, I can do it without blushing: some of the greatest suffering during and because of the Second World War was borne by Germans. When you comprehend the scale of the horrors suffered by the German people, as well as their (admittedly well-justified) guilt regarding the horrors they inflicted on others, in addition to the division of their country and its partial occupation by the Red Army, you can readily see why German people have typically been among the most enthusiastic supporters of the European project.

In contrast to these horrors, but still shocking, France lost 'only' about 800,000 people (around 2% of its population). A good deal of these casualties occurred in the German invasion of 1940, but about 50,000 were killed unintentionally by the Allies in the Battle of Normandy after D-Day, about 20,000 in the Calvados department alone. The city of Caen was all but obliterated by the Allies.

By contrast, during the whole war, the British got away with a comparatively modest death toll of just under 400,000 (0.8% of the population), combatants and civilians combined. Thinking of their experience over the whole war and not merely in the Battle of Britain, continental Europeans might readily understand how the British could believe that this was 'their finest hour'.

All of this European slaughter during the Second World War is widely believed to have been exceeded by the carnage of the First. In fact, as regards total losses this is not true: the Second World War was much bloodier. It is true for Britain, though, which lost more than 2% of its population in the First World War; more significantly, it is also true for France. Indeed, in the First World War France lost almost 2 million people, over 4% of its population.[1] Scarce wonder, then, that there was so much reluctance to staging resistance *à l'outrance* during the repeat run in 1940.

With these enormous losses during the First World War behind it, in addition to its not inconsiderable losses during the Second, as well as the humiliation of three times being mauled by German armies (including the defeat by Prussian-led forces in 1870), it is hardly surprising that in the postwar world, France also sought a European answer to the essential questions about national security.

Indeed, across Europe, after the devastation of 1939–45, both ordinary people and the governing elites inwardly pledged that nothing similar must ever happen again. Many believed that Europe's leaders had to evolve some pan-European entity that would tame and subdue the passions and rivalries of the nation states of Europe. Soon the pledge became explicit. Pledge turned into vision and vision into reality. This vision-inspired reality was a series of institutional structures that evolved into what we now call the European Union.

The founding fathers

One of the earliest supporters of the idea of European union was none other than Winston Churchill, who had talked of some sort of European 'commonality' as early as 1930. In a speech in Zurich in 1946, he uttered the words quoted at the beginning of this chapter: 'We must build a United States of Europe ... The first step in the re-creation of the European family must be a partnership between France and Germany.'

Some people have taken his remarks as an endorsement of the idea of British membership of such a union, but this is clearly not what Churchill had in mind. In the same speech he said: 'Great Britain, the British Commonwealth of Nations, mighty America and I trust Soviet Russia – for then indeed all would be well – must be the friends and sponsors of the new Europe and must champion its right to live and shine.' So he clearly envisaged Britain remaining outside such a European association.

The evolution of the EU owes much to two men who translated Churchill's vision of European union into action: Jean Monnet and Robert Schuman, widely regarded as the EU's founding fathers. Their legacy continues to live on in the EU today, particularly in its vision of the future.

Interestingly, at the beginning of the Second World War, Monnet, a French political economist and diplomat, advocated a full political union between France and Britain to fight Nazism. On 5 August 1943 he said:

> *There will be no peace in Europe, if the states are reconstituted on the basis of national sovereignty ... The countries of Europe are too small to guarantee their peoples the necessary prosperity and social development. The European states must constitute themselves into a federation.*

After the war, Monnet set about work aimed at the creation of a European Community. On 9 May 1950, Robert Schuman, France's Minister of Foreign Affairs, made the 'Schuman Declaration', which had been prepared by Monnet. It proposed to place all French and German production of coal and steel under one central authority. This laid the foundation for the European Coal and Steel Community, the forerunner of the European Economic Community. Indeed, that date is now celebrated as the EU's birthday.

The Schuman Declaration of 1950 laid out the key themes that were to dominate the evolution of European institutions. It said:

> *Europe will not be made all at once, or according to a single plan. It will be built through concrete achievements which first create a de facto solidarity. The coming together of the nations of Europe requires the elimination of the age-old opposition of France and Germany.*

Schuman was a proponent of further European integration. In 1958, he became the first President of the body that may be thought of as the predecessor of the European Parliament. When he left office in 1960, he was acclaimed the 'Father of Europe'.

The European Economic Community (EEC) itself was established by the Treaty of Rome in 1957. (In Britain the EEC was referred to as the Common Market, on membership of which a referendum was held in 1975.) Although its early ambitions may have seemed modestly economic, in the preamble to the founding treaty was enshrined the essential driving force. The signatories to the Treaty of Rome (the heads of state of the six founding members: France, Germany, Italy, Belgium, the Netherlands and Luxembourg) declared that they were 'determined to lay the foundations of an ever closer union among the peoples of Europe'.

Constant change

So, from its very inception, the Community was set up to become something more than it already was. There was a sense that the payoff for current efforts and sacrifices would only come in the future, when full integration was complete. Ever since then, being a member of the Community has amounted, not so much to acceptance of a certain set of conditions in the here and now, as to participation in a process that would lead on to the final destination. This is still the case today – and still the final destination has not been reached.

I will spare readers a detailed account of which treaties did what to whom. The key point, though, is that a succession of treaties has transformed the nature of the Union. In the process, the powers of the EU institutions have radically increased relative to those of the nation states. The major developments were the following:

♦ In 1957, the Treaty of Rome established the EEC.
♦ In 1965, the Brussels Treaty streamlined European institutions, laid down the composition of the Council and set

out which institutions would be located in the three Community centres – Brussels, Strasbourg and Luxembourg.

♦ In 1986, the Single European Act marked the watershed, since it extended qualified majority voting in council, making it harder for a single country to veto proposed legislation.

♦ In 1992, the famous Maastricht Treaty prepared for European Monetary Union and introduced elements of a political union (citizenship, common foreign and internal affairs policies). This is when the EEC dropped one of the *E*s in its abbreviated name and became simply the European Community (EC). This clearly marked the transition from a largely economic association to one with an obvious political dimension.

♦ In 1995, the Schengen Agreement came into effect, allowing travel without passport control between seven countries (later joined by others): Belgium, France, Germany, Luxembourg, the Netherlands, Portugal and Spain.

♦ In 1997, the Treaty of Amsterdam saw the UK agreeing to the 'Social Chapter' of the Maastricht Treaty. Moreover, the treaty created a new senior post, a sort of Foreign Minister for the EU, known as the High Representative for Common Foreign and Security Policy.

♦ In 2001, the Treaty of Nice replaced the need for unanimous voting with a qualified majority system in 27 different areas – again diluting the power of a nation state to block measures that it did not like.

♦ In 2007, the Treaty of Lisbon extended qualified majority voting to more areas, established a legal personality for the EU and created a new post: President of the European Council. For the first time in the history of the EU, included in the Lisbon Treaty was a clause making it clear how a state could exit from the Union.

But the story is not over yet. It has been widely mooted that before long, the post of EU President should be filled by the winner of a direct presidential election across the whole EU. The EU, of course, already has a flag and an anthem. Plans for a European army have been discussed. To the ultra-integrationists, the final destination is pretty clear: a United States of Europe.

Even if integration does not go quite that far, given the existence of the euro, matters cannot stay as they are. For, as I make clear in Chapter 4, if the euro is to survive, some sort of fiscal and political union will be necessary. So a United States of the eurozone, if not of Europe, is on the drawing board. Indeed, in January 2014, Viviane Reding, Vice-President of the European Commission, said: 'We need to build a United States of Europe with the Commission as government and two chambers – the European Parliament and a "Senate" of member States.' So the USE is not a mere pipedream; it is a realistic prospect – or, some would say, even a political necessity.

Geographical expansion

During the process under which the EU's role in each member country's affairs grew steadily greater, so the number of states belonging to the Union also increased dramatically. In her famous Bruges speech of 1988, the then British Prime Minister, Margaret Thatcher, drew a contrast between 'deepening' the Union and 'widening' it; that is, letting in more countries. She wanted less of the former and more of the latter. In the event, the EU delivered more of both.

Figure 1.1 shows the stages of the EU's expansion. The original six signatories to the 1957 Treaty of Rome were joined in 1973 by three more: Denmark, Ireland and the

Figure 1.1 The stages of the EU's expansion

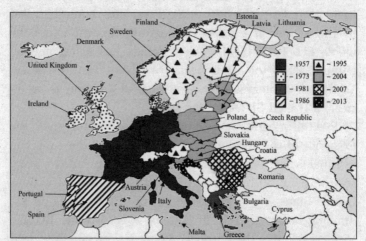

Source: www.europa.eu

UK. Greece joined in 1981, followed in 1986 by Portugal and Spain. In 1995, Austria, Finland and Sweden joined, making a union of 15 countries.

However, it was in 2004 that the EU was really transformed. This was the largest of all the expansions, bringing in eight former members of the Soviet bloc, plus Malta and Cyprus. In 2007, the accession of Romania and Bulgaria brought the total membership to 27 countries and in 2013 Croatia joined, creating a union of 28 countries – a far cry from the 6 that originally set out on this road in 1957. What is more, as I explain in Chapter 2, there are several other countries in the queue to join.

Centripetal forces

Why countries wanted to join the EU – and so many others still want to – requires an explanation. One of the reasons is quite simply that as the Union gets larger, remaining outside becomes more and more uncomfortable: diplomatically, politically and economically. Outsiders fear that they will be subject to the EU's overwhelming political power, but also that, if they remain outside it, they will be excluded from its enormous, and still growing, market.

It is almost like the decision facing investors as to whether or not they should stand aside from a great stock-market bubble, like the tech boom, as it continues to inflate. History relates that in the tech boom, as well as in a host of previous bubbles, very few investors did so. Even those who initially avoided it were, by and large, sucked in by the end. The bigger a bubble gets, the more powerful are the forces drawing others in.

Many critics of European integration suggest that as well as this 'sucking in' of new members, there have been some nakedly self-interested motives at work. They have a point – although, as I will show in a moment, this is far from the be-all and end-all of the motives behind integration.

The financial interest

Admittedly, though, several of the countries attracted to membership over recent years have had motives involving a decidedly pecuniary aspect. All of the new joiners have been relatively poor. Accordingly, they have benefited from substantial net injections of EU money, provided by the richer members, which are net contributors.

In 2015, according to the European Commission, the largest net recipient of EU funds was Poland, which received €9.5 billion, followed by the Czech Republic (€5.7 billion), Romania (€5.2 billion), Greece (€4.9 billion), Hungary (€4.6 billion) and Spain (€4.5 billion).

You can probably guess who the net contributors were: in ascending order, Luxembourg, Finland, Denmark, Austria,

Belgium, Sweden, Italy, the Netherlands, France, the UK and Germany (which paid €14.3 billion). The top five contributors – Germany, the UK, France, the Netherlands and Italy – paid 86% of the total.

Although it is the net rather than the gross figures that measure the true extent of a country's contribution to, or receipts from, the EU, this is not an accurate gauge of the extent of support that may be purchased through flows of money. For when the EU spends money – on regional development aid, for example, or road building – it makes a big thing of the fact that it is the EU that has funded the project, with frequent displays of the blue flag, bedecked with yellow stars.

Yet the funding for all of this is hidden in the national accounts of member countries. The ordinary taxpayer is not made aware of what they are themselves contributing to their countries' benefits, but are instead encouraged to believe that the EU's munificence has descended on them like manna from heaven.

The interests of elites

Moreover, the political elites of those countries that have joined the EU, both the founding members and more recent recruits, have had a clear self-interest in joining; that is, being able to participate in the governance of Europe and enjoying the benefits thereof in terms of interest, power, status and, dare I say it, money. (I comment on the pecuniary attractions of working for the EU in Chapter 2.)

This allure has been particularly strong for small countries, because the EU structure is specifically designed to give them more weight than would be justified on a pure count of GDP or numbers of people. So for many of the political leaders of small European states, the EU has been a wonderful career opportunity. It is as though they have gone from being an ordinary sitting member of the local parish council to Cabinet Minister. Jean-Claude Juncker, for instance, when Prime Minister of tiny Luxembourg, was twice President of the European Council, representing all EU member states. He is now President of the European Commission.

For the elites in the big three countries, Germany, France and the UK, it has been a different story. Nevertheless, each has had its share of benefits and inducements, pecuniary and otherwise. For Germany, to be accepted as an equal rather than a pariah was paramount. In order to secure this, over many years German leaders and officials were happy to take a shrinking-violet role in international affairs and, in particular, to play second fiddle to France; at least until recently.

By contrast, for France, the EU represented a way to bolster its power and influence in the world. France called the shots, but they were fired by a much bigger entity. As recently as 2012, the then French President, François Hollande, said: 'To be influential in tomorrow's world, to defend our values and our development model, France needs Europe and Europe needs France.' (The changing attitudes of France and Germany to the EU are taken up in more detail in Chapter 2.)

For British politicians and officials, the postwar world, characterized by loss of empire and pretty much continued relative decline, has been a trying time. While membership of the EU has been a rocky road, it has at least given the UK a forum through which its elites could seek to influence the world – or so they thought. This mattered a lot. For the UK's silky-smooth, Rolls-Royce diplomats and senior officials, groomed to run the world but in danger of being confined to running merely their own little island, it has at least meant that they continued to sit at the top table. This 'top table syndrome', as I call it, has exercised a profound influence over their views of the EU.

The guiding beliefs

Yet these cynical explanations are superficial. On the whole, particularly in great enterprises, people have to believe in what they are doing. This is where Anglo-Saxon free market economists so often miss the point completely and in the process greatly underestimate the strength of the integrationist tendency on the continent. Life is not all about profit or utility maximization – except in the justly notorious, desiccated mathematical models so beloved of American economists.

Human history is dominated by the doings of people who, for good or ill, believe in something other than themselves. Such a belief brings strength, endurance and determination. If necessary, it even enables you to kill. This is why army officers usually place so much importance on the state of their men's morale. And they are right to. In the end, it can make the difference between defeat and victory. Something similar is true in politics.

In Nazi Germany, although some of the perpetrators of its ghastly crimes were merely obeying orders, remarkably, huge numbers did what they did because they believed in the cause. Naturally, far fewer admitted to that subsequently.

For decades, many of the people who fought for the Soviet Union, either against its external enemies or against its supposed enemies within, did so not because they saw some self-interest in so doing, but rather because they believed in Communism. (Admittedly, just as at Stalingrad some troops were forced to fight by the machine guns aimed at their backs by the Soviet security police, so some people who worked for the Soviet interest in peacetime did so because they were made to.)

If the creation of the Soviet Union owed much to the power of belief, its collapse had similar roots. Of course, this was a complex matter, but surely prime among the causes of the Soviet Union's demise is that its people, leaders and led alike, had ceased to believe in its founding myth. Once this had gone, its various failings became insupportable.

The pursuit of European integration was, and still is, sustained by five guiding beliefs: the desire to avoid another European war; the idea that it is natural for Europe to be united; the concept that in economics and politics size really matters; the notion that Europe needs to be united to resist the competitive challenge from Asia; and the idea that European integration is somehow inevitable.

To a greater or lesser extent, these beliefs have been shared by people in all countries that have joined the European Union, both founding members and latecomers. But some countries have also been driven by other factors that need separate attention: the UK, members of the former eastern bloc, plus Finland, Ireland, Spain, Portugal and Greece. I briefly turn to these particular cases, after discussing the all-important guiding beliefs.

The avoidance of war

Avoiding war is surely a most noble motive and it would be quite wrong to be cynical about it. People in Britain in particular underestimate it at their peril. Whatever you may think of the widely held view that it is NATO, or the Americans, or fear of the nuclear bomb, rather than the European Union, that has kept the peace in Europe, the evolution of the next 60 years was not known in the early 1950s when European integration was being discussed.

And, as always, it would be wrong to read history

backwards. Who knows what alternative European histories could have played out if the European Union and its fore-runners had not been in place? After all, in the immediate postwar years it looked as though Italy and France were turning Communist. Meanwhile, Spain and Portugal were ruled by dictators.

The original six members of the European Economic Community consisted of three small countries (Belgium, the Netherlands and Luxembourg) and three big ones (France, Italy and Germany), which all had the war monkey firmly attached to their backs. For five of these countries, the primary fear related to Germany. For four of them, it was the fear of being overrun, dominated or humiliated by the Germans. This applied to France, the Netherlands, Belgium and Luxembourg. Given that it was only 20 years from the Versailles Treaty to the outbreak of the Second World War, it was perfectly understandable that after this second war these countries should fear a recrudescence of the same old problem before too long.

The fifth country was also afraid of Germany, for Germany was afraid of itself: afraid of what it would be like if it were left to its own devices and of what conse-quences would follow, both for itself and for others; as well as being afraid of its own isolation and international pariah status. It craved respectability among nations. During an interview with *Der Spiegel* in 2012, Germany's Finance Minister, Wolfgang Schäuble, was pretty blatant about this: 'Germany would have been prepared to relinquish powers to Brussels, because it was only through Europe that we received a new chance after World War II.'

The sixth country, Italy, was also afraid of itself, but for rather different reasons. It too had experienced a period of fascism, wartime destruction and immense suffering. But in addition, many Italians doubted the ability of the postwar

Italian state to deliver prosperity, stability and honesty in public life. Ugo La Malfa, the postwar leader of the Italian Republican Party, famously said about European integration: 'Chain Italy to the Alps, in order not to let it sink into the Mediterranean.' Subsequent developments have confirmed that such fears about the Italian state were well founded – even with Italy chained to the Alps.

Europe reunited

The second key idea was the sense that Europe had been falsely divided for centuries. It was eminently plausible to imagine that Europe's historical destiny was to be reunited. After all, under the Roman Empire, as Figure 1.2 shows, it had been united from the shores of Iberia in the west to the Rhine and Danube in the northeast, and from the Scottish Borders in the north to the southernmost Mediterranean islands.

Mind you, there were a few differences from today's

Figure 1.2 The Roman Empire in 117 CE*

* The Roman Empire was at its height in 117 CE following Rome's conquest of Mesopotamia.

Hibernia

GERMANIA

PARTHIAN EMPIRE

■ – ROMAN EMPIRE

ARABIA

Source: www.ancient.eu.com/Roman_Empire

concept of Europe. The Roman Empire was essentially built around the Mediterranean, *Mare Nostrum*. Interestingly, most of Germany and the northern part of what we would call eastern Europe were outside the empire. This was not because the Romans found the Germans too barbarian to stomach (a sentiment felt by some of their descendants today who are resisting German-inspired austerity). Indeed, the Roman historian Tacitus wrote a good deal in appreciation of German life and mores. Rather, they found Germany too difficult to conquer.

However, the southern part of eastern Europe, including some countries that are not yet members of the EU, was inside the empire, as well as, interestingly, all of Turkey, the north African littoral and much of what we would call the Middle East. Ironically, the successors to those who signed the Treaty of Rome now find these parts too hot to handle.

After the fall of Rome, there were several other attempts to unite Europe, but none matched what Rome had achieved. In the Middle Ages there was the concept of Christendom; that is, the countries under Christian rule. This covered broadly the same territory as the Roman Empire, with a few variations. Unlike the Roman Empire, after the Islamic conquests in the seventh century, the geographical limits did not reach North Africa or the Middle East, but they stretched further into eastern Europe, including not only the various German states, but also parts of Scandinavia, Ukraine, Bohemia, Poland and Muscovy (subsequently the core of European Russia); see Figure 1.3.

Of course, Christendom was not a political construct, more a description of a territory across which a certain set of presumptions and allegiances loosely held sway. On several occasions, though, the princes of Christendom fought alongside each other in defence of their religion (and the promotion of their own material gain) against the forces

Figure 1.3 Christendom in 1453*

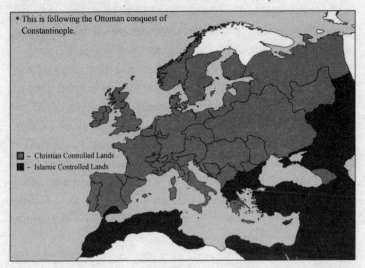

Source: commons.wikimedia.org, www.timemaps.com

Figure 1.4 The Holy Roman Empire at its peak c.1000

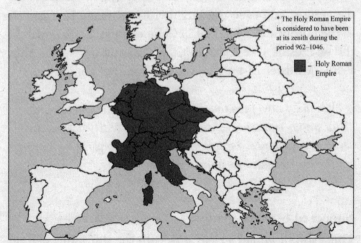

Source: www.britannica.com

of Islam. Even after the Reformation added another split in Christendom, so that it was divided into three (Catholicism, Protestantism and Orthodoxy), something of this loose idea of the association of Christian-governed lands survived.

The notion of a broad supranational European association survived also in the form of the Holy Roman Empire (depicted in Figure 1.4), even though, in the words of the famous quip, it was neither holy, nor Roman, nor an empire. More concretely, four European leaders sought at different times to establish hegemony across much of Europe: Louis XIV of France, Charles V of Spain, Napoleon and Hitler. Each succeeded for a limited period, but soon afterwards Europe returned to much like its prior constellation of small states and rivalrous empires.

In view of the continent's distant history, it was possible to regard the Europe of nation states that emerged after the end of the Napoleonic wars – and the somewhat different patchwork that emerged at Versailles in 1919, which was largely left intact after 1945 – as inefficient, illogical and dangerous; and even thoroughly un-European. In a speech to the European Parliament in October 1999, Romano Prodi, the ex-President of the European Commission and former Prime Minister of Italy, put it as plainly as could be:

We must now face the difficult task of moving towards a single economy, a single political entity ... For the first time since the fall of the Roman Empire we have the opportunity to unite Europe.

Squeezed between giants

This aspiration had a clear link with the third idea behind the impulse towards European integration: the importance of size. The decades immediately after the Second World

War were dominated by the Cold War. The world divided into two camps, led by their respective champions, the United States and the Soviet Union. Weakened by the war and now set to shed their empires, in comparison to these behemoths, even the former great colonial powers of Europe, Britain and France, appeared shrunken creatures, never mind the lesser lights such as the Netherlands and Belgium.

Of course, the countries of western Europe were part of the American-led 'West', and so they could remain. However, this put them in vassal status to the US, which seemed incompatible with their history and cultural depth. Moreover, to many people the US was far from being a paragon of virtue. If Europe could unite, it could look both the United States and the Soviet Union in the face. The world would also benefit from having a counterweight to these two overbearing giants, imbued with all the European virtues, distilled through the centuries.

Strikingly, even Margaret Thatcher subscribed to this view. Addressing an election meeting in 1966 she said: 'Europe has become a cornerstone of our campaign ... I believe together we could form a block [*sic*] with as much power as the USA or Russia.'[2]

This idea also had an economic aspect. The prevailing thinking in Europe was that in economics, size really matters. The size of the market determines the scope for economies of scale. Moreover, the size of a country, or a bloc of countries, has a major bearing on its power to negotiate economic relationships with other countries or blocs.

On both counts, opinion was doubtless heavily influenced by the example of the US. There was a strong case to be made that the essential reason for America's economic prowess was the size of its home market. If that was true, why could some combined European entity (whether the United States of Europe or something a little less than a full political union) not enjoy the same benefits? (In fact there are some good reasons why Europe cannot easily ape the US, which I discuss in Chapter 7.)

Interestingly, from an early stage, well before the advent of the euro, there had been an idea that America enjoyed an enormous advantage over Europe by being able to issue the world's currency, thereby greatly reducing its cost of finance. The French President, Charles de Gaulle, referred to this as America's 'exorbitant privilege'. (Having experienced the euro as a rival to the dollar, I doubt that many Europeans have felt 'privileged', but this subject must await the full discussion in Chapter 10.)

So the objective of building up, or belonging to, a large bloc of countries for security or defence reasons went hand in hand with the objective of promoting European prosperity. That in turn would help to promote Europe's influence in the world.

This European thinking about the benefits of integration was mirrored on the other side of the Atlantic. There have always been some members of the American establishment who have seen the emergence of a united Europe as a potential threat to American hegemony. Even so, from the start, the predominant US attitude to European integration was positive. Again, this was for both political and economic reasons. Politically, in the early decades of the postwar period the US was preoccupied by the Communist threat and saw a more integrated Europe as a bulwark against Communism.

The economic element came into the political equation too. The more economically successful Europe was, the less likely Communism was to spread. Quite apart from this, greater economic success would also help America economically, through trade and investment links and by helping to reduce the US contribution to global defence, aid and international bodies.

As to how to achieve greater prosperity in Europe, to most of the American establishment it would have seemed obvious that bringing down trade barriers and fostering integration would do the trick. In fact, America went further than this. For four years, starting in 1947, the Marshall Plan transferred over 1% of America's GDP each year to the stricken countries of Europe.

Yet once the European project was underway, it never seemed to occur to senior American officials and diplomats that if European institutions were badly constructed, and if the prevailing economic ideology was statist and interventionist, closer integration could actually harm economic growth. To be fair to them, just getting Europe growing again was the immediate priority. Moreover, at the time very few economists recognized the importance of institutions as opposed to 'simple economic forces' for bringing prosperity. It took the fall of Communism and the rise of emerging markets to cause the penny to drop. Perhaps more surprisingly, as a great democracy itself, the US was puzzlingly unaware of the looming democratic deficit at the heart of the EU.

Eastern challenge

Over recent years, with the Soviet Union having disintegrated and even the end of American hegemony now sighted on the horizon, a fourth factor has emerged: fear of the East. Supposedly, the world is going to be dominated by China and India, with perhaps some lesser powers, such as Indonesia, snapping at their heels. If Europe does not unite, then how will it be able to make its voice heard in the world? How will it compete? Indeed, how will it survive?

It is common for defenders of the EU to point out that

without the Union, in 20 years' time no single European country, not even Germany, would be able to sit at the table of the decision-makers, and that China would be able to divide and rule by negotiating with each European country individually. As the Italian Prime Minister, Enrico Letta, put it in a joint speech with David Cameron given at Chatham House in July 2013:

> *Today, size matters again. Member states need the collective strength of the European Union to have leverage; otherwise they will be without the power and wealth needed to matter in world politics. Either Europe is a global actor in economic terms and in foreign and defence policy, or each of the member states will struggle to maintain the role that it had in the past century.*

In practice, though, in 20 or 30 years' time the world is likely to be multipolar and with very different institutions, as I argue in Chapter 11. Nevertheless, the fear of European irrelevance and impotence if the EU does not survive has induced more tolerance of the EU's failings than it deserves.

Inevitability

The fifth idea behind the urge towards European integration is really the confluence of the other four: namely, the notion that European integration is simply *inevitable*. Inevitability confers a strange strength on those who are possessed by belief in it. It is strange because, strictly speaking, if you believe that an event or outcome is inevitable, this could be expected to undermine or weaken any impulse to action – since the 'inevitable' event or outcome is going to happen, *inevitably*, whatever you do or do not do. In practice, though, people seem to be goaded into action by the belief that what they are doing is in step with the march of history.

In *War and Peace*, Tolstoy questions why hundreds of thousands of men are moving across Europe towards the great clashes of arms of the Napoleonic wars. He gives all sorts of specific explanations for particular people, but he is clear that they are all simply cogs in a wheel. He sees the whole shifting canvas as the outcome of Fate.

Not that long after Tolstoy wrote his masterpiece, the idea of inevitability came to play a key role in the rise of Communism. Marx developed a theory of the evolution of the economy and society that made Communism 'inevitable'. Many of the revolutionaries who subsequently fought in Russia and elsewhere to bring Communism into being genuinely felt that its eventual triumph was inevitable. This hardened their will and made them prepared to do almost anything to turn the vision into reality.

European integration too has had an air of inevitability about it. It seemed to be the summation and healing of the past and the way of the future. Nation states were on the way out, *passé*. A united Europe would embody the best of European traditions while securing Europe's future in the modern world.

This feeling of inevitability even affected opponents of integration, who so often felt that they were up against a steamroller that would proceed to roll over them come what may. Even objections by the majority of the people were ignored. When referendums on the proposed European Constitution were lost in both France and the Netherlands, the euro elites simply carried on anyway to implement key elements of what had been rejected at the polls. They just refrained from using the C-word.

When Irish voters rejected the Lisbon Treaty in 2008, the question was subsequently put to them again in a second referendum. This time they approved it, but presumably if they had approved the treaty in the first referendum there would not have been a second one. The impression was left that they would be compelled to go on voting until they said yes; once they said yes, they would not be asked again.

Only in the last few years has the halo of inevitability begun to slip, for both supporters and opponents alike. In truth, further European integration was never inevitable, but now that it no longer seems so, it is in fact less likely.

So the European movement has had five guiding ideas, which have sustained the push for continued integration. They have inspired and driven the movement's supporters, filled them with a sense of moral superiority and given them the confidence that history is on their side.

Thinking more broadly, the movement has had not only its ideology, consisting of these five ideas, but also its sacred text (the Treaty of Rome), its patron saints (Monnet and Schuman) and its ultimate goal: the formation of a United States of Europe. In other words, it has had many of the trappings of a religion. This surely helps to explain the strength of mind of the supporters of further European integration and their determination to press on with their objectives even when millions of fellow citizens do not share their views.

Britain's awkward position

The five guiding beliefs – and the integrationist religion – had a major influence in Britain, as well as on the continent. There were also some key economic considerations affecting the UK's decision to join the EEC in 1973, which I defer until Chapter 3. However, there was one peculiarly British aspect to the geopolitics of the case – though it had a decidedly American twist.

Winston Churchill had successfully constructed the narrative of the two great Atlantic democracies, America and Britain, fighting the war together and then together laying the foundations of the postwar world, sustained by fellow feeling, common language and a shared heritage – as well as mutual advantage. There was a substantial element of truth in this, but there was also a darker side to the relationship. During and after the war, America had been keen both to seize commercial advantage over Britain in world markets and, relatedly, to ensure the dismantling of the British Empire.

Most Britons have never understood the tendency of informed Americans to see Britain, with its colonies abroad and the operation of the class system at home, including a hereditary monarch as head of state and the continuation as a political entity of the House of Lords, as not a true democracy. Moreover, the British generally do not recognize the extent to which, towards the end of the war, President Roosevelt sought to make common cause with Stalin, leaving Churchill isolated. For many of those who did know it, or learned it later, this had a profound effect. Even in its early stages, although the 'special relationship' was not a complete delusion and the favours, to some extent, flowed in both directions, it was nowhere near a relationship of equals. Moreover, the US meant to make it more unequal. For America fully intended to reduce Britain's standing in the world – and, of course, it succeeded.

The Suez disaster of 1956, when the US effectively pulled the plug on the joint British/French attempt to seize the Suez Canal back from Egypt's President Nasser, provided the *coup de grâce*. Suez was a profound national humiliation. After that, the choice for Britain appeared to be between becoming an American lapdog or throwing in its lot with Europe.

After Suez, the new British Prime Minister, Harold Macmillan, liked to see Britain's options as much less stark. He fondly envisaged Britain at the centre of three key relationships: with the US, Europe and the Commonwealth, as Britain's former empire now became – a sort of international equivalent of the House of Lords. This triangular situation, he thought, made Britain a crucial country, whose experience and sophistication in world affairs rendered it especially valuable to America. As he put it, he saw Britain playing Greece to America's Rome.

But as the years went on and European integration deepened, this complacent view seemed increasingly wide of the mark. Did the UK want to sign up to the European project or not? Much of the British establishment now saw throwing Britain's lot in with Europe as 'inevitable'. As it turned out, President de Gaulle of France said 'Non' to British overtures. In the end, though, once De Gaulle had departed, Britain did join the European Economic Community, without most Britons realizing they were signing up to the project of 'ever closer union'. They thought they were merely joining a Common Market. Meanwhile, Britain continued to be an American lapdog just the same.

Escape from Communism

For several of the newer EU members, the centripetal forces drawing them towards membership have been quite different, although their story also involves a relationship with a much larger country. These are the members of the former eastern bloc, which, under Soviet domination, experienced a long period of exclusion and separation from the West. After the Soviet collapse, they now longed to be part of the western club and to be regarded as normal. On a more negative note, they continued to fear that a re-expansionist Russia would at some time seek to gobble them up. In varying degrees, this applies to Poland, the Czech Republic, Hungary, the Baltic states of Latvia, Estonia and Lithuania, Slovakia, Slovenia, Croatia, Bulgaria and Romania.

It also applies to Finland, which was at war with the Soviet Union for most of the period between 1939 and 1944. What is more, Finland had been part of the Russian empire between 1809 and 1917. This, as well as Finland's ethnic and linguistic heritage, marks it out as different from the other Nordic countries that have either stood outside the EU (Norway) or, like Britain, have been in the EU but kept their distance from the euro (Sweden and Denmark).

For all of these countries, membership of the EU was a sign of realignment with the West and appeared to make a clear warning statement and to raise the stakes, if Russia at some future stage turned belligerent. (All of the former members of the eastern bloc, but not Finland, also joined NATO, which provided concrete protection without compromising national sovereignty; see Chapter 11.)

Although it was not originally envisaged that the EU would perform this role – or indeed, that it would be possible – the European Union acted as a receiving house for the countries of the former eastern bloc as they emerged from the nightmare of Soviet domination. Aspiration to membership of the EU provided the drive and political rationale for pushing through painful political and economic reforms. It has also helped to check any tendency towards backsliding since. For this achievement, if for nothing else, the EU can be said to have been a success and to have served humankind well.

Other countries, other motives

For what we now call the Republic of Ireland, anxiety focused not on a bear but rather on a mangy old lion. The southern part of Ireland, Eire, became an independent state in 1922. However, it was not until 1948 that the remaining duties of the British monarch were dropped and the country became a republic. Even then, the UK continued to loom large in its affairs; Ireland did not break the link with sterling until 1979. Membership of the EU represented a real escape from the UK's influence and Ireland's coming of age as a country – not the loss of sovereignty and national identity but rather their clear assertion.

Interestingly, three of the Union's troubled southern members also saw the EU as the giver and guarantor of freedom, although not freedom from outside domination but rather freedom from arbitrary rule and oppression. For these three countries are refugees from dictatorship, albeit not of the Communist variety. In 1974, Greece emerged from a seven-year period of rule by the Colonels. Spain was governed by a fascist dictatorship from 1936 until 1975, for most of the time under General Franco. And Portugal was under a dictatorship from 1926 until 1974.

For these countries, the ceding of power to Brussels did not have the sinister ring that it did to many people in Britain. On the contrary, it represented a sort of liberation and escape, an apparent guarantee of democracy and the rule of law at home, and membership of the club of respectable nations abroad.

A history of achievement

So the EU was forged from a variety of motives, some common to almost all joiners and some specific to individual countries. Some of the motives have had an economic aspect to them, namely that new members thought that they were joining an economic success story – and that their own economic performance would improve as a result. (I will deal with the EU's economic performance separately in Chapter 3.) But many, if not all, countries joining the EU had a decidedly political motivation – in keeping with the political origins of the Union.

In that regard, leaving economics to one side for a moment, in relation to what was hoped for and expected of it, in so many ways the EU can be described as a success:

♦ There has been no European war.
♦ In particular, France and Germany are close allies.
♦ The EU has helped countries from the former Soviet bloc to be reabsorbed into the West.
♦ There is a queue of countries waiting to join.
♦ The EU has leveraged the power and influence of member countries on the world stage.
♦ The institutions of the EU seem to be at the point of transformation so that it, or rather a large part of it, is ready to realize the original dream of a United Europe.

The trouble is that since the original vision of the founding fathers, things have changed. Is the EU really what Europe needs now? Or is it one of Europe's main problems?

2

The Trouble with the EU
as a Political Institution

*I believe in political union. I believe in political Europe.
I believe in the Europe of integration. I believe in a
Europe where we have the economy, culture and the
politics brought together.*
— Nicolas Sarkozy, President of France, 2007

When a cow is born in a horse's stable, it is still a cow.
— Anon.

To an increasing number of contemporary observers, the
EU's successes seem to relate to the past. With regard
to the present, however, and even more to the future, it has
several key defects:

◆ It suffers from a profound identity crisis.
◆ Its institutions are mainly badly structured and badly run.
◆ It is focused on a largely irrelevant agenda, driven by
  the objectives of harmonization and integration, which
  produce excessive regulation and smother competition.
◆ It is alienated from its electorates.

One major result of the EU's defects is a tendency for it to
come to bad decisions, which then affects, among other things,
economic performance. I analyse that in the next chapter.
Here, I discuss the political and institutional character of the
EU. I start with a discussion of why institutions matter before
going on to review the failings of the EU's institutional structure, starting with the essential matter of identity. I then

consider the EU's institutions themselves and analyse the changing views of the member countries' electorates.

The importance of governance

For most of our history, human beings have had virtually no say over how they were governed. They were governed the way they were because that was how it had been before – until some other arbitrary power came along and usurped the original one. Dynasties and empires came and went without much of a rationale, except the exercise of brute force, alternating with the passive power of tradition, law and custom.

It should not be forgotten that this long history of arbitrary power also coincides with a long history of next to no economic growth. While the reasons for this, of course, are complex, the point to emphasize here is that governance really matters, not only for human freedom and happiness – surely the most important objectives – but also for economic growth. Accordingly, it is no accident that when growth began to emerge in western Europe in the seventeenth and eighteenth centuries, it was associated with the limitation of arbitrary power, the acknowledged power and sovereignty of the law and the development of a vibrant civil society.

The reasons for the Industrial Revolution happening first in England have been endlessly debated by scholars over the last couple of hundred years and doubtless this will continue. But let me put it this way: it was not all about the availability of coal and water power. Changes in the world of politics and institutions – as well as in the world of finance – played a major role.

Looking back over the last four centuries, three key revolutions were closely associated with disagreements about the legitimacy of the existing sovereign power raising money from the people. The English Civil War, which saw Charles I lose his head and England briefly become a republic, began initially as a result of Parliament's objections to Charles raising taxes to fund his wars. The French Revolution of 1789 was similarly partly inspired by a rejection of punitive taxation. The American Revolution of 1776 was also spurred by the issue of taxation, with the revolutionaries' cry being 'no taxation without representation'. And in the case of both Britain and its then colonial offshoot, the United States, the limitation of sovereign power, specifically the limitation of its economic aspects, played a major role in bringing about subsequent economic success.

Institutions really matter – for both good and ill. In their recent book *Why Nations Fail*, Daron Acemoglu and James Robinson stress the distinction between *inclusive* institutions, which serve the public interest, and *extractive* ones, which essentially serve the interests of the rulers or some special interest group. (This is a similar distinction to the one I draw in *The Trouble with Markets* between *creative* and *distributive* activities.) Societies only progress when inclusive institutions predominate over extractive ones.

The economist and Nobel Laureate Douglass North[3] has stressed that the institutions that matter are not only the formal ones. What matter too are what he calls 'informal institutions', such as sanctions, taboos, customs, traditions and codes of conduct. He points out that after independence, Latin American countries virtually all adopted carbon copies of the US Constitution, although this did not ensure good governance. North says that the reason is that nearly all Latin American countries had been Spanish colonies and were thus infused with Spanish informal institutions, in which 'personalistic' relationships 'are the key to much of the political and economic exchange'. By contrast, the United States had begun life as a British colony and benefited from British informal institutions, which permitted complex impersonal exchange.

So how do the institutions of the EU stack up? Are they well structured? Is there embodied in the EU treaties and the surrounding arrangements a clear limitation on arbitrary power? On what we know, are its institutions likely to operate in a way favourable to the promotion of economic growth? And are the institutions likely to command the loyalty and affection of the people under their sway? The place to start to answer these questions is by looking at the fundamental issue of identity.

What is it to be European?

The EU suffers from a profound identity crisis, which goes right back to the foundation of the Union. Despite the teleological nature of the integrationist project, the founding fathers of the European Union did not have a well-defined idea of the feasible, or desirable, extent of the Union. Because they set about their project during the Cold War, when the Soviet Union loomed large and the idea of eastern Europe being able and willing to join what we now call the EU was a mere pipedream, they probably did not need to consider the issue seriously. But it does need to be considered now.

What is the point of the EU? Is it to link together countries and peoples that are 'European'? Is it to link together countries and peoples that are geographically close together? Is it to link together countries that conduct themselves in a certain way and are prepared and able to obey EU law? Or is it simply to carry on expanding as far as it can, because bigger is better, so that the EU can be regarded as an early progenitor of global government?

Without a clear answer to these questions, it is difficult to see why the EU should not contemplate expansion to nations that are geographically close, such as Israel or the countries of North Africa, even though they are not strictly European. (Interestingly, the remit of the European Bank for Reconstruction and Development (EBRD) does extend into the Middle East and North Africa.) Or if the key concept is cultural, what about countries that are European in character and history but are far distant, such as Canada, Australia or New Zealand?

This question is of existential importance. For if there is no clear answer to the question of how far EU membership should spread, perhaps it should be restricted to a smaller territory – or indeed, perhaps the EU should not exist at all.

Formal criteria

It is clear that EU membership is not open to any old country. According to the Copenhagen criteria (laid out by the European Council in Copenhagen in 1993), to be a candidate for EU membership, a country must:

♦ have stable institutions guaranteeing democracy, the rule of law, human rights and respect for and protection of minorities;
♦ have a functioning market economy and the capacity to cope with competition and market forces in the EU;
♦ have the ability to take on and implement effectively the obligations of membership, including adherence to the aims of political, economic and monetary union;
♦ adopt the common rules, standards and policies that make up EU law.

This still leaves unclear which countries can, and which cannot, become members. As we shall see in a moment, there are a number of hard cases.

As the European Union developed and the fall of the Soviet Union made it possible to imagine the unification of Europe, the idea gained ground that the EU represented the quintessence of Europe. Accordingly, its extent should be dictated by the extent of Europe itself. That sounds easy enough – until you start to look at these hard cases.

Figure 2.1 shows the extent of further possible expansion. It has already been decided that Europe includes the second wave of former members of the Soviet bloc, Romania and Bulgaria, and Croatia became the 28th member of the European Union in July 2013. In addition, there are five countries that are formally acknowledged to be candidates for EU membership: Iceland, Macedonia, Montenegro, Serbia and Turkey. (Turkey is an important subject in itself, to which I will come in a moment.) There are three others that are not formally acknowledged as applicants but are widely recognized as potential candidates: Albania, Bosnia and Kosovo.

Figure 2.1 Potential expansion of the EU

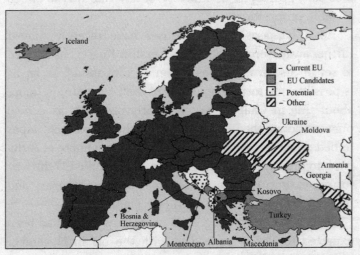

Source: www.europa.eu

More serious issues concern two countries that are not yet even in the line-up of potential candidates, but ultimately could be, namely Ukraine and Russia. These countries can be regarded as part-European, but they have also been outside mainstream European political culture for some time and cannot be regarded as full western democracies governed by the rule of law (although that did not stop Russia being included in the G-8). Moreover, they are both very large. Ukraine has a population of about 45 million and Russia over 140 million.

Of the two, Ukraine is the more plausible candidate for membership. Its population may be large but it could just about be absorbed, although surely not without even greater angst in the capitals of western Europe than accompanied the accession of Romania and Bulgaria. Even if Ukraine were successfully to complete a reform programme, the combination of very low levels of GDP per capita and a dubious political culture would make Ukrainian entry extremely difficult for the EU to swallow. These same points, plus size, geography and history, surely rule Russia out as a viable proposition.

As it happens, both countries have recently moved further away from possible membership. Russia has decided to set up its own customs union encompassing, so far as is possible, the former republics of the Soviet Union (more about this in Chapter 11). It clearly sees this as a rival organization to the EU and, by establishing it as such, hopes to bed down former Soviet republics in its sphere of influence, to prevent them being drawn towards the EU the way former eastern bloc Soviet satellites such as Hungary and the Czech Republic have been (see Figure 2.2).

Which way Ukraine goes is in the balance. It had been expected to sign a trade deal with the EU in November 2013 at a summit in Vilnius, Lithuania. But at the last

Figure 2.2 The former Soviet Union and its satellite states

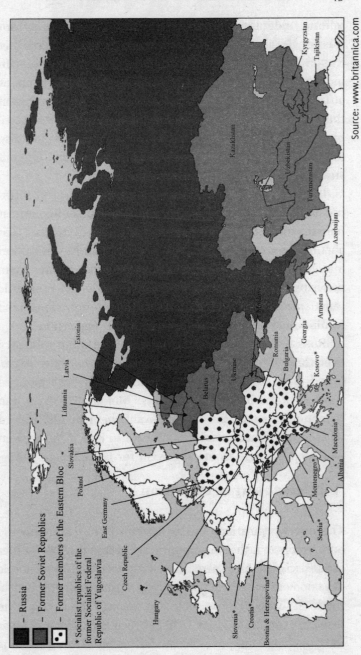

Source: www.britannica.com

minute, under intense economic and political pressure from Russia, Ukraine withdrew. Subsequently it emerged that Russia had offered Ukraine substantial economic aid, including buying its bonds and providing energy supplies at below market price. It was evidently Russia's intention that Ukraine should join its Eurasian Union and that, accordingly, it should be prised away from the EU. This gave rise to considerable unease in Ukraine, with riots and demonstrations in the streets.

In 2014, Russia seized Crimea from Ukraine and incorporated it within Russia, while apparently fomenting unrest in eastern Ukraine, supposedly intending to destabilize that part of the country, possibly leading also to its absorption into Russia. These actions prompted major military manoeuvrings on both sides and the imposition of economic sanctions on Russia by the West. This whole episode seemed to mark a clear limit to the EU's eastern expansion.

Russia's intentions may similarly have a big influence over three other former Soviet republics that have established close relationships with the EU but have stopped short of full EU candidate status: Moldova, Georgia and Armenia. Whether the EU will want them in, and indeed whether they themselves would want to join, is being overwhelmed by Russia's evident wish for them not to join.

A different sort of expansion

The size of populations and the attitude of Russia are not the only factors to take into account when thinking about further expansion of the EU. There is also the critical issue of economic development, for which per capita GDP is a reasonable benchmark. It cannot be emphasized enough how large the disparities are in levels of GDP between the current EU and the candidates and potential candidates for EU membership.

Figure 2.3 shows the GDP per capita of the six founder members of the EEC in 1957. Excluding tiny Luxembourg, the richest country was the Netherlands. Its per capita GDP was not quite double the poorest country's, namely Italy. Over the next few decades, the gap gradually closed. Moreover, in the first expansion of membership in 1973, the new members, Denmark, Ireland and the UK, had a per capita GDP broadly in line with existing members.

Figure 2.3 GDP per capita in 1957 of the six founder members of the EEC (excluding Luxembourg, in US$ at PPP, 2011 prices)

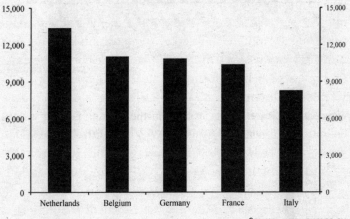

Source: www.europa.eu

This was most certainly not the case with the large expansion that took place in 2004, as Figure 2.4 shows. The per capita GDP of the poorest new member was about a third of the richest (excluding Luxembourg). When Bulgaria and Romania joined in 2007, they were even poorer. Similarly, as Figure 2.5 shows, with the exception of Iceland, present and potential candidates all have a per capita GDP that is a fraction of the EU average.

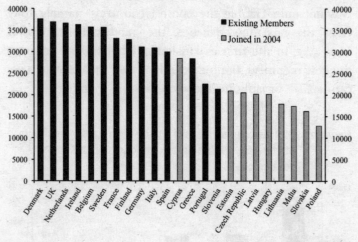

Figure 2.4 GDP per capita in the existing 14 members of the EEC in 2004 (excluding Luxembourg) and the new members that joined that year (in US$ at PPP, 2011 prices)

Source: www.europa.eu

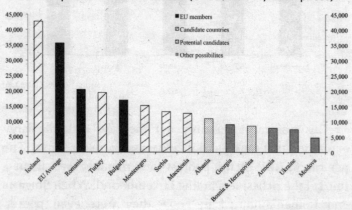

Figure 2.5 GDP per capita in 2015 in the existing EU and various possible new members (in US$ at PPP, 2011 prices)

Source: www.europa.eu

As the EU has spread eastward, it has taken in countries at a very different level of development. This has caused significant problems, most notably with the central idea of free movement of people within the Union. The result has been a level of migration that has seriously upset the indigenous populations of older member countries and not only fanned anti-EU feelings, but also sparked an ugly upsurge of racism and xenophobia.

This issue did not arise when the EEC was formed, or with the 1973 expansion, since there was a smaller discrepancy in development between the founder members. However, the 2004 and 2007 expansions were different. Future expansions seem set to follow this more recent pattern.

It is almost as though the people generating these two parts of the EU agenda – the free movement of labour and the urge to expand – do not talk to each other.

The Turkish question

The level of development is not the only, or even the main, issue confronting the EU over its most challenging potential entrant: Turkey. The issue of possible Turkish membership goes right to the heart of the EU's identity crisis.

In many ways Turkey belongs naturally in Europe. Unlike Russia, it is a member of NATO and competes in the Eurovision Song Contest and in European football's Champions League and Europa League. Geographically, while most of Turkey is in Asia, part of it is clearly in Europe. Famously straddling both is Istanbul, its major city (although not its capital), one of the cradles of European civilization. Under the name Constantinople, reflecting its foundation by the Roman Emperor Constantine, it was the capital city of the eastern Roman Empire and, under the name Byzantium, capital of that part of the Empire that survived the fall of Rome until the eve of the modern era, succumbing to the Turks in 1453.

On the Asian shores of what we now call Turkey stood the cities of Troy, Ephesus and Halicarnassus, which have figured so large in the European historical imagination. Across the plains of Anatolia (Asiatic Turkey), Alexander the Great fought and defeated the armies of the Persian king Darius, in the process Hellenizing much of the Middle East, in a way that had major consequences, not least for the subsequent spread of the Christian Gospel. It was on the shores of Anatolia that Alexander ordered his Macedonian troops to 'burn their boats' – an expression that has passed down to us in English today. All of that seems pretty European to me.

Moreover, Istanbul is only a few miles further from Brussels than Athens is; and it is not much further distant from Brussels than Helsinki or Lisbon. However, in other matters it is much further apart. When Byzantium fell to the Ottoman armies in 1453, in cultural terms what we now call Istanbul shifted eastwards. Having moved westwards again during the twentieth century, Turkey has recently been moving eastwards once more. Today, it is a predominantly Islamic country. It is still a secular state, but even that does not seem secure. And it has a history of coups d'état and sketchy adherence to the rule of law.

So should Turkey be part of the EU? Several European countries may have large Muslim minorities living within their borders, but that is quite different from admitting to the EU an Islamic country and one with about 76 million people now and, according to the Turkish Statistical Institute, set to have over 90 million people 20 years hence. The EU has reacted to this challenge by dragging its feet on Turkish membership, with the result that the Turks are themselves cooling towards the idea.

Turkey is a litmus test. Is the EU meant to be the modern reincarnation of Christendom? Or is it a union of geographically close states that fulfil certain dry membership criteria? If the EU merely exists to bring together neighbours, how can such a union be close and based on shared values? At its heart, the EU suffers from a profound identity crisis.

The Union's limits

Interestingly, France's former President, Nicolas Sarkozy, recently made some pretty clear statements on the question of European identity and specifically on whether Turkey should be admitted to the EU. He said:

> *What is Europe? Europe is not a sub-region of the United Nations. It's a political project, an integration. We have to constantly give thought to what's happening as regards the enlargement and integration of Europe. I want an integrated Europe, in other words, a Europe that has borders. Turkey is in Asia Minor. Russia is not Europe either, but the Balkan states, they are part of Europe. And what about Ukraine? We would have to take in Ukraine. And then we're going to have a Europe that's so enormous that nobody will be able to do anything in Europe and we've already got the United Nations for that.*

In these remarks, over and above matters of compatibility and shared interests, Sarkozy raised the question of whether there is an upper limit to the size of the Union for it to function properly with an effective democracy and institutions that command the respect (if not the affection) of its citizens. And he was right to do so.

Surely there must be some upper limit to the size and type of union that allows (and indeed requires) the free movement of people within its borders. This alone must rule out Turkish membership, but it must also pose a serious question mark over Ukraine (never mind Russia). Either that, or the Union must change into something utterly different from the dreams of the founding fathers, who were driven by the prospect of 'ever closer union'. (I take up this subject in Chapter 11.) The free movement of people within the EU's borders has been a fundamental principle of the Single Market, but it is incompatible with a membership of countries with huge disparities in income and culture.

The European Union now has a membership whose size and diversity are out of keeping with its institutions, its ambitions and its own sense of what it is and what it is there for. The European Union has stumbled into this position without adequate forethought. It has continued to nurse the idea of ever closer union while expanding its geographical horizons well beyond what the EU's founding fathers could ever have imagined and beyond what has a reasonable hope of being effective.

In many ways, this problem is the result of success: umpteen countries have wanted to join the EU (for a variety of motives) and for the Union it was agreeable to be wanted and to grow larger. Nevertheless, to avoid becoming a horrendous monster, the EU needs to make a choice. It could continue with its current membership or even expand further, but not pursue full integration and ever closer union. Or it could retain this objective but for a smaller group of countries – perhaps those currently belonging to the eurozone. Yet, as we shall see in a moment, to make even that successful will be a tall order.

Institutional structures

The EU is a grouping of countries that is on the verge of becoming a state, but it is not quite there yet. The consequence is that it has emasculated the role of nation states in a number of areas without fully supplanting them. The result is a mess.

There is now a proposal for the eurozone to have its own president. In fact, this would be the EU's fifth president of sorts. There is already the President of the Commission, the President of the European Council, the President of the Council of Ministers (i.e. the rotating Country Presidency) and the President of the European Parliament, not to mention the EU's High Representative (recently the UK's Baroness Ashton). This puts into context Henry Kissinger's quip that since Europe consists of so many nation states, there is not a single telephone number he can call to get something done. Even if he tried to make contact with the EU, as distinct from its member states, it might take four, or even five, calls to do the trick.

The rotating country presidency, which is held for six months before the role is passed on to some other country, is distinctly odd, because countries such as Germany or the UK get treated the same as Luxembourg or Croatia, whose senior civil servants and diplomats are both much less numerous and, in general, less capable and experienced.

On foreign policy, the President of the European Commission, Mr Juncker, attends meetings of the G-7, alongside the Prime Ministers and Presidents of the member countries. However, that does not mean that there is an agreed European policy on any of the issues to be discussed. Indeed, EU members of the G-7 – France, Germany, the UK and Italy – are at liberty to pursue their own foreign policies, and they often do.

Although the European Commission is the EU's embryo government, its composition is dictated by the multinational nature of the Union. There are 28 Commissioners, one for each member of the EU. The Commissioners are supposed to represent all EU citizens and not simply their own country, but in practice, countries do look to their own Commissioner to argue their case. And the Commission itself is a strange animal. A research document published by the pro-EU think tank the Centre for European Reform describes it as a 'political body that initiates legislation and also brokers compromises among member states; a technical body that evaluates the performance of the member-states' economies; a quasi-judicial authority that polices markets and enforces rules; and a regulator of common policies on behalf of the member states'.[4]

There is also the Council of Ministers, where national leaders meet with each other face to face. In this forum, countries are supposed to be able to protect their national interests, but membership is now so big that even large countries have difficulty in achieving this. For instance, the UK's share of the vote is now down to 8% and its ability to influence, let alone block, measures affecting its interests is decidedly limited. In practice, many key decisions are taken in bilateral meetings between Prime Ministers and Presidents. Given that France and Germany are widely accepted as the motor of the EU, the most important of these meetings concern the French President and the German Chancellor.

The European Parliament is not meant to function in the same way as national parliaments. It can propose or amend legislation, but its decisions are not binding on the European Council. European constituencies are very large and there is little connection between MEPs and ordinary people back home. The fact that constituencies for the Parliament are all chunks of one member country, rather than stretching across countries, reinforces the Parliament's position between the nation states and full union. And although there are seven cross-country political groupings in Parliament, given the large linguistic and cultural differences between different country representatives, these make little impact in the member countries themselves.

Similar problems afflict the European Court of Justice (ECJ). Each country, regardless of size, supplies a judge. This scarcely enhances the Court's performance – or its reputation. Admittedly, some of the Court's judgments have been widely acclaimed. Perhaps the most celebrated is the 1979 Cassis de Dijon ruling, which established the principle of mutual recognition, such that any good marketed and sold in one state is to be allowed to be marketed and sold in another. Nevertheless, a raft of judgments have caused consternation. One of the most controversial was the 2011 ruling against gender discrimination in insurance, which *The Economist* called 'pretty bonkers'. Its result was to prevent insurance companies from discriminating in favour of young female drivers, who tend to have fewer accidents than young men. The ruling also forced insurance companies to give the same annuity rates to male and female pensioners, even though men and women have markedly different life expectancies.

More generally, the Court has been criticized, not just in the UK but in several other member states, for 'judicial activism'; that is, a tendency to go beyond its remit and to advance European integration. (Note that the ECJ is not to be confused with the European Court of Human Rights (ECHR), which was set up under the European Convention on Human Rights, which is also referred to as the ECHR. To distinguish between the two, the European Court, as distinct from the European Convention, is sometimes referred to as the ECtHR.)

The European Central Bank (ECB) is arguably an exception to the list of institutional failures. In technical terms it has worked well. Nevertheless, with its national representatives who are meant to set monetary policy for the eurozone as a whole, it is prone to many of the same difficulties besetting other European institutions. Indeed, many of its policy actions – and more particularly inactions – have been highly questionable. Admittedly, though, it has been saddled with a herculean task in trying to manage the euro. (I discuss the problems of the single currency in Chapter 4.)

The democratic deficit

The result of these institutional structures is that the electorates of individual countries no longer have the power to exercise the ultimate control over their rulers. Even in a country with a strong democratic tradition such as the UK, democracy has never amounted to an ability to shape, let alone veto, particular laws or governmental practices. Fundamentally, democracy in Britain – as elsewhere – has been about the power to turf out the party of government and its leader when they choose, or are forced, to seek the endorsement of the electorate. Now British people have to accept laws imposed on them as a result of Byzantine intrigue between the unelected European Commission and the leaders of the other European member states. This represents a negation of centuries of British history, a central theme of which has been the gradual transfer of powers from the crown to the elected representatives of the people, who can be removed by those people at elections.[5]

Indeed, it is not widely recognized how deep-seated the democratic tradition is in Britain. The Anglo-Saxon kings were elected; not, admittedly, by universal suffrage, but from among the nobility and by the vote of an Advisory Council, the *witenagemot*. After the Norman Conquest in 1066, kings of England were more like dictators and before long they succeeded by primogeniture, not by being elected. But even then, they had to govern with the consent and counsel of the barons, and gradually the authoritarianism of the Normans was moderated by the influences of the Anglo-Saxon tradition and by the increasing authority of parliament.

In 1327 parliament deposed Edward II and in 1399 it deposed Richard II for assuming absolute powers not recognized by the English people. Subsequently, other notable moments occurred with the deposition of Charles I and James II and the establishment of clear parliamentary supremacy under the 'Glorious Revolution' of 1688. The rest, as they say, is history. It is striking that today the European Commission has greater powers to ignore parliament than did most English kings.[6]

Of course, the relative impotence of the British parliament – and indeed, other national parliaments – vis-à-vis the governance of the EU need not be viewed as a fatal flaw if one simply accepts that the size of the political entity that is subject to these democratic constraints has increased. Just as the people of Croydon cannot, by themselves, overturn a British government, so it may seem appropriate that the people of Britain, either directly or through their parliament, cannot, by themselves, overturn a European government.

In fact, this is far too indulgent a conclusion to come to, because even the European electorate as a whole cannot turn out the European Commission, while the European Parliament is a supine and ineffective institution. Moreover, as I argue in Chapter 10, even if the EU's political institutions were radically reshaped, there are good reasons why a European democracy would not work very well.

Administrative failures

Given its evolution and the stresses and strains in its institutional structure, it is hardly surprising that much of the EU does not work efficiently. Admittedly, bad and even chaotic government is not restricted to the EU. Professors King and Crewe have produced a fascinating, though hair-raising, account of blunders made by British governments over the years, including the Thatcher government's programme in the 1980s and early 1990s to encourage people into private pensions, millions of whom were ill-advised to switch out of their existing schemes.[7] Massive compensation payments followed.

The complaint heard particularly strongly in the UK, but also in other member countries, is not so much that the EU is especially incompetent or prone to outright blunder, but rather that it imposes too many regulations without any regard for the cost of enforcing them, or the knock-on effect throughout the system. Moreover, when such regulations are imposed across the EU as a whole, even if they are broadly appropriate and practical in some countries, they may be completely inappropriate in others. What is more, it is widely believed that many of the EU's actual or proposed regulations are extremely petty, so that the irritation factor is much higher than any quantifiable economic cost.

For example, in May 2013 the European Commission proposed a ban on olive oil being served in saucers or jugs in restaurants, for public health reasons. After a reaction of widespread outrage and incredulity across Europe, the Commission President killed off the proposal.

The dispute that emerged in June 2012 over the European Commission's plans to implement reform of data protection laws is an interesting example of the frustrations that European businesses endure. Across the EU, businesses were up in arms about the increased costs they would have to bear if the measure went through. What was so infuriating – and this was just the latest example – was the sense that those who had designed the measure in Brussels were completely out of touch with the real world and were oblivious of the consequences that might flow from the proposed measure.

Irrelevant agendas

The above complaints, frequently heard from eurosceptics, are serious, but not serious enough to make a real difference to economic performance. Yet there is something essentially political that does: the prevailing ethos of the EU pushes it towards interventionism. In the interests of closeness (as in 'ever closer union'), the EU establishment has been keen to harmonize arrangements and outcomes across a broad swathe of economic and social affairs. Given that the countries of the EU come to this association with substantial differences in histories, structures, circumstances, tastes and preferences, the urge to harmonize naturally implies intervention and the suppression of national differences.

I will discuss the economic implications of this in the next chapter, but it is important to note that this leads the EU into obsessing about various sorts of trivia, while being unable or unwilling to make a meaningful difference to the substantive matters that its citizens care about. The energies and attentions of the European governing elites, which should have been devoted to laying the real foundations for economic growth in the same way as happened in the Asian Tiger economies, were instead diverted onto whatever the pet integrationist scheme was at the time.

To be fair, sometimes the European elites have

recognized the need to focus on the real factors underpinning economic success. However, they have never been able to bring the same energy and drive to implementing effective economic measures as they have to the various political projects.

The alienation of voters

One serious problem with the idea of a fully integrated EU is that this notion is increasingly out of touch with what people want. Of course, most major established political parties are europhile, but this is no longer the whole story. We all know that euroscepticism proved to be so strong in the UK that it prompted the British electorate to vote for Brexit. But there are now major eurosceptic parties in the Netherlands, Italy, Austria, Greece, Finland, France – and Germany. In some cases their scepticism extends to the euro only, while they continue to support the EU. In other cases, EU membership itself, as well as the euro, is in question.

Naturally, the emergence of these political parties has been both cause and effect of a shift in public opinion. As the euro elite has moved forward to ever closer union, by and large European electorates have been moving in favour of ever looser union – or no union at all. As I document below, this is a massive change from earlier decades, when the EU commanded widespread support and even, in some cases, enthusiasm. This loss of popular support is relevant for two main reasons:

♦ It shows how, either because the EU has changed, or because its citizens have, or both, the EU no longer corresponds to what its citizens broadly want. In a democracy, that ought to give cause for concern.

♦ The lack of popular support for the more integrated, more intrusive EU makes it difficult to function and highlights the danger of creating an alienated citizenry if the EU proceeds to full political union.

Elections provide a measure of voter attitudes. In the latest EU parliamentary elections, average voter turnout across the EU was 43%, down from 62% in 1979. In the UK in 2009, the turnout was less than 35%. In the last two EU parliamentary elections, the turnout in Slovakia was below 20%.

Another way to measure the general support for EU membership is to use the Eurobarometer, a European Commission survey that examines public opinion in the member states. The survey taken in April 2017 showed support for the EU only slightly above the 50% mark in France and Portugal and well below it in Greece, Italy and Austria.

German and French opinion

While there have been some significant differences in popular opinion in different EU member states, in most countries the degree of support has declined markedly over the years. Given that France and Germany are the two main drivers of the European project, how public opinion towards the EU develops in these countries is critical to the future of the Union. And in both countries opinion has shifted substantially.

The German policy and business elites always have been, and still are, fully aware of the apparent benefits that the EU has brought to their country: new markets for German exports, the ability to act on the world stage and friendly neighbours. Nonetheless, they are increasingly detached from the case for more European integration. Among politicians, the traditional cross-party consensus for more integration is fragmenting. The federalists complain that whenever they want to push for more integration, other EU members are against them.

German public opinion has also shifted significantly. During the Cold War, the German public saw membership of the EU as a barrier to the Soviet threat and a way of integrating into the western world. The majority still believe that membership of the EU is a good thing. However, an increasing number now believe that greater EU integration was a sacrifice made for the benefit of other EU members. During the euro crisis, increasing euroscepticism has been propelled by bitter anti-EU and anti-euro campaigns in the German mass media, something that has never been present before. And now there is a eurosceptic party, AFD, to reflect and stir up anxieties.

Meanwhile, France has been becoming steadily more eurosceptic. The 1992 referendum on the Maastricht Treaty was a turning point. The far right and left political parties opposed the Treaty altogether. In the end, it was voted through with only 51% support. The French public had another shock in store for their leaders when they rejected the European Constitution in a referendum in 2005. Their priorities were focused on national interests, with clear limits to support for the European integration project. Although the eurosceptic Marine Le Pen lost the 2017 French Presidential election, she won more than a third of the votes cast.

Interestingly, French cooling towards European institutions and the objective of further integration is, on the whole, for opposite reasons to the ones that prevail in the rest of northern Europe, especially the UK. Many French voters opposed the draft European Constitution because it was seen as too liberal and insufficiently protectionist!

So it looks as though a split is opening up between the EU's two driving powers, France and Germany. It is not only that French views have changed; they have started to look less like the prevailing attitudes in Germany and more like those in Spain, Italy and Greece. What is more, as I argue in Chapter 4, the French economy is moving in the same direction.

Right from the start there was something profoundly odd about a system in which one country (Germany) punched well below its weight and paid a disproportionate amount of the bills and another (France) punched well above its weight, because of the events that besmirched the European continent some decades ago. Most importantly, there has been an overarching contradiction at the heart of the EU between a country that, partly because of its history, is prepared to subdue its own national identity into a new Europeanism and another that, partly because of its own weakness but also because of its history, wants to cling on to its identity as a proud nation state.

Changes in Italy

Italy, politicians and people alike, has traditionally been among the strongest supporters of the European Union. Alcide De Gasperi, the founder of the Christian Democrats, said that Italy was 'ready to transfer wide powers to a European Community, provided that it is democratically organized and gives guarantees of life and development'.

Support for deeper European integration underlay the political agenda of all subsequent governments. Even the Italian Communist Party took a pro-European stance in the mid-1960s. In the past, the Italian public has frequently viewed the EU as a provider of democracy and stability, attributes that Italians usually associate with other countries.

The centre-left governments led by Romano Prodi, the former President of the European Commission, have openly supported all major aspects of European integration. By contrast, although the centre-right governments led by Silvio Berlusconi supported EU membership, they also voiced criticism about issues such as immigration and new climate change rules. In April 2013, the Italian government launched an unprecedented critique of the EU, going so far as to question Italy's EU membership. This followed the refusal by the European Commission to grant temporary protection for migrants from North Africa. Berlusconi was direct: 'Either Europe is something concrete, or it would be best to part ways.'

Among the Italian public, support for the EU has fallen since the early 1990s and especially over the last decade. The present EU, with new and less prosperous member states, is no longer seen as a prerequisite for democracy. More recently, the pressure put on Italy by Germany and other northern countries to reform and enact austerity measures has led to growing resentment and scepticism towards both the euro and the EU. Indeed, all three of Italy's main opposition parties are against the euro.

Growing unpopularity in other countries

Among the smaller EU members there have also been significant shifts of opinion compared to when countries first joined. The Netherlands has traditionally been among the most enthusiastic of EU members, but there were always limits to how far people wanted integration to go. The broad political consensus for deeper European integration began to fall apart in the 1990s. Successive governments stated that the Netherlands was contributing too much to the EU budget. The rejection of the European

Constitution in a referendum in 2005 highlighted the shift in people's attitudes towards EU integration. While the majority of the government supported the Constitution, 61.6% of people voted against its adoption. What is more, in June 2013, the Dutch government released a list of 54 powers that it wanted to remain at the national rather than European level. This was the most significant step in the country's recent political shift towards a more sceptical stance on European integration.

By contrast, Belgium has always been more inherently europhile. Mark Eyskens, who served as Prime Minister in 1981 and as Foreign Minister during the years leading up to the signing of the Maastricht Treaty, summed up the prevailing Belgian mood as 'Europe is like a fatherland to be loved'. The vast majority of Belgian voters continue to favour their country's membership of the EU and the euro.

In Spain and Portugal, however, popular opinion towards membership of the European Union has been changing radically. The outbreak of the global economic crisis, the collapse of the housing bubble, the deep recession, rising unemployment and the austerity measures have all soured people's mood, with the EU frequently being blamed. Since 2007, Spanish approval of the EU has almost halved, and in Portugal public support for the EU is among the lowest in the EU, together with the UK and Greece.

In Finland, the eurosceptic True Finns party became the largest party in parliament after the 2015 election and took part in a coalition government. In Sweden and Denmark, euroscepticism has focused on the euro and the common foreign policy, both of which have been opposed by the vast majority of the population since the beginning of the crisis. In Denmark, a poll by Ramboell/Analyse Denmark, released on 25 January 2013, showed that 47.2% of voters

surveyed favoured a review of Denmark's relationship with
the EU.

During the early 1990s, across the former eastern Europe
both politicians and the public displayed a marked willingness to join the European Union. Indeed, many people were
ecstatic about EU membership. But the outbreak of the recent
economic crisis led to large shifts in public attitudes. The
majority of citizens in these countries still favour the EU,
partly perhaps because of the large sums received from the
EU budget. Nonetheless, support for the EU, and especially
the euro, has still diminished significantly.

The Swiss exception

Perhaps the most significant development with regard to
public opinion has occurred in a country that is not even a
member of the EU: Switzerland. Despite its non-membership,
Switzerland has enjoyed a very close relationship with the
EU, while retaining some national freedoms. Many Swiss
people, including a good number of business leaders, hoped
that Switzerland would proceed to full EU membership in
due course. Equally, many eurosceptics, including in Britain,
hoped that the Swiss arrangements would provide a model
for a new sort of relationship for countries, like the UK, that
might decide to leave the EU.

Yet in a referendum in February 2014, the Swiss people
voted to restrict immigration into Switzerland, including
from the EU, thereby violating the country's treaty with
Brussels. This cannot be reconciled with the EU as currently
constituted. Either the EU will have to change and reform
on the issue of the free movement of labour, or Switzerland
is going to move further away from the EU. What is particularly significant is that Swiss voters have expressed a view
that is shared pretty much throughout the EU.

A changed world

So what should we make of these shifts in opinion? What we now call the EU, together with the associated process of further integration, has always been a project conceived at the top of European society. It has been the idea of the European elites. Nevertheless, for most of its existence, across nearly all member countries, it has enjoyed a considerable measure of popular support. But not any more. A dangerous divide has opened up between the governing elites and the governed. European history teaches us to be extremely wary of such developments.

Of course, one could assume that popular disillusion with the EU is based on a misapprehension of the situation and of people's own interests. Nevertheless, that would not be a wise, or a well-justified, assumption. The truth is that when Monnet and Schuman were dreaming their dreams – and putting some of them into action – the world was a very different place. Most important of all, the memory of the Second World War loomed large over everything people thought and did. By contrast, in 2017, it is 72 years since the end of the war. It is remarkable that we are still trying to escape from its shadow.

Yet it was in that shadow that the shape of the EU was cast. Most importantly, after the war Germany was a divided country, with scant hope for reunification. In addition, the Soviet Union dominated European security concerns. The Cold War raged and people lived with the ever-present fear of nuclear annihilation.

At this point, as coming economic and political powers, China and India were nowhere to be seen on the radar, both still mired in poverty. Although Japan had already begun its rise to global success, no other significant Asian countries were following.

From a technological point of view, travel by aircraft was possible, but it was far from being a frequent occurrence for most people. Similarly, there were telephones and televisions, but not many people had them. Most importantly, there were no computers; or, more accurately, none available to ordinary people. And, of course, that meant no internet and no email. Forget the emerging markets or globalization – no one had even heard the expressions. Compared to today's world reality, this was more like the Dark Ages.

Over subsequent decades, during which the world was changing, the EU was also changing – but not in a way that made it more congruent with the changing reality outside. Its membership, of course, greatly increased and became more diverse. Moreover, its pretensions to statehood became more and more obvious and, except in Germany and a few other countries, were widely resented.

At the same time, some of the diverse fears that bolstered initial support for the EU faded: fear of another European war, fear of the Soviet Union, fear of dictatorship. These have largely been supplanted by new ones: fear of recession and unemployment, fear of immigration, fear of crime and disorder, fear of social breakdown and, most importantly, fear of the impotence of government in the face of these threats.

In 2014, the Russian seizure of the Crimea and the apparent attempts to destabilize eastern Ukraine, with a view to absorbing it into Russia, briefly raised a flicker of interest in the EU as the saviour and guarantor of European security.

Nevertheless, this did not last long. It was widely believed that the EU had partially caused, or at least facilitated, President Putin's aggression by cuddling up to Ukraine and dangling the prospect of EU (and possibly, by extension, NATO) membership in front of a country that could legitimately be regarded as part of Russia's 'sphere of influence'. Moreover, it quickly became clear that in relation to the idea of confronting Russia, the leading states of the EU were seriously divided. In particular, with its heavy energy dependence on Russia and its strong trade ties, Germany was decidedly unenthusiastic about taking a tough line.

So even in 2014, when push came to shove, with regard to their security the countries of Europe looked not to the EU, but to NATO. In other words, they were still militarily dependent on America.

The Great Recession and the crisis of the euro obviously increased the disaffection with European elites, but these are not to be regarded as accidents completely outside the responsibility of political leaders. After all, their actions and inactions laid the groundwork for the Great Recession in Europe as well as America; as for the euro, that was completely their doing.

So it is not inappropriate or unfair that European politicians and policies are widely believed to be responsible for the mess that so many Europeans feel they are now in. In this respect, the EU itself is widely regarded as either the source of much of the problem or, even if it is not, as too incompetent or distracted to do anything about it. There is much to be said for both conclusions. The result is that the EU's citizens are increasingly disillusioned and dissatisfied with an institution that, despite its failings, continues to get larger and more intrusive.

From politics to economics

You might readily believe that whatever its political shortcomings, the EU justifies its existence by delivering superior economic performance. That is the subject of the next chapter, so I will not steal its thunder here. Nevertheless, I must say this. However much you, the reader, are surprised by what you glean there about the EU's economic record, you should be ever mindful of the roots of this economic performance – in the politics of the European Union, its institutions and its prevailing ethos, derived from its foundation in the 1950s, in the shadow of a terrible conflict just concluded, and in the foreshadow of a new and more terrible one that might soon commence.

Part II

The Economics of the EU

3

Has the EU Been an Economic Success?

Above all it is important to point out that we can only maintain our prosperity in Europe if we belong to the most innovative regions in the world.
　　　　　　　—Angela Merkel, German Chancellor,
　　　　　　　to the *Financial Times*, July 2005

The EU may have been established primarily for political rather than economic reasons, yet even so, much of its early development was focused on economic integration. Moreover, both for its own citizens and for those abroad, how it performed economically was a prime arbiter of whether or not it was judged to be successful; and it still is. So it is about time that we took stock of whether the EU has been an economic success.

The image of success

To the casual observer, it may seem obvious that the EU has been successful. After all, it is the world's largest economy and trading bloc. It accounts for almost 30% of global output, 15% of trade in goods and about 24% of overall global trade.

What is more, its people are prosperous, with standards of living that their parents and grandparents could only dream about. On the face of it, the average European citizen has all the trappings of material success – as well as generous social benefits and ample leisure to boot.

In fact, this does not prove very much. Size alone is not decisive; after all, the Soviet Union was big. It is on income per capita that the issue turns. On that score, the EU's record is not outstanding. Most countries in the world, including those in Europe that do not belong to the EU, enjoy living standards much higher today than those of 30 or 40 years ago, not to mention umpteen stars of the economic firmament, spread around the world, whose citizens have seen their lives not so much improved as transformed.

Perhaps the very least we can say is that the EU has not been an outright failure. Whatever it has done and not done, it has not produced the sort of abject poverty that exists in parts of Africa today. Nor have its citizens suffered the enforced squeeze of living standards that exists in North Korea, side by side with a prosperous South, nor the juxtaposition of material degradation and advanced science that one can witness in Cuba.

Nevertheless, that is not saying a great deal either. The issue is how much of the success of EU members, and how much of their failure, is down to the EU itself. We will never be able to be sure of the answer, because we lack what economists call the 'counterfactual'; that is, we do not know what would have happened in the absence of the EU. The best we can do here is to look at the performance of EU members compared to non–members and speculate about how the EU's actions and inactions may have contributed to this result.

In what follows, I start by noting the EU's early success and then move on to its more disappointing recent performance. I then briefly review some excuses for the EU's economic failure, including the idea that it is the policies of national governments, rather than the EU, that are responsible. (I do not discuss the euro as a cause of Europe's woes, since that has a whole chapter devoted to it, straight after this one.)

The core of the current chapter concerns the key areas in which the EU has a major bearing on economic performance. It tries to identify where the EU has gone wrong, including analysing the central idea that the Union should bring benefits to its members as a result of its sheer size. The chapter concludes with a discussion of the importance of competition between governments – which is, of course, the polar opposite of what is achieved through harmonization and integration.

Early success

Early on, the EU certainly showed plenty of signs of success. The first couple of decades of the Community's existence were characterized by very strong economic growth. From 1957 to 1973 (when the UK joined the Community), Germany grew at an average annual rate of 4.7%, France by 5.2%, the Netherlands by 4.6% and Italy by 5.3%. The six countries that formed the European Community in 1957 – that is, the above four plus Belgium and Luxembourg – grew at an annual average rate of 4.9%. By comparison, over the same period the UK grew at an average annual rate of only 2.8%.

Although 2.8% was extremely high by British standards, the fact that the UK was losing ground to the continent was one of the driving forces behind the case for British membership. Implicitly, the British establishment accepted the idea that there were major advantages in being members of a large bloc – or at least this bloc. And they feared that outside it, Britain would be left behind.

In fact, this strong growth among the Six did not establish very much about the benefits of being in the Community. All of these countries were enjoying rapid growth as they made good the effects of war destruction. Several of them also benefited from the one-off surge in productivity that occurs when large numbers of people leave the land and gain employment in cities.

By contrast, the UK had not been that badly damaged in the war, its agriculture was relatively small and efficient and – as countless studies have documented over the years – there were many factors making for relative economic decline that had nothing to do with Britain's exclusion from the Community.

The reasons for the UK's slow growth revolved around the more fundamental, and inherently very tricky, issues of excessive trade union power, weak management, under-investment and poor economic structure. When the UK finally addressed these problems under Prime Minister Thatcher, its relative growth performance improved, not because it was by this stage inside the EU, but rather because it had finally got to grips with many of the real factors that had held the country back.

Indeed, just to prove the point that it was not membership of the then EEC that made all the difference, other countries outside the Community were also growing nicely over the period leading up to the UK's accession (1957–73). Switzerland and Sweden grew at an average annual rate of 4.3%, the United States by 3.8%, Norway by 4.1%, Australia by 4.8% and Canada by 4.6%.

The simple fact is that the main reason for the rapid growth of Community members was not their membership. However, it was typical of some of Thatcher's predecessors, and of some of the languid, often incompetent British establishment, that they thought the solution to the nation's problems was to join a club.

Recent slowdown

By contrast with early apparent success, over the last couple of decades the growth of most EU members has been disappointing. Not only has the growth rate fallen back in comparison to their own past histories, but economic growth has also been low relative to the US and even low relative to their fellow EU member the UK, never mind the rapidly growing countries of Asia. (Some EU members have done well, though: Sweden is a notable example.)

Between 1980 (Thatcher's first full year in power) and 2007 (just before the financial crash), the average annual growth rate was 2.2% for France, 1.9% for Germany, 2.6% for the Netherlands and 1.8% for Italy. These figures compare with 2.5% for the UK and 3% for the US.

If the period is extended to 2016 to include the full impact of the Great Recession (which affected the UK particularly badly) and the subsequent recovery, the UK's lead over the EU average is still there. Over the period, the EU Six, the original signatories to the Treaty of Rome, grew at an annual average of 1.6%, compared with 2.1% for the UK. And by the middle of 2017, although the US, UK and most of Europe were recovering, some members of the eurozone were struggling to emerge from recession. Admittedly, headline growth numbers have to be adjusted for changes in the number of people and the number of hours they work, adjustments that have the effect of making the EU look better compared to the US, but they do not close the gap entirely.

Until very recently, the rest of the EU has been losing ground to the UK and the US. Moreover, as I shall detail in a moment, quite apart from weak economic growth, the EU has become one of the world's unemployment hotspots; hardly the hallmark of an economic success story.

At least by the middle of 2017, there had been some sort of economic recovery across Europe, including the eurozone, and on some indicators it seemed as though the peripheral countries were making some much-needed adjustments, prompting many observers to believe that the crisis of the euro was over. However, this is only the superficial picture. In the peripheral countries unemployment remains appallingly high and GDP is flat or falling. Since these countries are continuing to run government budget deficits, this means that the all-important debt-to-GDP ratio is still rising. The eurozone crisis is not dead, but merely sleeping. (I take up this subject in more detail in Chapter 4.)

Moreover, the fundamental economic problems besetting Europe remain as serious as ever. Even the German Chancellor, Angela Merkel, recognizes their seriousness. In an interview with the *Financial Times* on 11 December 2012 she said:

> *If Europe today accounts for just over 7 per cent of the world's population, produces around 25 per cent of global GDP and has to finance 50 per cent of global social spending, then it's obvious that it will have to work very hard to maintain its prosperity and way of life.*

Admittedly, the EU is by far the world's most popular destination for Foreign Direct Investment (FDI). Over the past decade, though, the share of global FDI going to the EU (including intra-EU investments) has declined substantially from 46% in 2005 to 33% in 2016, as the share going to emerging markets has risen. Interestingly, two European countries that are not members of the EU, namely Norway and Switzerland, have been just as successful at attracting FDI as most EU members and much more successful than some, such as Italy.

Excuses for economic failure

So much for the facts of relative economic performance. What about the reasons? One excuse for comparatively poor

economic performance is the idea that the countries of the
EU, or at least many of them, are caught in the equivalent
of the so-called middle income trap. Many countries in Latin
America are experiencing a growth slowdown and they are
not the only ones. All of the BRICs (Brazil, Russia, India and
China) have recently experienced decidedly slower growth.
Yet this is wholly inadequate as an excuse for disappointing
growth in the EU. For a start, EU growth has not slowed
down recently but has been poor for a good while. Moreover,
when the countries of the EU began to struggle, they were
not in a 'middle income' position.

Indeed, sometimes poor European performance is put
down to the rather different idea that Europe's standard
of living is so high that further advances from this level
are not easy to achieve and/or are not avidly desired by
the people. In my view this does not stack up either. Living
standards are as high as, or higher than, the EU average in
Switzerland and Norway and yet GDP there is still increasing
at faster rates than in the EU. Singapore has a level of GDP
per head that is higher than in the UK, France and Germany,
yet over the last four years its economy has still grown by
about 3% per annum, well above the average – or even
the best – EU rate.

The argument is also sometimes put forward that it is
inappropriate to judge the EU by its economic performance
because, from the start, European integration has been an
overtly political project, designed to achieve peace and
stability in Europe. What is more, in that respect it can be
regarded as a success.

In Chapter 1, I have already given due weight to the
political origins of the EU and to the strength of the political forces holding it together. However, this does not mean
that economic performance does not matter. To believe that
would be to let the leaders of the EU off much too lightly.

Although the original driving force behind the foundation of the EU was political, it was always envisaged that there would be economic advantages too. That was the whole point about market size and the reduction of trade barriers.

There was also a belief that central EU authorities would be bound to make better decisions for Europe as a whole than would competing nation states. The prevailing ethos was that competition between nation states, or at least European nation states, was wasteful.

There was never a time at which the leaders of Europe said to the European people: 'This is a political project that is necessary to preserve peace in Europe, but it will cost you a great deal of money.' On the contrary, they trumpeted the idea of economic advantage – which was easy to sell in the early years because economic growth was so strong.

And that was the whole point about being able to stand tall on the world stage, able to look America in the eye. This would not be possible simply by cobbling together a group of European states. No, the idea was that European integration would make Europe more prosperous and hence able to face America as an equal.

Only in recent years has the idea that there was a price to be paid for European unity come to be widely argued and partly accepted. That case has been argued specifically in relation to the euro, especially in Germany. The idea has been advanced by the elite that preserving the euro may cost money – particularly if you are German – but that the euro is necessary for the survival of the EU itself. Yet that idea was not present before the foundation of the euro, or even in the euro's early years. It has emerged only during the euro crisis of the last few years.

Poor EU economic performance is not the result of a rational choice made by rich, well-provided-for Europeans who have a different set of values from mere material advancement, including the funding of inefficient EU institutions for political reasons. Nor is it the well–anticipated price to be paid for integration and security. It is, quite simply, the result of relative economic failure, brought on by bad policies.

Still, there is massive resistance to acknowledging this, not least among the European elites. It is often argued, for instance, that if laws governing employee protection and macro policies including quantitative easing (QE) are the keys to success, then it is puzzling why the UK has only recently started to recover and why its performance after the crisis of 2008 was so poor. This view puts the cart before the horse. No one is suggesting that UK economic policy has been a paragon of virtue. Indeed, the weaknesses of the UK economy are substantial, particularly regarding the poor level of education and skills attainment. By contrast, in much of continental Europe these aspects of economic policy are more robustly addressed by public policy.

But these aspects of economic performance are deep-seated and difficult to shift. If they cannot be easily shifted, then a critical issue surrounds how economic policy is conducted despite these shortcomings. The point is that in spite of its supply-side inadequacies, the UK has been able to put in a decent macro performance. That is largely due to policy. By contrast, in spite of substantial initial endowments of human and physical capital, the macro performance of much of continental Europe has been disappointing, mainly because of bad policy.

Not everything is down to the EU

Can some of this relative economic failure be explained by factors other than the EU? Yes. In many EU member countries, the factors holding back investment and inhibiting employment and productivity stem from national, rather than EU, legislation. As a consequence, the EU is often wrongly, and unfairly, blamed for economic failures that are national in origin.

This can be seen in the very different levels of unemployment in different EU member countries. In 2016, the Netherlands had an unemployment rate of 6% and Germany 4.2%, while the rate in France was 10%, that in Greece was 23.5% and that in Spain 19%. Yet all these countries are subject to the same EU laws and regulations. Admittedly, some of the high unemployment in Spain and Greece is due to a lack of price competitiveness associated with membership of the euro; more on that in the next chapter. Nevertheless, a good deal of it is down to structural factors and different national laws and practices.

Indeed, the differences between various EU members with regard to labour market regulation are startling. The OECD compiles Employment Protection Indicators that attempt to measure how easy (and expensive) it is to dismiss individuals or groups of workers and the procedures involved in hiring workers on fixed-term or temporary work agency contracts. The higher the reading, the greater the difficulties and costs involved. In 2015, for the key indicator covering individual dismissals, the outcomes varied from 3.0 for Portugal down to 1.2 for the UK, with all other EU members scattered in between.

Similarly, the extent of social security spending (including out-of-work benefits) varies enormously across states. The average for the EU 28 is just under 30% of GDP, but that varies between 18% for new member states such as Bulgaria, Latvia and Romania to over 33% for France and Denmark.

So whatever ails European economic performance is not all down to the EU. Much of it is self-inflicted by national governments. Yet some of what holds EU member countries back does derive from the EU, both directly and indirectly.

The indirect role of the EU has been to lull national elites into a false sense of security, making them think that however badly they run their economies, other EU member countries would be running theirs similarly and that in any case, in some sense 'Europe' would bail them out. In practice, poor decisions at the level of individual nation states have been compounded by more poor decisions in Brussels and Strasbourg.

There are five main areas in which the EU has directly impinged on economic performance: trade; the movement of capital and people; labour law; competition; and the raising and spending of considerable amounts of money. Insofar as the EU has not been a great economic success, presumably it is because in these five spheres of competence it has not done a good job and/or because whatever benefits have accrued have been overwhelmed by other factors. As I hope you will see after I have examined each of these factors in turn, both answers are part of the story.

Trade

The most important of the EU's direct economic contributions concerns trade. Various EU treaties lay down requirements that member countries abstain from imposing tariffs or other trade restrictions on other member countries. More than that, external trade with non-member countries is governed at the EU level. The EU imposes a common external tariff on imports from the rest of the world. In 2014, the simple average tariff rate was 6.4%, but the range was huge. Dairy products, for instance, suffered a 36.1% average tariff, whereas imports of metals and non-electric machinery were subject to an average tariff of 1.9%.[8]

To the extent that the EU increases trade, this can be

supposed to bring economic benefit through all the usual channels. Trade increases efficiency by fostering a better allocation of resources and, by encouraging specialization, it opens up gains through increased economies of scale (that is, the tendency for average unit costs to fall as the number of units produced increases).

Yet the promotion of trade within the EU is not an unalloyed blessing. The EU is not merely a free trade area, one within which there are no tariffs, quotas or other restrictions on trade. Rather, the EU is a customs union, an area within which there is internal free trade but which imposes common restrictions on trade with countries outside the union (the common external tariff).

The economics of customs unions are well established and the early debates about British membership featured some of the conclusions. Essentially, customs unions create trade within the union, but they also divert trade from countries outside the union. A priori, it is impossible to tell which is greater, the gains from trade creation or the losses from trade diversion.

The evidence on trade creation within the European Union is mixed. Various academic studies suggest that trade creation has more than offset trade diversion.[9] Nevertheless, the record shows that although trade between EU member countries has greatly increased over the years, this increase has been exceeded by the growth of trade with non-EU members. Consequently, as a share of total exports, EU member countries' exports to other EU members fell from 68% in 2002 to 64% in 2016.

The reason is that the gains from trade creation within the EU have been comparatively minor beside the massive gains occurring from the growth of trade made possible across the world as a whole, first by the GATT agreements on liberalizing trade and later by the process of globalization as China and other emerging markets rapidly developed and enjoyed high rates of GDP growth.

The key point is that the benefits dreamed up by a group of European bureaucrats for members of a European customs union were overwhelmed by the reality of economic benefits arising naturally on a world scale once the huge, formerly backward and isolated parts of the world were linked into the global market economy.

Capital and people

Similar benefits from EU membership are supposed to derive from the free movement of capital within the EU's borders: a potentially better allocation of resources and enhanced competition. There have been some gains of this sort, as borrowers have been able to draw on a larger pool of capital and investing institutions have had uninhibited choice about where to invest their money.

However, the benefits unleashed by the free movement of capital have probably also been overdone. Insofar as there have been such benefits inside the EU, it must be recognized that capital mobility is occurring simultaneously on a global scale. Being able to reallocate capital across several over-regulated, slow-growing countries, held back by an anti-business culture, is not exactly a game changer compared to investing in only one of these countries.

The free movement of people is a different story. Clearly, this has had a huge effect on some EU members. The UK, for one, has experienced substantial net immigration from eastern Europe. Has this been a good thing? This is a tricky area and there are evidently some significant losers from the process, not least the indigenous workers who now find themselves in keener competition with immigrant labour. (I take up this subject in more detail in Chapter 9.)

Moreover, with some eastern European countries now denuded of much of their local labour force, does the fact that these people are now to be found in the West really represent 'an improved allocation of resources'?

Admittedly, the benefits of the free movement of goods, services, people and capital, in addition to the attractions of being inside the tariff wall, may help to attract FDI into the EU. Nevertheless, as I pointed out earlier, in this regard the EU is less than an overwhelming success.

Labour law

If one of the benefits of the EU is intended to be the freedom of people to move across the Union, other benefits are supposed to flow from its imposition of *restrictions* on freedom in the labour market. Although, as I pointed out above, there are substantial differences between different member countries' labour laws, the EU does impose some Union-wide restrictions. The spheres that it covers comprise gender equality; working time; the Social Charter, which provides guidelines on working conditions and intervention in favour of groups such as minorities and women; and atypical employment contracts, such as contracts affecting part-time, agency and temporary work.

With regard to this area of EU economic competence, how you view the EU's interventions will depend greatly on who you are. Doubtless, plenty of people think they have been helped by the EU's actions. However, speaking as an economist who believes in markets (while acknowledging that not all economists do), I think that the EU's interventions in the labour market have been a disaster. The Commission has implemented a series of regulations that make it more expensive to employ people, more difficult to use them flexibly while they are employed and more expensive to sack them when they perform badly.

The Working Time Directive (WTD) is one of the most debated of EU regulations. It lays down maximum daily and weekly working time (an average of 48 hours per week over a span of 4 months), minimum daily rest, minimum breaks during the working day, minimum paid annual leave and extra protection for night workers.

Employer federations in the UK and the Nordic countries have strongly criticized the WTD. The think tank Open Europe has estimated that EU social policy costs British business and government about £8.6 billion (0.5% of GDP) a year, with WTD being the 'most expensive' of EU social laws. (Having said that, it is open to individual workers to opt out of the WTD, which virtually all City workers and UK doctors now do.)

The Agency Workers Directive, which came into force in October 2011, is also widely criticized. It lays down that temporary staff are entitled to the same salaries, holiday pay and overtime pay as their full-time equivalents. This change has significantly reduced the flexibility of the labour market and, in particular, has placed an extra burden on small firms, many of which especially need flexible arrangements for temporary staff.

Admittedly, EU directives are often exceeded in their anti-business bias by national labour regulations. Moreover, the major variation in unemployment rates and general economic progress across the EU is clear evidence that this is not a problem that can be put down to the EU alone. Still, that is not to excuse the EU dimension.

Furthermore, companies operating in the EU know that its tendency to over-regulate labour markets is deeply embedded and is likely to strengthen over time. So this depresses business confidence and inhibits business investment.

Competition policy

Nevertheless, not all of the EU's interventions operate against the grain of the competitive market ideal. With regard to competition policy, its interventions are designed to ensure a more competitive framework across all member countries.

The EU's involvement in competition policy only arises when trade between member states is affected, so national competition authorities deal with competition issues within member states. Where trade between member states is affected, EU competition policy comes into play across six main areas: restrictive practices; abuse of dominant market position to squeeze out competitors; mergers; market liberalization; state aid; and ensuring that EU competition law is applied equally across member states.

In this area of its activities, the EU has probably, on balance, been beneficial. The European Commission has carried out numerous investigations of anti-competitive practices in industries such as airlines, chemicals, energy and computer games. In 2015, helpfully to coincide with the run-up to the Brexit referendum – surely a coincidence? – it secured the abolition, to be fully implemented by mid-2017, of the much-hated 'roaming charges' by mobile phone companies. And the EU has been effective in blocking state aid to domestic industry. As an article published in *The Economist* on 18 February 2010 put it:

> *Over several decades the European Commission's competition directorate has evolved into perhaps the most important regulator of its kind in the world. It has been rigorous in the development of antitrust theory and an energetic enforcer of the law.*

Two key failings, however, are that the European Commission has placed too much emphasis on competitors and not enough on consumers, and that it has become too big for its boots. *The Economist* went on to say:

> *Critics, whose concerns have increased with the ferocity of the sanctions imposed, say that by acting simultaneously as investigator, prosecutor, jury and sentencing judge, the Commission is denying defendant firms the basic right to be heard by an impartial tribunal. They are right.*

Spending money

This brings us on to the fifth area of EU economic competence, the raising of a considerable amount of money from member countries and the spending of it in different proportions to national contributions. In 2015, the EU's total expenditure was about €145 billion, or roughly 1% of the EU's GDP, including spending on the Common Agricultural Policy (CAP).

In the wider scheme of things and certainly compared to the size of national budgets, this is pretty small beer. Mind you, 20 years earlier, in 1991, the budget had been only €56 billion. And the direction of travel is clear. If europhiles get what they want, the size of the EU budget will increase consistently over time.

Given the budget's comparatively small size, its contribution to economic performance must all be down to microeconomics. Insofar as the EU successfully identifies deserving causes that would not otherwise receive funding, then, provided that the raising of money does not cause substantial distortions and disincentives, this activity may boost GDP. Well, that might happen in the fairytale version, anyway.

In practice, this is an area in which the EU has been close to a disaster. With about 80% of its money spent on farming and regional aid, the Union's budget does not do much to promote economic growth. Moreover, the EU dishes out money as if it comes from another planet. Due diligence and the careful husbanding of resources are not high on its agenda, with the EU instead being a byword for poor husbandry and extravagance. The British think tank Open Europe has compiled a list of examples of wasteful spending by the EU.[10]

Admittedly, national governments are no strangers to wasteful spending. In Britain, one of the most notorious examples is the project to create fully computerized records for the NHS, which was scrapped in 2011 after it had reportedly cost £10 billion.[11]

Some of the best examples of EU extravagance concern pay and employment policies. The EU is a lavish pay-master for thousands of people who earn salaries – tax-free – plus perks and pensions beyond all comparison with what they might earn back home.

The EU is not only an especially bad spender of public money, it is also bad at accounting for what it does. Between 1994 and 2006, the auditors failed to pass the EU accounts as sound. From the 2007 EU budget until now, the accounts have been counted as 'sound', but the European Court of Auditors has never declared the EU budget free from material error; that is, with an error rate of less than 2%. In the 2015 EU budget the error rate was 3.8%, meaning that out of a budget of €145 billion, over €5 billion was in question.

The gains from specialization

Thus, in the five areas of intervention and competence directly related to economic performance, the EU's record has been less than stellar. Yet one of the key economic ideas behind the integrationist theme was that the sheer size of the EU would bring benefits. Some of these ideas were related to trade, which I discussed above, but there were also other supposed benefits. What has happened to them? Have the gains simply been so small that they have been overwhelmed by the negative influences described under the five headings above? Or was there something wrong with the original analysis? Doesn't size matter?

The answer is that it all depends. One of the oldest precepts in economics is the importance of scale. In the eighteenth century, Adam Smith emphasized the division of labour as the source of prosperity. The more specialized production was, the more producers would gain expertise. He also argued that the extent of the division of labour was limited by the size of the market. Accordingly, international trade was a huge driver of increased prosperity because it permitted increased specialization.

It is easy to understand this in more homespun terms. At the most basic level of a one-man subsistence economy, Robinson Crusoe has to do everything himself. He has no ability to specialize at all. But once Man Friday appears, he has the ability to specialize and this capability continues to grow as more and more people appear on the scene.

If we go to the opposite extreme and imagine the whole world as a single economic unit, the capacity for specialization is enormous. However, for an economic unit as large as the world, with all its complexities, specialization and exchange do not simply happen in a vacuum. At the very least, specialization needs to be conducted across not only distances, but also language barriers and legal systems, and, above and beyond the narrow economic issues, it needs to be governed. In practice, these issues of coordination and governance appear in some shape or form as soon as human beings work together, so the economic benefits of specialization start to interact with, and perhaps conflict with, other considerations.

Part of the case for the EU is that it tears down the barriers to trade within the Union and hence promotes the benefits of specialization. Yet, as the above discussion makes clear, this is not the end of the matter. The EU also represents the suppression of national sovereignty and the assertion of a supranational authority in umpteen economic and political spheres across a wide territory, which involves a considerable amount of harmonization and regulation. We need to delve deeper to investigate why this is not necessarily optimal.

Size in theory

Governments have a natural tendency to inhibit trade and commerce, because by definition their jurisdiction extends across a certain territory. They assert themselves as entities by affirming their borders with regard to the movement of both things and people. Borders can easily become barriers.

This innate presence of authority at the borders naturally affords the opportunity to raise tax revenues at this point. From the earliest times, governments have obtained a good part of their revenues from taxes on trade; in many cases they still do.

Therefore, a system of many small sovereign states is liable to become a system of sharply divided economies, with tariffs and other trade barriers locking up economic activity within political borders and hence restricting the benefits of trade and specialization.

The removal of such barriers has on several notable occasions throughout history led to the growth of prosperity. This is what happened with the *Zollverein* (customs union) in Germany, established in 1834 under Prussian leadership. And to the American generals and officials worried about Soviet intervention or Communist revolution and concerned to get the European economy going after the Second World War, the biggest economic threat they saw lay in the patchwork of small states across Europe enforcing their own petty sovereignties at the border through the imposition of significant tariffs, quotas and other trade restrictions.

Now suppose that there is open trade between states. In that case, the gains from specialization can be enjoyed by even small political units. Of what advantage is greater size then? There is a considerable academic literature on this subject.[12] The general thrust is to see the increasing size of political entities as potentially bringing economies of scale in the provision of public goods (e.g. defence), but also greater heterogeneity and a tendency to damaging disputes (and bad policies) with regard to the distribution of costs and benefits. Just about everybody, however, recognizes the importance of open trade and economic integration in making it possible for smaller political units to operate successfully. Interestingly, this result, which is confirmed in several academic studies, runs completely counter to the off-the-cuff assumption of many commentators that globalization and economic integration automatically favour the establishment of larger political units.

So, on the face of it, the EU's tendency to transfer powers to itself from nation states operates against the prevailing trend in the rest of the world towards globalization and integration. As authors Alesina, Angeloni and Schuknecht put it in a wonderfully academic way: 'European-level institutions are involved in areas where economies of scale are far from obvious and heterogeneity of preferences among European citizens are high.' In other words, the EU is involved in too many things that it should leave to national governments.

Even so, these academic analyses concerning size do not necessarily point to the superiority of political units consisting of existing nation states, for the self-same arguments can then be advanced for at least the partial break-up of existing states into subregions or nations. Examples include the possible secession of Scotland from the United Kingdom and Catalonia from Spain.

At this point, purely abstract analysis tends to get us nowhere. Much depends on the specifics of the cases in question, on the history and the quality of government. The United Kingdom may or may not be the 'optimum' size for a unit of government according to academic criteria, but these criteria cannot be allowed to be the arbiters of political association. For a start, different assessments of the optimum size may come up with different answers and these answers may change over time. States cannot – and should not – be dissolved and reformed on the basis of such results.

More fundamentally, whether institutions and political associations work is usually the result of non-systematic factors to do with their historical development. Although there is clearly a powerful secessionist tendency in Scotland, by and large the UK and its institutions work well. By contrast, we can have no idea how well new institutions in Scotland and the remainder of the UK would function if the UK did break up. In particular, during the campaign leading up to the referendum on Scottish independence in 2014, it became clear that establishing a satisfactory currency regime for an independent Scotland would be extremely problematic, echoing many of the difficulties of the eurozone that I discuss in Chapter 4.

Subsidiarity

What point marks the best division of sovereignty? It is clearly not the individual, and not the street or local community. At some stage, probably at a point that shifts over

time in response to changing attitudes, economic realities
and technologies, borders are required to separate one polity
from another.

In reality, it is not necessary for all decisions to be taken
at one level, whether that is the nation state, a federation
of nation states, a region, or a local authority. Different sorts
of decisions are best taken at different levels: arrangements
for rubbish collection at the local level, defence at the
national or supranational level.

However, there is a host of in-between cases where the
answer is not clear. Should the structure and content of
school curricula, for instance, be left up to individual state
schools, controlled by local authorities, or laid down by
central government? The right answer will differ between
countries and over time, depending on the effectiveness of
local and national authorities and on national objectives
for educational attainment.

The EU's approach to the issue of the appropriate level
at which to take decisions is in theory very appealing. It is
governed by the principle of 'subsidiarity', the idea that a
decision should be taken as close to the citizen as possible.
Except in the areas that fall within its exclusive competence,
the principle is that the Union should not take action unless
it is more effective than action taken at the national, regional
or local level.

The trouble is that this principle is honoured more in
the breach than in the observance. This is for two good,
and related, reasons. First, there is a struggle at the heart
of the EU between those who want to establish full political
union and those who do not and who therefore wish to
preserve the powers of nation states. For the former group,
any opportunity to wrest powers from nation states tends
to be regarded as a step in the right direction. Accordingly,
the EU ends up poking its nose into matters that, on a

practical and less political analysis, would not be regarded as lying within its proper sphere of competence.

Second, the implementation of subsidiarity runs counter to the objective of harmonization and may lead to competition. Yet harmonization is deeply embedded in the objectives of the EU. Accordingly, the default position of the Union is to resist subsidiarity.

Size in practice

Is there in fact a marked tendency for large economic and political units to do well compared to small ones? The evidence is not conclusive. The chief example of the beneficial effects of size is the United States. From quite early in its history, it achieved a high level of economic success and a high standard of living. Admittedly, it had a huge territory per head of population, giving it a wealth of arable and grazing land per capita, as well as considerable endowments of minerals and oil.

Nevertheless, this is not necessarily decisive. After all, other countries have had these advantages without reaching such high standards of development. The old Soviet Union possessed them and, to a lesser extent, Russia still does. Argentina, Australia and Brazil also enjoy similar advantages. Yet the results have been mixed.

Clearly, how a territory is governed is of major importance. What is necessary for success is a government strong enough to ensure that the law is upheld and a country's wealth is not filched by minority interests, or continually fought over, bringing loss and destruction. However, it also has to be a government that does not inhibit the growth of industry and commerce by excessive taxation or interference. This, and not just the abundance of land, was the secret of America's success.

It is very striking, nevertheless, that many of the world's richest countries are small. By 'small' I mean either small in territory or number of people, or both. According to the IMF, the five countries with the highest GDP per capita in the world are Qatar, Luxembourg, Singapore, Norway and Brunei – all of which have populations of less than 6 million.

Singapore is a particularly interesting example. At independence, the view of the British government was that it should throw in its lot with the much larger Malaysian Federation – which it did. When Singapore was expelled in 1965, it must have seemed that its future was bleak. Now look at it. Never mind Malaysia, Singapore has a higher income per head than the UK. Why? The essential answer is good government – by Singapore for Singapore.

There are several examples of small-country success in the Middle East, but one might argue that their relevance to the rest of the world is limited because their success derives pretty much entirely from oil and natural gas. I refer, of course, to the Gulf states of the UAE, Bahrain, Qatar, Kuwait and Oman. Even in these cases, though, there is a case to be made that their (admittedly non–democratic) governments have managed their affairs rather well. Their oil wealth has not been squandered.

In Europe, successful small states do not have oil at their root – apart from Norway. Switzerland is the best example, but other noteworthy ones are Belgium, the Netherlands, Luxembourg, Denmark, Sweden and Finland. (These last six are, of course, members of the EU, although they were pretty successful before they joined it.)

Democracy and competition

Why might these small political units have done well? In some cases it is largely because they are established as tax havens. Accordingly, their success is distributional; that is, they are in the business of transferring income and wealth from other entities, rather than that of wealth creation. As such, they have little relevance to the question of how the division of sovereignty best promotes overall prosperity.

However, in most cases of small-country success, tax advantage is only a part of what they do and their achievements are much more widespread and broadly based. Even where success is due to them acting as tax havens, this serves the cause of jurisdictional competition. The issue is all about what makes governments behave in the best interests of their countries and their citizens.

Competition can provide a more effective restraint on governments than democracy. We are used to the idea that competition within economies brings benefits and to the associated idea that preserving competition may require intervention to ensure that no large firms dominate the market. We are also used to the idea that competition between countries brings benefits in the shape of the gains from trade. We are less used to the idea that competition between sovereignties also brings benefits, although it most assuredly can.

The gains concern good governance. Without such competition, governments can carry on with economically destructive policies for ages. Where jurisdictions are in competition, however, the benefits of different policies show up more quickly. The result is to encourage pressure for best practice.

This is closely related to the issue of size. In essence, small countries feel vulnerable and, as a result, their governments are limited in the degree of damage they can do without suffering serious consequences. By contrast, in large countries governments can maintain the trappings of success and power at the international level even if, in per capita terms, their people are seriously poor. This was true of the Soviet Union, for instance.

Europe's golden age

Interestingly, the era when Europe was strongest and most prosperous compared to the rest of the world was a period when it was divided into small states, which competed vigorously with one another. The great explorers set forth not from a united Europe, but from Spain, Portugal, England, the Netherlands, France and the various city states of Italy, including Genoa and Venice. They did so in a spirit of rivalry.

Admittedly, this rivalry sometimes found its expression in war. Revulsion against this form of competition is one of the strongest emotional arguments against the return to a Europe of competing nation states. While the fear is that competition between such entities is bound to be destructive, as it was before, this throws the baby out with the bathwater. It is possible to make institutional arrangements that prevent further European wars while maintaining rivalry in other ways – including in economic competition, just as happens already in everything from football to popular music.

So we have discovered a more fundamental reason for the EU's under-performance that goes beyond the accountants' totting up: the EU has suppressed competition between nation states. More than that, it has smothered them in a suffocating balm of harmonization and convergence. Simply to allude to this or that aspect of bad decision-making or mismanagement misses the point. These defects are systematic. They derive directly from the essential nature of the EU – which is most assuredly not the same as the essential nature of Europe.

The EU's poor economic record

Let us not get this out of perspective. The EU is not an economic disaster – yet. But in economic terms it is a considerable disappointment to many of its supporters. And, internationally, it is an under-achiever. The rapidly growing countries of Asia do not look to the EU as an example; they regard it as showing what they need to avoid.

What explains this under-performance? I have put forward eight reasons:

♦ The EU's designers put far too much importance on size alone as bringing benefits.
♦ In the process, they underestimated the growth of the world economy outside the EU.
♦ They underestimated the importance of good governance as the key to economic success.
♦ The agenda for harmonization and regulation involved too much interference in business.
♦ The European social agenda with regard to labour laws and benefits was, and was believed by firms to be, anti-business.
♦ Europe's leaders paid insufficient attention to getting the basics of economic success right – unlike so many of their equivalents in Asia.
♦ They spent the EU's (admittedly not enormous) funds badly.
♦ The very objectives of harmonization and integration hid the consequence of bad economic policies and smothered the natural rivalry between countries that could have produced better economic performance.

Arguably, these failings would not necessarily have held back the European economy if it had already embarked on a dynamic growth path in a relatively stable world. But, the world of the last 20 years has been anything but stable. Two great revolutions have shaken the modern economy to its foundations – information technology and globalization – and they required flexibility and adaptation. That is precisely what the institutions of the EU are bad at delivering, hence the EU's relative decline. It is surely because the US adapted better to these forces that partly explains why it has recently outperformed the EU.

There is something else as well. As the EU has continued in sharp relative decline, the concentrated effort of the European elites should have been directed towards the requirements to raise productivity, employment and investment. Instead, European leaders have been obsessed by further harmonization and integration, by treaty change and, of course, by that ultimate form of integration – the euro.

4

The Trouble with the Euro

When you come to a fork in the road, take it.
                                        —Yogi Berra,
                        US baseball player and philosopher

The European single currency, the euro, has become the focus of European integration – and it could yet prove to be the cause of the EU's disintegration. If this happens, it would be deeply ironic, for it was not imperative to have a single European currency and the enterprise was embarked on too early and with insufficient preparation. It was an integration too far and too soon.

It is, therefore, the best example yet of bad decision-making in the EU. But, as with so much else, the bad decision did not emerge accidentally. Rather, it derived directly from the EU's history and its essential nature. Much of what went wrong with the euro is now so well known that it is pointless to dwell on it. It is on why it went wrong, and what this tells us about the EU, that the euro saga has so much to teach us.

In what follows, I begin with the origins of the single currency and a discussion of how it ran into trouble, how it was supposed to adapt to difficulties in theory and what happened in practice. I then discuss the political lessons to emerge from the euro's travails. I conclude with an assessment of the eurozone's relative performance since 2008, including its growing trade surplus, before discussing what policies could be deployed to save the eurozone economy – and its currency.

Figure 4.1 The split between EU members using the euro and not using it in 2017

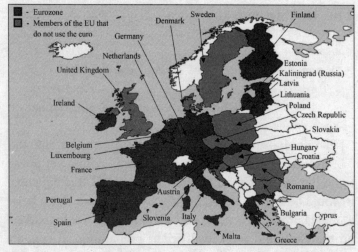

Source: www.europa.eu

The beginnings

A European single currency was debated as early as the Werner Report of 1970, which set out a three-stage process to achieve European Monetary Union (EMU) within a ten-year period. The final objective would be the irreversible convertibility of currencies, the free movement of capital and the permanent locking of exchange rates – or possibly a single currency. To achieve this, the report said there would need to be closer economic policy coordination, with interest rates and the management of reserves decided at Community level and, showing remarkable perspicacity and far-sightedness, agreed frameworks for national budgetary policies.

Subsequently, two European exchange rate schemes were implemented that built on these foundations and acted as

forerunners of the euro. The Basel Agreement of 1972 introduced the 'snake in the tunnel' and, in March 1979, a new
European Monetary System was formed using an Exchange
Rate Mechanism (ERM) to reduce fluctuations between the
currencies of member states. Neither of these currency
systems was the real McCoy, though, and the ERM, already
a shrunken creature compared to the early days, was
replaced in January 1999 when the euro came into being
in 11 member states. After 7 more countries joined it, the
eurozone comprised 18 countries, leaving 10 EU members
outside the zone. With the accession of Lithuania in 2015,
the eurozone has expanded to 19 members, leaving 9 EU
members not using the euro. (See Figure 4.1.)

The lure of monetary union

It is easy to see why the formation of a single currency
would be a key objective for those who wanted to unite
Europe. A common currency would lead to a common state.
There are examples of different states using the same
currency, but they are all cases of small countries sharing
a currency, such as some of the Caribbean islands, or of a
small country using a larger one's currency without having
any say in the issue or management of that currency;
Panama's use of the US dollar is an obvious example.
However, I cannot think of any example of major states of
roughly equal status sharing a common currency – apart
from the members of the eurozone.

The nineteenth-century Gold Standard is sometimes
quoted as a counter-example, since it united umpteen
different countries at fixed exchange rates. But it does not
really count, since the Gold Standard was not itself a
currency, or even a system for managing currencies, but
rather a regime that left countries in charge of their own

economic and financial management, albeit with little room for manoeuvre if they wanted to stay in the system. Most importantly, the Gold Standard did not remove national sovereignty, not least because it was possible to suspend it or leave it, as the UK did twice, in 1914 and again, having returned to it in 1925, in 1931.

Currencies and states are closely linked. The taxing power of the state is one of the sources of assurance that money will be worth something. Equally, when things go wrong, it is the state that can and often does pick up the tab for failing assets and banks, as recent experience in Europe and America can attest.

The danger in sharing your currency with a neighbour over which you have no control is that it will operate policies that will undermine the currency. These may cause either a spike in bond yields, a currency collapse, an upsurge of inflation or a banking crisis – or any combination of the four – with obvious costs for your economy. That surely means that, if you are going to share your currency with other countries, you will reasonably demand some sort of control over their fiscal (i.e. budgetary) and financial policies. And if one country is going to have oversight over another's fiscal policy, how can that be done without also having some form of political union that will enable joint, or at least shared, control of fiscal policy?

So when the architects of monetary union put in place the single currency without arrangements for fiscal or political union, they were in fact constructing a halfway house. It was European integration lite.

Yet this was not entirely a case of blindly stumbling towards an unsatisfactory half-answer. Many of the euro's progenitors fully understood what they were doing. When the euro was still no more than a glint in the eye, a debate raged between the so-called German and French schools.

The 'German' school argued that economic integration and full convergence should come first and then monetary union would be the coping stone that finished off the whole structure. The 'French' view was that, since political union was going to be so momentous and difficult to reach agreement on, insisting on it first would delay the whole process and perhaps even make it impossible. It would be better to start with monetary union. Admittedly, this would inevitably lead to crises, but out of these crises would come the political will to forge fiscal and political union.

As matters stand, it is too early to say which of these views was correct. While the depth of the crisis in which the single currency has been embroiled suggests that the German view was spot on, we do not yet know the final act. The euro crisis has indeed, as the French view upheld, spawned an effort to forge fiscal and political union. It may yet be successful. We shall have to wait and see.

How it happened

In economics textbooks, countries decide whether or not to form monetary unions with other countries on the basis of their economic suitability to each other. Are they subject to similar economic shocks? Where they are not, are their structures flexible enough to be able to absorb different shocks without massive dislocation and unemployment? Are countries able to live together and produce full employment without needing recourse to exchange rate changes, different interest rates or exchange controls?

A whole literature, enough to keep you busy for the best part of a lifetime, was developed by economists to answer questions such as these, culminating in the crowning glory, the Theory of Optimum Currency Areas; that is, a theory about the best (i.e. most efficient) grouping of countries to form single currency blocs. And this theoretical edifice is a pretty impressive structure, well worthy of a Nobel Prize or two.

As you may have guessed, however, this vast literature had next to no bearing on how the euro came into being or how it was structured. As things turned out, the pace of currency union was forced by events – and not even economic events at that. In November 1989 the Berlin Wall came down and just over two years later the Soviet Union disintegrated. These events made possible the reunification of Germany after nearly 50 years of separation. But not everyone saw this as an unalloyed blessing. What would Russia think? It still had nearly 400,000 troops stationed on German soil. What would France think? And what would be the UK's view?

At first, UK Prime Minister Margaret Thatcher was dead against reunification and was in close communication not only with the Soviet leader, Mikhail Gorbachev, but also with America's President, Ronald Reagan.

If reunification was going to happen, West Germany had to have the support of France, but that was not a foregone conclusion. French fears of German dominance were very real. Why make things worse, France might reasonably think, by letting Germany get bigger and stronger? After all, the French writer François Charles Mauriac had said in the 1960s that he was so fond of Germany that he was glad there were two of her. He surely spoke for many Frenchmen – and people of other nationalities.

In the event, French President François Mitterrand did agree to reunification, but he exacted a price. Germany would have to agree to submerge the deutschmark into a new European currency, subsequently to be called the euro, and in the process emasculate the Bundesbank, which had ruled the roost over the European economy for the last few decades. West Germany's Chancellor Kohl agreed to this price and so the euro was born. The greatest monetary experiment in the history of humankind happened when it did, and how it did, because it appeared to make political sense at the time.

Trouble right from the beginning

As might be expected from the difficult circumstances of its birth, right from the start the new currency was plagued by serious design failures. In order to ensure that the countries admitted to the union were capable of coexisting in a monetary union without recourse to currency changes, different levels of interest rates or the use of capital controls, certain conditions were laid down in the Maastricht Treaty of February 1992 to govern eligibility to join. These included a 'reference value' for the ratio of government debt to GDP of 60%. Countries were expected to be at or below this reference value.

A country could still be admitted even if its ratio was above this level, provided that the ratio was falling and was approaching 60% 'at a satisfactory pace'. In the event, Italy and Belgium, and later Greece, were admitted to the currency even though their debt ratios were well above the 60% level and even though they did not convincingly pass the qualifying test. The reason, of course, was political. Europe's leaders simply regarded it as unacceptable to keep them out.

No arrangements were put in place for a fiscal union, but instead there was a no-bailout clause in the Maastricht Treaty, which stated that there would be no external or Union-wide support for any national government that got into financial difficulties. This was supposedly to instil a sense of responsibility in individual fiscal authorities and a sense of caution in those in the financial markets who might lend to them.

Moreover, the countries of the currency area agreed to a Stability and Growth Pact, which laid down limits to their fiscal deficits. Unfortunately, this pact was very far from watertight, as both France and Germany proceeded to exceed the deficit limits without incurring any penalty. (Admittedly, one could argue that without the pact their fiscal slippage would have been greater.)

Both the no-bailout clause and the Stability and Growth Pact were paper tigers. So, in practice, there was no effective fiscal union to accompany the monetary union that was unleashed by the euro. There was no political union either. The nation states of the eurozone simply sailed on much as before.

Nor did the arrangements for the new currency involve any form of banking union. There were no agreements covering what to do in the event of a sovereign default or banks getting into trouble. In fact, the architects of the euro seemed to know very little financial history, since their restrictions and agreements regulating the criteria for entry to the euro referred solely to the fiscal realm; that is, the level of government deficits and debt.

As events turned out, when problematic conditions were encountered, although for some euro members this was because of fiscal profligacy (Greece being a prime example), in Spain and Ireland the fiscal numbers were in great shape until the recession caused by the financial crash of 2007–09 sent their fiscal deficits through the roof. Their problem was centred on a private-sector credit boom, closely associated with a property market bubble. Of this sort of disturbance the architects of monetary union seemingly had no inkling whatsoever. They certainly made no provision for it.

So when the good ship *Euro* set sail, she was equipped

for moderate winds and a calm sea. When she instead encountered the violent storm unleashed by the world financial crisis of 2008, she proved to be a most unseaworthy vessel.

The anatomy of trouble

The problems of operating a single currency did not emerge at once. On the contrary, the launch of the euro in 1999 was a massive technical success and, for a time, the different economies seemed to be adjusting well to it.

Mind you, this is not surprising. The case against monetary union for ill-assorted members with substantial rigidities, poor institutional structure and a susceptibility to divergence was always that problems would build up over time – and would be exposed in a crisis. So no one should have been taken in by the fact that at first, the new currency seemed to be going swimmingly. Nevertheless, they were.

Initially, in the peripheral countries that were subsequently to be in such trouble, there was a boom. People went on a spending spree. These were countries that had traditionally tended to have relatively high interest rates and now they were able to luxuriate in a rate set by the European Central Bank (ECB) that was similar to the low rates previously enjoyed by Germany under the Bundesbank. If you like, this was a combination of British-style inflationary habits and a German cost of finance. The result was an explosion of credit and economic activity in Spain and Ireland and an associated boom in the property market with regard to both prices and levels of construction. In Greece, new-found security and the absence of an exchange rate to worry about gave the government free rein to indulge in a burst of excessive expenditure. To be alive in those days was very heaven!

Significantly, German exporters who were beneficiaries of this spending, and also German workers who, by and large, did not gain much direct benefit, did not throw their money around extravagantly.

The competitiveness gap

Then reality began to strike home, not suddenly, but stealthily. In all of these peripheral countries, costs and prices continued to rise faster than in the Germanic core of the union. They had always had this tendency, but the difference was that in the past the exchange rate had been able to depreciate to offset any lost competitiveness. Now the exchange rate safety valve had been closed off. The result was a huge loss of competitiveness in the periphery that manifested itself in large and growing current account deficits (broadly speaking, an excess of imports over exports). Meanwhile, in the Germanic core, there were large and growing current account surpluses.

At the most extreme point, the current account deficits in Ireland, Spain, Portugal and Greece were 7.7%, 10.4%, 13.4% and 16% of GDP, respectively. Correspondingly, at their highest point, the surpluses for Germany and the Netherlands were 9.3% and 12.2% of GDP, respectively.

Yet the euro elite seemed to subscribe to some equivalent of Brownian economics: there would not be a crisis because the euro had put an end to boom and bust. That was just as well. For cynics of the old persuasion, including yours truly, this was an accident waiting to happen.

Let me make one thing clear, though. Having your own currency is not a panacea for all economic problems. Moreover, umpteen countries have on occasion suffered from destabilizing exchange rate changes. In addition, the peripheral members of the eurozone had much more wrong with them than simply the fact that their costs and prices were out of line. Nevertheless, having your own currency is really important in those once-in-a–generation crises when relative prices need to adjust by 20–50%. The crisis that broke upon the world in 2007–08 was one such occasion. And just when exchange rates were needed to take some of the strain, the countries within the eurozone had to face the fact that national currencies had just been abolished.

The debt problem

When the Great Recession engulfed the world immediately after the financial crisis of 2007–08, all economies were hit badly, but the impact on the eurozone's periphery was catastrophic. As is usual in recessions, governments' budget deficits soared and this, combined with falling GDP, caused debt-to-GDP ratios to rise sharply, taking them into territory that signalled a serious risk of default. Accordingly, bond yields rose to levels that were ruinous for governments to borrow at.

Predictably, the remedy offered by the politicians was an alphabet soup of support mechanisms, typically beginning with the magical letter *E*, and more of the balm that supposedly overcomes all ills, political will. In other words: don't panic, it will be all right on the night.

But it wasn't. At the worst point in 2012, it looked as though the euro was going to break up or, at the least, some of its most vulnerable members were going to leave it. Indeed, Greece came perilously close to being expelled as the other member countries, especially Germany, were completely exasperated with it. It was only the fear that a Greek expulsion would result in a financial crisis that would bring the whole eurozone down that held Angela Merkel back.

Then came a declaration in July 2012 by the ECB President, Mario Draghi, that he would do 'whatever it takes' to save the euro. In the event, this took the form of a programme to launch so-called Outright Monetary Transactions (OMTs); that is, ECB purchases of the bonds of troubled countries, potentially without limit.

This was a stroke of genius. Bond yields fell dramatically without the ECB having to buy a single bond. Nevertheless, Draghi was sailing very close to the wind. In order to keep up the pressure on governments to improve their finances and to reform their economies, he laid down that OMTs could only be deployed to buy the bonds of countries that had entered a European bailout programme. The point was that if they were in such a programme then, as a condition of the bailout, their finances would already be subject to outside control. That was designed to placate the German Bundesbank as well as other critics.

As it happens, the two largest vulnerable countries, Spain and Italy, were not in a bailout programme and their governments were unlikely to accede to one. Their government bond yields fell all the same. Even so, the German Bundesbank President objected that the ECB programme amounted to monetary financing of governments and, as such, was illegal. In effect OMTs were a remarkable confidence trick, which has paid off – so far.

Back to the 1930s

Meanwhile, without an exchange rate to take the strain, how were the peripheral countries to regain competitiveness and thus hope to restore growth to their economies while reducing their budget deficits? The orthodox European (and especially German) answer was through austerity. Afflicted countries were to cut government spending and raise taxes in order to reduce their budget deficits, much in the way that one might do in a household.

The trouble is that economies are not households. When person A cuts their spending, this reduces the income of person B, who cuts their spending, and so on and so forth. All the while, GDP will be falling and the deficit may remain the same, or even get bigger. This Keynesian criticism of austerity economics is well known: sometimes it is justified; and sometimes it is not. There have been many times when it seemed well justified for the eurozone.

There was a second flaw to the austerity solution that was more telling. The idea was that austerity would not only improve the public finances but would also restore competitiveness, since the release of resources from the public sector as a result of spending cuts, as well as the reduction in private spending brought on by increased taxes, would reduce aggregate demand and increase unemployment. In the usual way, the resulting excess supply in the economy and increased pressure to win business and keep jobs would lower costs, prices and wages, thus improving competitiveness.

This was straightforward deflation of the sort that had been tried (and found wanting) in the 1930s. This being the EU, however, if the politicians involved could not quite alter history or blot it out, they could at least give the policy a different name. They did: they called it 'internal devaluation'. But the change of name did not make the process any the less painful, or any the more effective.

This process of 'internal devaluation' would inevitably be extremely slow. Even deflation of 1% or 2% a year would be very difficult to achieve and extremely painful. Yet some of the peripheral countries had suffered a loss of competitiveness of 30% or 40%. They would be condemned to decades of deflation. The 1930s had demonstrated that this is a recipe for misery and destruction on an epic scale. And we all know what happened subsequently, partly as a result of this economic misery.

More importantly, this strategy of deflation suffered from a huge economic weakness: deflation worsens the debt ratio. It reduces nominal tax revenues and nominal incomes and hence nominal GDP, while the outstanding value of the debt remains the same.

The danger is that the experience of prices falling leads people to expect them to go on falling. As I said all those years ago in *The Death of Inflation*, if this happens, deflation has got into the most dangerous place of all; that is to say, it has entered people's minds. And, just as with inflation, once deflation is established there, it is devilishly difficult to shift. That is exactly what happened with Japan and it could easily happen in the eurozone, thereby worsening economic performance and intensifying the problems confronting the eurozone's policy-makers.

Now the eurozone has both a competitiveness and a debt problem. To the extent that it improves the former through domestic deflation, it worsens the latter. By the middle of 2017, several of the peripheral countries had reduced their competitiveness gap against Germany – although interestingly, in Italy progress had been very slow – but the debt ratios of all peripheral countries continued to climb, and unemployment rates remained obstinately high. In Spain and Greece the rate fell a little, but it was still almost 20% in the former and over 20% in the latter. The eurozone's adjustment mechanism turned out to be rather like the use of a corset by someone trying to deal with obesity. The fat is still there; it just bulges out in different places.

As it happens, the eurozone has just about escaped the deflation trap so far. By the middle of 2017, with the

economy recovering, eurozone inflation was not far off the
ECB's 2% target. So panic over, for now. But another major
economic downturn could see the return of deflation – with
serious consequences for debt ratios.

Economic loss as the price of political gain?

While I have argued that the euro has been a failure, not
everyone will agree. Some people may assert that, as with
everything else to do with the EU, the essence of the project
is political. To a large extent this is true – certainly as
regards its origins. However, this does not mean to say that
the euro had been expected to incur huge economic costs.
On the contrary, the progenitors and supporters of the euro
did not favour it simply as the route to political union. They
believed – and asserted – that it would boost economic
performance and in the process increase prosperity and
create jobs.

Writing about the prospective benefits of EMU in
the *Europe Quarterly* in 1999, the late Wim Duisenberg,
then President of the European Central Bank, said: 'The
introduction of the euro and the single monetary policy
will result in higher economic growth in the euro area,
while maintaining price stability.' He went on: 'It removes
the risk of serious exchange rate misalignments within
the euro area. This will contribute to economic growth
and help to avoid any misallocation of resources.' And
he concluded: 'The true benefits of the euro derive from
the fact that it is a unique opportunity to shape a macroeconomic environment conducive to stability, growth and
employment.'

As late as May 2008, the European Commission was still
claiming that the currency union had been 'a resounding
success. It has brought economic stability, promoted

economic and financial integration, generated trade and growth and [provided] a framework for sound and sustainable public finances.'

It is quite clear that the euro elites did not see the euro as an economic price that had to be paid to secure the political benefits of a full union across the eurozone, but rather as the route to both political and *economic* advantage. They could not have been more wrong.

Economic performance in theory

Their key argument for the euro increasing prosperity was that currency variability reduces economic efficiency. Supposedly, it inhibits trade because firms are burdened with either increased uncertainty about relative prices and costs or the extra costs incurred by dealing with it (unsatisfactorily) through some financial hedging mechanism. Also, consumers find it difficult to compare prices across different currencies. The result is a series of nationally segmented markets that, from the standpoint of the wider group as a whole, reduces efficiency.

Meanwhile, in these conditions, capital and money markets are segmented as well. The possibility of currency changes means that interest rates and bond yields are increased by having to incorporate an uncertainty premium. Moreover, the fact that these financial markets have to be separate eliminates the advantages of large size, which again raises costs and reduces efficiency.

Equally, on the side of macro management, having umpteen national currencies rather than a single one brings problems because individual countries operating on their own risk being blown off course by events in the exchange markets. Under a single currency, therefore, governments would be able to borrow more cheaply and that too would help economic performance by allowing either lower taxes, increased public spending or lower borrowing.

It is true, the euro's proponents conceded, that giving up national currencies would remove the exchange rate safety value, but they argued that the gains from this were largely illusory. For a start, far from absorbing volatility, the exchange markets created a good deal of it themselves. Even when disturbances were generated in the domestic economy, the ability of exchange rate flexibility to offset or absorb them was limited. It is extremely difficult, they argued, to get a change in the so-called *real* exchange rate by varying the nominal rate. Any attempt to adjust to a problem in the real economy by resorting to devaluation ends in tears because inflation just moves up in tandem, leaving no real advantage.

In any case, they asserted, in a properly constructed monetary union, costs and prices would not get out of line between member countries precisely because everyone would know that there was no safety valve and macro-economic policies would be aligned between members.

Performance in practice

If that was the idea of how the euro would pan out in -theory, things have worked out very differently in practice. The gains from reduced uncertainty over exchange rates and increased market size and efficiency have proved to be very small, as some of us argued all along that they would. Trade grew no faster between eurozone members than it did between members and non-members; about which more below.

Meanwhile, again in accordance with the sceptics' fears, costs and prices did continue rising much faster in the historically high-inflation countries than in the German-led core. The result was very weak performance in the peripheral countries, thus, given only moderate performance of the core countries, making for poor performance overall.

The German economy did fairly well, but was heavily reliant on exports. Germany generated little increased domestic demand itself and its propensity to save remained high. Instead, it benefited from demand created elsewhere (which I discuss in more detail below). Meanwhile, the workings of the euro, allied to political pressure, pushed the peripheral countries into austerity programmes.

So the euro has had a strong deflationary bias, with the pressures for adjustment entirely on the deficit countries. Far from bringing a jobs bonanza, it has led to appallingly high unemployment. This is precisely the criticism of the Gold Standard made by Keynes in the 1920s and 1930s. Indeed, deflationary bias was exactly the potential problem he was so keen to avoid when designing the Bretton Woods fixed but adjustable exchange rate system for the postwar world. The euro has proved to be a modern incarnation of the Gold Standard, with all of its vices and few of its virtues.

Disappointment all round

Thus, the reasons for expecting improved macro performance from the eurozone were weak and the arguments for expecting worse performance were strong. The facts tell a clear story. (Remember that the euro was formed in 1999.) During the years 1980–98, the average annual economic growth of the area that we now call the eurozone was just over 2%. Admittedly, this was below the growth rate achieved in Australia, Norway, the US, the UK and Canada, but it was about the same as Sweden and a little higher than Switzerland. Over the years

1999–2016, however, the eurozone's average growth rate slipped to about 1.3%.

Now, it is true that over this period, the economic environment was more difficult and many countries experienced much weaker growth. Nevertheless, it is the relative performance that is significant. Between 1999 and 2016, the eurozone's average growth rate was the lowest in the above-mentioned group of countries.

It is a similar story on the unemployment rate. Over the years 1980–98, eurozone unemployment was high, but it was below the rates in Canada and the UK. From 1999 to 2016, eurozone unemployment shot up to be the highest in this whole group, and by a decent margin.

One might think that despite disappointing macroeconomic performance overall, at least the eurozone countries would have enjoyed greatly increased trade with each other. It must surely be that, for whatever reason, this has not contributed enough advantage to outweigh whatever economic disadvantages the euro has brought. In fact, that is not what the data show. Since the creation of the euro, exports from eurozone economies to the non-eurozone have increased at a faster pace than exports to other members of the single currency bloc, for all member countries except Ireland.

Economic catastrophe

The acute problems of the eurozone first became crystal clear during the financial crisis of 2008. That crisis spawned what is now being referred to as the Great Recession, which saw output fall across just about every country in the developed world. By the end of 2014, however, some parts of the developed world were recovering nicely – but not the eurozone.

If we compare the performance of output from the beginning of 2008 to the end of 2016, thereby encompassing the crisis period, the recession and the subsequent recovery, the extent of the disaster in the eurozone becomes clear. From the beginning of 2008 to Q4 of 2016, the US economy grew by 13%, while the equivalent figures for the UK, Canada and the world as a whole are 8.5%, 14.4% and 21.2%. By contrast, the eurozone economy grew by only 2.5%. Within that total, Germany managed growth of 7.8% and France 4.6%. The equivalent figures for Spain, Portugal, Italy and Greece were *minus* 1.1%, 4.1%, 7.4% and 27.3%. This catastrophic fall of Greek GDP is roughly the equivalent of the drop that occurred in the US and Germany during the 1930s.

By the way, the figures for other continental European countries that are not in the EU are interesting. Over the same period, Norway and Switzerland grew by 9.4% and 10.4%, respectively. But the comparison that really lays bare the extent of the European crisis is with China. Over this period of just nine years, the Chinese economy has grown by 100%. Putting this another way, the increase in China's GDP has been roughly equal to the level of GDP in Germany and Italy. That's right: in nine years the Chinese economy has added another Germany and Italy combined.

You might readily seek comfort in the idea that this is all about Chinese exceptionalism. To some extent this is right. Comparisons with other countries are less startling – but they are still pretty shocking. Over this period, India's GDP has risen by 80%, while the equivalent figures for Hong Kong, Korea, Malaysia, Singapore and Taiwan are 22.6%, 29%, 53.4%, 41% and 22%, respectively. Something may or may not be wrong in the state of Denmark, but there is clearly something catastrophically wrong in the would-be state of Europe.

The contrast between Germany and France

For most of the euro's existence, the German economy has done reasonably well. This has not been because domestic demand has been strong, but rather because German exports have grown well.

The situation in France is intriguing. In the early years of the euro, the French economy performed more or less in tandem with Germany. Whatever variable you look at, the numbers were very similar: growth, unemployment, inflation, the public finances. Even the external accounts were similar. Germany ran a larger current account surplus, but France was in the black as well. Then from about 2006 this started to change, with French relative performance falling back on all counts.

There seem to be two fundamental reasons. The Hartz labour market reforms in Germany in 2003–05 appear to have made a big difference, enabling German unemployment to come down and to stay down. By contrast, France has made hardly any reforms at all. Second, and perhaps relatedly, German companies have done extra-ordinarily well in keeping costs down and hence gaining in competitiveness.

As France's performance has started to diverge from its erstwhile close partner, increasingly it is coming to resemble the peripheral countries rather than the Germanic core of the monetary union. Moreover, without deep and fundamental reforms, it is difficult to see matters changing. Since such reforms would strike at the essence of the French model, and would be seen by many in France as an abandonment of the 'French way', they seem politically impossible to implement. In short, not only has the 'Franco-German motor' stalled, but the vehicle has been shunted off the road.

With the election of Emmanuel Macron in 2017 some analysts, and many members of the public, believed that at last France had a President who would reform the economy. Time will tell. But on past experience President Macron will find radical reform extremely difficult. The French have a habit of stopping reforms, not in the National Assembly, but on the streets.

Trouble disguised in the periphery

The story of the peripheral countries is more nuanced. One country stands out from all the others: Ireland. Its output has started to recover strongly. It still has its major problems, notably in the public finances and the banking sector. But as a small, open economy, it has benefited from the improvement in competitiveness brought on by a period of domestic deflation that included huge cuts in public sector pay – and from growth in its two main markets, the UK and the US. In 2015 exports grew by 13%.

The other four peripheral countries present a rather different picture. Greece continues to be a disaster, with GDP down by 27% since 2008. In Spain and Portugal, on some measures there has been a quite impressive recovery in competitiveness – thanks to domestic deflation, including wage cuts.

In fact, this improvement seems more impressive than it really is. It is true that in all the peripheral countries there has been a massive turnaround in the current account that has shifted it from large deficit to small surplus. What is more, this has happened partly because exports have revived. (This supports the improved competitiveness story.) However, a large part of the turnaround in trade performance is due to the deep depression of imports, which is simply a response to the collapse of domestic demand. Indeed, when, in 2014, domestic demand in Spain and Portugal started to revive, imports soared and the current account deteriorated.

Admittedly, though, in both these countries the economic situation has improved. GDP has risen and unemployment has fallen. And the reductions in the government's fiscal deficit have been astounding. Yet, for the reasons explained earlier in this chapter, this has done nothing to reduce the debt-to-GDP ratio. Indeed, in all three countries it has continued to climb. After all the painful austerity they have endured, this is a bitter blow. They have been running faster and faster in order to go backwards. In Greece this has led to a new crisis. At the end of 2014, Greek bond yields spiked up, anticipating an anti-austerity Syriza government in Athens – despite the evidence that the Greek economy had turned the corner. Syriza did win; it buckled to German pressure; and the Greek economy fell back into recession.

The country that stands out from the other peripheral nations is Italy. It has had the same experience of the debt ratio climbing; indeed, the ratio is now about 132%. But unlike the others, Italy has not undergone a painful deflation of prices and wages and there is no sign of an improvement in competitiveness. Accordingly, GDP has recovered only modestly (and thanks mainly to low oil prices) and un-employment is almost 12%. Moreover, there seems no realistic prospect of the radical reforms that would be needed to set the country on the right path. Rather like France, the political system seems incapable of delivering what the country needs. It is as though Italy is frozen in its current state. Interestingly, Italy's three main opposition parties are against the euro.

Turning Teutonic

The German tendency to save rather than spend, and accord-ingly to run up large current account surpluses, has been well known for some time. I wrote about it earlier in this chapter. For most of the eurozone's existence, these surpluses have been mirrored by deficits in the peripheral countries, thereby leaving the eurozone as a whole with its trade pretty much balanced. With the depression of demand in the periphery, however, and the improvements in some peripheral countries' competitiveness, this has all started to change. Now the eurozone as a whole is running a significant current account surplus of the order of about 0.5% of world GDP. In 2016, this was roughly double China's surplus and was, by far, the largest surplus in the world.

This is highly significant, not just for Europe, but also for the world. In my previous book, *The Trouble with Markets*, I attributed much of the blame for the factors that led up to the financial crisis of 2008 to the world's tendency to save too much, with several countries 'over saving' and building up large current account surpluses. In recent years, though, this situation has changed greatly. The Chinese surplus has halved, and the oil producers' surpluses have been extinguished. Just as this has happened, however, a new source of imbalance has emerged – the eurozone.

The euro has turned the whole eurozone Teutonic. Contrary to what some German opinion might hold, this is not a badge of honour. These countries are not Teutonic in their productivity performance; and their current account surpluses are created mainly by their domestic demand being bludgeoned. But the result for the eurozone – and the world – is Teutonic, just the same.

This has now become a serious problem for the world economy. It would be far healthier if the surplus disappeared thanks to higher domestic demand leading to a burst of imports than through a collapse of exports.

Just teething trouble?

There is a view that the difficulties of the euro and the associated poor economic performance of eurozone members are merely temporary. Accordingly, the only policy response required is to sit tight and wait. In any case, no monetary union is perfect. In the US and the UK, differences between different parts of those unions persist, but the unions themselves have carried on. Might the euro not be the same? Moreover, the euro has begun in most inauspicious times. In a better era, whatever difficulties remain, surely the countries of the union, and the union itself, will fare better. Why cast it asunder now?

There is something in this view. If the wider benefits of European cohesion, if not a fully integrated fiscal and political union, are that great, it could be worth putting up with some temporary costs brought on by monetary union. However, even if they are of a temporary nature, the costs seem to be absolutely huge, not least in the shape of a whole generation of young people in southern Europe without work and without hope.

Moreover, these 'temporary' effects can have long-lasting consequences. In depressed economies, there is no incentive to invest heavily in plant and equipment, so the capital stock ends up lower than it would otherwise have been. In addition, the result of large-scale unemployment will be loss of skills and motivation on a massive scale. This could lead on to huge social problems – drug abuse, alcoholism and family breakdown – not to mention fostering the rise of racism and fascism. Even if the incompatibilities and inflexibilities that meant countries like Italy and Greece were ill-suited to joining a monetary union with Germany were eventually sorted out, the bad effects of the current euro depression would linger for years, if not decades.

In this regard, there is an example from history that is quite disturbing. For centuries, Italy was a patchwork of city states and kingdoms (see Figure 4.2). When it was unified in the 1860s, along with this political unification came monetary and fiscal union. Ever since, the south, which broadly corresponds to the Bourbon Kingdom of the Two Sicilies, has been depressed. After unification, the south's industry was ruined and its agriculture was sent into decline. Many of its people were so poor that they were forced to leave. Over the next two decades, millions of people from Sicily and the southern mainland gave up on Italy and emigrated to North and South America. Indeed, there are disturbing parallels with Greece today, where the working-age population has fallen to its lowest level since the country joined the euro.

According to historian David Gilmour,[13] many southern Italian leaders came to see unification as a serious mistake. He quotes Sicilian priest Luigi Sturzo, who became the inspiration for the future Christian Democratic Party:

> *Leave us in the south to govern ourselves, plan our own taxes, take responsibility for our own public works and find our own remedies for our difficulties ... we are not school children, we have no need of the North's concerned protection.*

Transfers for how long?

The position of southern Italy is closely connected with the issue of 'fiscal transfers' within a fiscal and monetary union. The economic literature about such transfers is extensive. The dominant paradigm concerns so-called asymmetric shocks; that is, economic events that affect different regions, or countries, differently. The idea is that within a monetary

Figure 4.2 Italy in 1820*

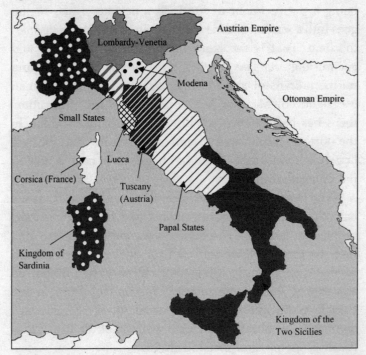

Source: www.europa.eu

and fiscal union, when country (or region) A goes through a bad patch, country (or region) B helps it out. And then when country (or region) B goes through a bad patch, country (or region) A helps it out in return.

This happens automatically, and on a large scale, within sovereign states, including the US, the UK, Germany and Italy. Such transfers clearly help to cushion the blow whenever a temporary setback of some sort causes regional GDP to fall.

Sometimes what happens between different countries or regions does roughly correspond to this paradigm, but often it does not. Rather than a region going through a bad patch followed by a good patch, and therefore going from being a net recipient of funds to a net donor, the region goes into a serious decline and stays in that state for decades to come. That is the story of the former industrial and coalmining districts of Belgium, northern France and northern England, and it is especially the story of the Italian Mezzogiorno. More or less continually since unification, there has been a constant flow of money from Milan in the north to Naples in the south, where it has disappeared, largely without trace. There has hardly ever been a flow in the opposite direction.

Why is this? It is far from clear that long-lasting transfers help the suffering region to adjust and recover when the problem is structural, especially since such transfers often take the form of financial relief for unemployment. Much needed though this is, if it is too generous it can inhibit full adjustment. Despite the ability to sustain consumption at a basic level, the affected region continues to be characterized by high levels of unemployment, with all of the usual associated economic and social ill-effects.

Furthermore, if the transfers take the form of some sort of assistance to companies, the danger is that this confirms and reinforces an inefficient industrial structure. Consequently, the money will effectively be wasted. The dangers are even greater if the transfer of money goes direct to governments, which have a congenital habit of spending it badly, or even counterproductively.

The Austrian, or Hayekian, solution to such problems, of course, is to let the awful current events that have caused a sharp fall in regional GDP, whatever they are, play themselves out. While I would not go that far, there is certainly much validity in the Austrian critique of attempts to ease current pain by financial palliatives.

The problems of adjustment are even worse when

there is the possibility of significant corruption. Famously, this is often the case in Italy. For decades now, huge amounts of money from Rome have regularly headed south for a variety of infrastructure projects, with much of the dosh being siphoned off along the way. The result is that whatever gets built is late, badly done and over budget – if it gets built at all. The fact that so much money is available from the state increases the rewards for corruption and so there is more corruption. The strengthening of corrupt individuals, institutions and practices then makes it more likely that corruption envelops other activities in the region.

Outside Europe, we have learned so much about how international aid, especially of the intergovernmental variety, can increase corruption and strengthen the very forces that are holding a country back. That was essentially the conclusion of the great economist Peter Bauer's life's work. Yet much the same logic applies within Europe.

We also know from countless studies that high levels of corruption are a major inhibitor of economic growth. In the case of Italy, a significant part of the factors that are holding back the south is bound up with the flow of transfer money from the north.

The attraction of a region being able to adjust via a lower exchange rate is that this gives it the chance to keep unemployment down and economic activity up through net exports. Admittedly, all of us who criticize the rigidity of the euro must recognize that exchange rate changes are not the answer to a maiden's prayer. Nevertheless, if the Kingdom of the Two Sicilies had been able to run a separate monetary policy after unification, might its history have been different? A lower exchange rate for the south and the ability for it to go still lower might have kept southern industries in the game and hence boosted investment in the south. Mere fiscal transfers are no real substitute for this and they may well have made matters worse.

The German nightmare

At the opposite end of the eurozone money-go-round is Germany. Clearly, most German citizens are anxious about the financial burdens they are being asked to shoulder to support the periphery. Their true contribution, and their exposure to future losses, is shielded from them by the opaque way in which assistance is given – by the Bundesbank through the mysterious Target 2 balances, or through an alphabet soup of support funds, ESM, EFSF and many more. (See the Glossary for a brief explanation.) Meanwhile, they hear their leaders talk of a banking union, a fiscal union and a transfer union. They can easily be bamboozled by this variety of support mechanisms. Indeed, the politicians intend them to be confused and overwhelmed by the complication of it all so as to disguise the true cost.

In practice, German citizens can put all these niceties aside. There are only three key concepts that they need to understand and decide whether they can accept:

♦ Overspending and over-borrowing by the peripheral countries in the past, to be paid for by Germany.
♦ Overspending and over-borrowing by the peripheral countries in the present, to be paid for by Germany.
♦ Overspending and over-borrowing by the peripheral countries in the future, to be paid for by Germany.

Even if they are prepared to sign up to the first of these – that is, to write off a good proportion of the debt that is owed to them – agreeing to fund current excess is a different kettle of fish. And surely, agreeing to arrangements that would put them on the hook to fund future profligacy in the periphery is the ultimate no-no.

Yet without really tight controls over spending and borrowing throughout the union, that is what fiscal union would imply. German citizens need to take a long and hard look at Italy and ask themselves whether they are prepared to play Milan to southern Europe's Mezzogiorno. It is surely a scene worthy of Dante's *Inferno*.

A fiscal response?

So something must be done to rebalance the eurozone economy and revive the economies on the periphery. But what? One possible policy option is for the weaker members of the eurozone to engage in fiscal expansion, or at least to go slow on the pace of further fiscal consolidation. But nearly all of them are facing a serious fiscal problem as already huge ratios of debt to GDP head even higher. Even with a free hand, there would be clear limits to what they could do. And they do not have a free hand. The Stability and Growth Pact and their agreed targets for deficit reduction limit what they can do. The German government is standing over their shoulder watching for any sign of backsliding.

By contrast, there is considerable room for manoeuvre by Germany. For the next several years Germany is due to run a structural budget surplus and its debt ratio is set to fall from just over 68% of GDP in 2016 to under 60% in 2019. Moreover, there is an urgent need for the country to spend more on public investment. As a share of GDP, public investment in Germany is running at only about 2%, remarkably, less than in the UK.

Even so, the chances of a major fiscal relaxation by Germany look slim. Part of the problem is that German politicians and officials seem not to accept the Keynesian approach to aggregate demand, preferring the precepts of Gladstonian finance, or even thinking of the finances of the state in the same way they would a household. Another element in German thinking is that they believe that their country has to be tough on itself, because if it is not, weaker states will open the floodgates and deficits and debt levels will soar, destabilizing the eurozone and potentially landing Germany with some heavy costs.

When it comes to understanding the Keynesian arguments about aggregate demand, it seems that the Germans just don't get it. The German response to all economic difficulties, regardless of type, seems to be that we must all make painful structural changes and cut back. This approach reminds me of those doctors who, when you visit them about an ingrowing toenail, tell you to drink less and lose weight.

On this aspect of economics, so many German officials and economists seem to have a mental block. They appear to believe that if only the rest of the world could be like Germany, all would be well. There are many respects in which this might be true, but not with regard to current account surpluses. For every surplus there must be a corresponding deficit. Accordingly, for Germany to be able to enjoy surpluses, someone, somewhere, needs to be running deficits.

Herr Schäuble, the German Finance Minister, told the *Financial Times* on 20 May 2010:

> *I hear from Tim Geithner (the US Treasury Secretary), that Germany must do more for growth. But I must ask: what should I do to grow faster? It cannot be by building up bigger deficits, contrary to the stability and growth pact. That is crazy. I must reduce my deficit.*

And that is exactly what Germany has done. In 2013, just as the peripheral countries were in dire need of extra European demand, Germany was busy tightening its budget. So although, in 2017, a major German fiscal relaxation may be both feasible and desirable, it also looks decidedly unlikely – at least on any scale.

The ECB to the rescue?

Accordingly, the spotlight falls on the ECB. Faced with the conditions that exist in the eurozone today, the classic (I cannot quite say orthodox) Anglo-Saxon response would be to flood the system with money; that is to say, for the central bank to buy up assets, paid for with newly created money. The colloquial name for such a strategy is 'printing money', although in the modern world hardly any money is actually printed. Rather, it is created electronically as the central bank credits the sellers of securities with deposits at itself. In this process the balance sheet of the central bank increases.

This policy is an extension of trying to stimulate the economy by lowering interest rates (the price of money). That too has been pursued, even to the point of taking interest rates into negative territory. QE is typically pursued when rates cannot be lowered any further. (The eurozone is close to this limit.) Accordingly, the central bank switches from trying to influence the price of money to influencing its quantity. That is why the policy is now known as quantitative easing, or QE. (When Keynes advocated this in the 1930s, it was called 'open-market operations'.)

This is the strategy pursued by the Federal Reserve in the US and by the Bank of England in the UK. It is also the strategy pursued hesitantly by the Bank of Japan over the last 20 years and now embraced more wholeheartedly as part of 'Abenomics'. But it had been largely eschewed by the ECB – until it announced in January 2015 that it would, finally, go ahead with QE. It did so and, at the time of writing in August 2017, the ECB is continuing to buy €60 billion worth of financial assets per month. It is set to continue doing this until the end of 2017 and to taper its rate of asset purchase thereafter.

Opinions differ on how effective QE has been. Mario Draghi thinks it has been very effective. Indeed, he has suggested that roughly half of the pick-up in eurozone GDP since the middle of 2014 has been due to monetary policy (QE and low interest rates). What the policy has not achieved, though, is any diminution of the economic gap between Germany and its satellites on the one hand and the peripheral countries on the other. This, and the associated deflationary tendency, are at the root of the trouble with the euro.

Political lessons from the euro's failure

The countries of the eurozone are at a crossroads – and they know it. To make the currency work, they now have to press ahead with arrangements for fiscal and political union. However, that is not an easy assignment. Imagine what is involved: umpteen sovereign countries with different fiscal, political and parliamentary traditions have to agree on how each other's fiscal policy should be run and coordinated, and on political institutions for the whole eurozone that will exercise this power, while being democratically accountable.

We are where we are because of the astounding arrogance and incompetence of the European political elite. The saying is that democratic electorates get the leaders they deserve; heaven knows what the peoples of Europe have done to deserve their current leaders.

Nevertheless, they cannot say they were not warned. Largely, but not exclusively, from the UK, eurosceptic economists have waxed lyrical about the dangers of uniting so many disparate countries in a monetary union without real convergence and without robust, common fiscal and political institutions; interestingly, in private, senior officials of the German Bundesbank argued much the same. Although the eurosceptics were vilified by the establishment, both in the UK and on the continent, they have been vindicated.

Faced with the evidence of the failure on a huge scale of a project that was both unnecessary and badly structured, the response of the euro elites should by now have been fully predictable; namely, to push on with it, regardless of the economic costs, believing that sheer political will is going to see them through. But no amount of political will can enable you to reach the moon with a peashooter.

The conclusion is that the euro has been a disaster from the beginning. It shows the quality of EU decision-making at its worst, driven by national politics, horse-trading, considerations of national prestige and childlike visions of future European unity – with scant regard for economic reality.

One of the most important issues to emerge from the analysis of this disaster, though, is what the euro's survival or break-up would imply for the future growth of the EU. Could the end of the euro be part of the EU's salvation? And if not, what could?

5

Europe's Economic Future

Prediction is very difficult, especially if it's about the future.
— Niels Bohr, Nobel Laureate in Physics

It is impossible to know the future, whether about the EU or indeed anything else. The EU may have a very bright economic future or it may not. It is for statements like this that economists are justly notorious, yet they and other forecasters make a living by peering into the future. At the very least, we have the past, and current trends, to guide us. There can be no certainty, but there are things that can be said about the likely shape of the future.

When analysing the likely future growth of the EU economy, first of all I discuss the prospects of economic performance improving, assuming that the euro remains in situ, before going on to discuss how a break-up of the euro could improve matters, including the effects on the two key countries, France and Germany. I then turn to a non-economic subject with huge economic implications: Europe's demographic outlook. This enables me to come up with some plausible scenarios for Europe's long-term GDP prospects in comparison with the rest of the world.

Prospects for higher economic growth

The key point is that, as I showed in Chapter 3, the EU has been a comparative economic failure, with persistently low growth rates compared not only to the emerging markets, but even to other developed economies. Could this change?

It could. My analysis in this book is that weak growth is fundamentally due to bad policies at national and Union level. But these policies could change. The key issues concern labour market regulation, as discussed in Chapter 3: the EU needs to raise its rate of productivity growth and the employment rate. Although the latter in itself would not raise labour productivity – in fact, initially it would do the opposite – it would raise the level of output per head of the population and that would stimulate investment. Moreover, greater labour market flexibility would also encourage companies to expand.

Equally, it is possible to imagine a programme of tax reform to stimulate investment and employment. Furthermore, it is possible to imagine that when the state of the public finances allows this, taxes could be cut. It is even possible to imagine a shift in austerity programmes in France and Italy towards more emphasis on expenditure reduction and less emphasis on tax rises. Or, to be less prosaic, it is possible to imagine the EU actually implementing the so-called Lisbon Agenda.

It is possible to imagine all these things, but do they seem likely? For the EU to move in this direction would require fundamental reform of the EU itself, almost to the point of changing its very nature. In Chapter 9, I address the question of whether the EU could successfully reform itself. The answer is that of course it could, but it is unlikely to do so. As I have shown, there are systematic reasons why the EU tends to make bad decisions that suppress economic growth. The euro episode, which I related in Chapter 4, tells the story. Bad decisions are the natural outcome of both the structures of the EU and its dominant ideas.

Accordingly, many of the sources of weak economic performance are likely to continue, or even to get worse. Later in this chapter I will show what 'no change' would imply for the EU's relative importance in the world economy. First, I discuss something that could improve the EU's performance – the break-up, or partial break-up, of the euro.

How an end to the euro could improve economic performance

While this is not the place to debate the likelihood of the euro surviving or breaking up, it is important to recognize that it could break up, either partially or wholly. After the Greek crisis of 2012, it is impossible to pretend that the euro is necessarily for ever – all for one and one for all. We now know that it is possible for a country to leave the euro. What is more, during the Greek crisis the then French President, Nicolas Sarkozy, said as much, as did the German Chancellor, Angela Merkel. In addition, not least thanks to the essays submitted in pursuit of the 2012 Wolfson Prize, which my firm, Capital Economics, won, we know *how* it can be done. The 19 musketeers may not stick together after all.

That said, my interest here is solely about the economic consequences of the two possible scenarios: euro survival and euro break-up. Most people, both among the public at large and in the financial markets, now believe that the euro is going to survive. They may prove to be right. Despite its obvious difficulties, it is still perfectly possible that the euro will be saved by a deal involving lots of zeros, accompanied by handshakes and smiles all round.

If this does happen, all the ways in which the euro is holding back economic growth in the EU, which I analysed in Chapter 4, would remain in place. The peripheral countries would be stuck with extremely high unemployment and locked into austerity while Germany continued to 'set an example'. That would provide no basis to hope for stronger economic growth in Europe.

What if my own view – namely, that the euro is likely to break up – proves correct? It is widely believed, even accepted as beyond contention, that, in the spirit of *1066 and All That*, euro break-up would be a bad thing; indeed, that it could be disastrous, not only for Europe but for the world as a whole. There is no doubt that it could cause a financial crisis greater than anything yet experienced – Lehmans on steroids. Yet, for reasons I will spell out in a moment, there are good reasons why a euro break-up would bring improved economic performance in the medium term. So here, I am arguing, is something that could plausibly sustain a hope for better European economic growth in the future: the break-up of the euro.

Overturning the conventional wisdom

This idea will appear shocking to many readers. Nevertheless, the long-term results of a major economic crisis are often the complete opposite of the immediate impression registered at the time, by both people at large and the intellectual and policy establishments.

In 1931, just about all members of the UK's National (i.e. Coalition) government subscribed to a programme of extreme austerity – or at least, they thought that there was no alternative. When Britain was forced off the Gold Standard in September 1931, this was widely believed to be a disaster. Yet the economy was able to benefit immediately from low interest rates and was to benefit over the next several years from a more competitive exchange rate, which ushered in the fastest economic growth in Britain's history. As Sidney Webb, a former Labour Minister, said, 'Nobody told us we could do that.' In fact, this was, to put it charitably, a misunderstanding. Keynes had been saying it for years.

It was the same story in 1992 when the UK was trapped inside one of the euro's forerunners, the Exchange Rate Mechanism (ERM). Trying to keep the pound above the specified minimum against the deutschmark required the UK to set interest rates at a level much too high for the domestic economy. It was obvious to all but those blinded by an intellectual obsession that something had to give. Unemployment was soaring, businesses were going bust by the thousand, the economy was in recession and inflation and the rate of wage increase were low. Nevertheless, the Treasury and most of the commentariat said that if the UK came out of the ERM, the results would be disastrous. Bizarrely, they claimed that interest rates would have to rise and the recession would intensify.

Meanwhile, a few independent-minded economists, including, I am proud to say, yours truly, argued the exact opposite. We claimed that outside the ERM interest rates would fall, inflation would hardly rise at all and might even drop, and the economy would benefit from a vigorous recovery, just as it had after the financial crisis of 1931.

When the UK was forced out of the ERM on 16 September 1992, even though this was widely regarded as a catastrophe, the minority counter-view proved to be correct. Interest rates fell and, before too long, a decent economic recovery was underway. A date originally known as Black Wednesday became White Wednesday and finally Golden Wednesday.

It could be just the same with the break-up of the euro.

How could the euro break up?

There are several ways in which the euro as currently constructed could break up. It is important briefly to consider these, because they might have different economic consequences.

Leaving from weakness

The most frequently discussed form of partial break-up is through the chosen departure of a weak country. The most often considered candidate has been Greece or, more recently, Cyprus. If one country leaves, of course, it may be that more countries follow later. I have always thought that much would depend on whether the first leaver succeeded outside the single currency. In that event, forces pushing the other weak peripheral countries out would be irresistible.

I know it must seem incredible that a country like Greece, which has been so badly governed for so long, could successfully manage an exit and an accompanying large devaluation. Nevertheless, Argentina achieved something similar when it broke the peso's peg to the dollar in 2001. Greece might be able to pull off such a feat – or Italy, or Spain.

If any of these countries left the euro, doubtless the initial impact would be to create chaos. For a time at least, the leaders of other peripheral countries could say to their people: 'Look, we must go on taking Mrs Merkel's ghastly medicine, or we will end up like Greece (or whoever).' But if Greece (or whoever) was doing well outside the euro, the people would be likely to reply: 'Please, let us end up like Greece (or whoever).'

Of course, a weak country could be *asked* to leave. This possibility has been admitted over the last few years by Wolfgang Schäuble, the German Finance Minister, who wrote in an article in the *Financial Times*:

> *Should a Euro-zone member ultimately find itself unable to consolidate its budgets or restore its*

competitiveness, this country should, as a last resort,
exit the monetary union while being able to remain a
member of the EU.

And because by definition, in some sense or another, each
vulnerable country is dependent on outside funds, being
asked to leave would effectively kick it out. Once it was
denied financial support, the only way to prevent complete
economic and financial collapse would be to leave. There
were times over the last few years when the French and
German governments came to the point of complete exas-
peration with Greece and might have decided that they
would be better off without it. Although they recovered from
these feelings, they could easily return at some future stage.

Leaving from strength

Alternatively, a strong country could choose to leave. The
most obvious candidate is Germany, although the Netherlands
and Finland are other possibilities. For the time being, it
seems unlikely that Germany could choose to leave, but
the longer the crisis of the euro continues and the more
Germany is asked to pay to keep it together, the greater
becomes the chance that Germany could leave. The euro is
far from being wildly popular among the German public,
many of whom would like to see a return to the deutschmark. However, many have bought the line that the euro
has been good for Germany because it has helped German
exports, an argument I disputed in Chapter 4.

Moreover, quite a few people believe that the euro in
particular, but also the EU in general, is the key to German
security. For peace and stability they are prepared to pay a
heavy price. This is why the revelation that Germany is
paying an awful lot to keep the euro show on the road
has not already provoked such outrage as to force it out of

the system. Because of this, the size of the bill that would persuade Germany that it must leave is that much greater than it would be for a normal country. Still, 70 years after the end of the war, Germany is not quite a normal country.

Mind you, the size of the bill is rising all the time and the German psyche is gradually changing. It is interesting that finally, after many years during which the eurosceptic cause hardly found any voice in Germany, a new party, Alternative für Deutschland (Alternative for Germany), has been founded on an anti-euro ticket. It may not win many votes yet, but the journey of a thousand miles begins with a single step.

North–south splits

Perhaps the most appealing form of euro break-up is a split of the eurozone into two, euro-north and euro-south. What is particularly intriguing about this idea is the scope it gives for different outcomes for the euro as a currency, and what it implies about the problems of managing a new currency, depending on which countries leave the existing euro.

Suppose that the southern countries, Italy, Spain, Portugal and Greece, leave the euro and set up their own new currency. That currency would certainly be weak and these countries would still be saddled with enormous debts denominated in euros. They would have to default on a very large scale, thereby probably triggering a banking crisis across Europe, if not worldwide.

By contrast, if Germany and the other northern core countries departed, leaving the southern members to continue with the euro, the position would be much more comfortable. In this case, the euro would be a weak currency and the new northern one would be a strong currency. The group of strong countries would have to grapple with the problems of establishing a new currency. Meanwhile, in the south default would not be automatic, because their currency would continue to be the one in which their debt was denominated, the euro.

While this is an appealing solution to the problem of the euro, as things stand it is not very likely, not least because of the difficulty of effective coordination between the northern countries. Perhaps a more probable scenario is one in which Germany leaves and then the other northern countries leave later to join it. Even that, though, looks to be a long way off.

The French connection

Since Germany has been so closely twinned with France for the last 60 years, thinking about the German situation (which I will discuss in more detail in a moment) leads naturally to wondering about the future of France. I have always thought that the really interesting question about France is not why it is doing so badly, but rather why it is doing so well. By that I do not mean to suggest that France is a spectacular success – which it isn't — but rather, that it seems to operate some extremely destructive policies and yet somehow the results do not seem to be too bad. Indeed, if the UK ran its economy the way the French run theirs, it would have gone bust long ago.

I have been troubled by this question for some time, without coming up with a wholly satisfactory answer. I find myself juggling with four (not necessarily contradictory) possible answers. First, France is a large, inherently strong country. Second, even the daft things it does (such as the 35-hour week), it manages to do well. This links to my third possible reason: both the French managerial class and its cadre of senior civil servants are extremely well trained and hugely effective in promoting French interests.

So far it sounds like cause for a quick chorus of 'Vive la France!' However, my last reason is much less comfortable: it takes a long time for things to go badly wrong. Moreover, when the deterioration does come, it is not necessarily obvious. This sounds somewhat like Adam Smith's pronouncement: 'There is an awful lot of ruin in a nation.' But once the rot does set in, it is difficult to stop. The decline of the British Empire is one distant example, with Japan's fall from grace in the 1990s and the collapse of the Soviet Union being more recent cases. If France continues on the current path, it is difficult to see anything except persistent relative decline, not only against the rising powers of Asia but also against Germany and even the US and the UK. And it could be a good deal worse. Finally, finally, *les poulets* are coming home to roost.

One of my favourite factoids is that there are roughly as many British people living in France as there are French people living in the UK. The crucial difference is that the British living in France are mostly old and retired, whereas the French living in the UK are mostly young and employed. That speaks volumes. France may have (at least in the south) a better climate and an attractive, even beguiling, way of life. But for the young and enterprising and for anyone wanting to start a business, the country is a nightmare.

France has made a very large bet on its relationship with Germany and their joint construction of monetary union. While the euro may have been a French diplomatic triumph, in economic terms it has worked in favour of Germany. Furthermore, it has created a Frankenstein's monster of a currency that could yet pull down the whole of Europe, France included.

So if the euro were to split, which way would France go? Would it stick with Germany and be part of the strong northern core? Its current economic performance does not compare well with Germany's. Its fiscal deficit, at over 3% of GDP, is much higher than Germany's, and slightly higher than the UK's. The government debt ratio, at 97%, is about 8% above the UK's, and France is going to struggle to get this ratio lower as economic growth remains sluggish. Meanwhile, the unemployment rate runs at roughly double the German equivalent.

If France stayed tied to Germany in a northern euro, then I suspect that French economic performance would be really dire. A German-led northern euro – or new deutschmark, call it what you will – would soar on the exchanges, thereby making France even more uncompetitive, causing its GDP to slump and unemployment to rocket. Now that would make French politics really interesting.

If, by contrast, France broke with Germany, it could either operate its own currency or be part of a southern euro. Either way, it could lead the southern countries in what, encompassing Italy and Spain, would be an economic bloc as large as, or even larger than, the German-led north. And either way, if France broke the link with Germany, its economy would enjoy an immediate improvement in competitiveness, just like Italy and the other peripheral countries.

This choice mirrors the one France faced in the 1930s with regard to the disastrous currency regime of the day, the Gold Standard. While Britain left it in 1931 and enjoyed a rapid economic recovery, France stayed on and languished.

I have no doubt that if the French establishment were confronted with the choice now, it would choose to stay with Germany. Moreover, it would do so pretty much unthinkingly. Therein lies much of the problem. Whether the German establishment would want France in, however, is a different question.

Effects on third parties

Suppose the euro did split into north and south, or in some other way disintegrated, what would be the effect on European countries not in the euro, such as the UK, Sweden and Switzerland?

First of all, their exchange rates would go in opposite directions against the two groups. Let us take the UK as an example. The pound would go up against the southern euro and down against the northern euro. There is no way of knowing, a priori, how the balance of these two opposing movements would pan out for overall competitiveness.

However, the opportunity to expand aggregate demand in the south, and the possibility of a more relaxed fiscal and monetary policy in the north (more on this in a moment), holds out the likelihood of net benefits to the UK. At its simplest, the interests of the UK, and of other European countries, are best served by having a prosperous economy in the countries that currently constitute the euro-zone. As I have argued here, the most plausible way to achieve those conditions is for the euro to break up.

Just to emphasize the point, when I say that the euro is one of the causes of Europe's weak economic performance, I am not using 'Europe' loosely as a stand-in for 'the countries of the eurozone'. The weak performance of the countries locked in the euro straitjacket is an important factor restraining the economic growth of other European countries, like the UK, that have close and extensive trade relationships with the eurozone.

The economic benefits of euro break-up

Whatever form the break-up took, if the euro were to split there would be a boost to economic performance from two related sources. First, the peripheral economies (perhaps joined by France) would regain competitiveness immediately as their currencies fell. They would enjoy a boost from exports. Moreover, improved economic activity would increase tax revenues and thus lower fiscal deficits. Accordingly, it might be possible to ease up on the austerity drive. Where appropriate, it might even be possible for some of these countries to launch their own programmes of quantitative easing, which would enable indirect central bank funding of government borrowing.

These possible gains are clear enough. However, suppose that, for a variety of reasons, a let-up in the austerity drive and/or the adoption of QE is not possible. Then we would be left with exchange rate changes as the only source of benefit. Yet gains in competitiveness from exchange rate changes are a zero-sum game; that is, for the system as a whole, what is gained on the swings is lost on the round-abouts. If the countries of the periphery enjoyed improved competitiveness as their currencies fell, the flipside would be that the countries of the core would suffer reduced competitiveness as their currencies rose. So how would this bring an improvement overall?

This is where we come on to the second factor. As I pointed out above, we must presume that after any departure of the weaker countries or a full break-up, the exchange rate of Germany (and the other northern core members) would rise sharply. This would tend to reduce German exports and increase German imports, thus reducing German GDP and increasing German unemployment. As a by-product, the German inflation rate would fall. These changes would alter the balance of the German economy. As prices in the shops fell, German workers' real incomes would rise. As a result, they would increase their spending.

It is important to realize that since the euro's formation,

the German economy has been seriously unbalanced. It has performed quite well, although not spectacularly well by its own past standards, nor in comparison to other developed economies around the world. However, its success has been heavily dependent on exports, to both the rest of the eurozone and countries outside it. The combination of restraint on wages and the German exchange rate being kept down by the existence of the euro has transferred real income from wages to profits, from workers to companies. Companies have tended not to spend much of their extra income, while workers have restrained their spending.

If Germany somehow left the euro or the euro disintegrated, these factors would go into reverse. It is possible that the mere transfer of income from companies (which are, in current circumstances, reluctant to spend) to consumers (who would tend to spend a good proportion of their increased income) would boost aggregate demand sufficiently to more than offset the blow to GDP from reduced German exports. If so, German overall GDP would be higher. And that would mean, of course, that it would be higher for the current eurozone as a whole, since the boost to competitiveness for the peripheral countries would increase their GDP.

However, if this effect were not strong enough – as it might well not be – then there would be scope for economic policy to give it a push. German fiscal policy could be relaxed and there would be a case for Germany to adopt QE (which the Bundesbank might now agree to). At the very least, monetary policy could be kept looser for longer.

In this regard, the effect of a strong exchange rate in reducing inflation is critical. It would give Germany the ability and the encouragement to try to expand domestic demand. What such a development would do is return Germany to the sort of position it was in with the deutschmark, before the advent of the euro. That was hardly a period of economic failure.

Indeed, the deutschmark was central to the success of the German economy and the participation of ordinary German workers in that success. Just as it is now, under the deutschmark Germany was brilliant at manufacturing and exporting, and its businesses were successful at keeping the rate of increase in costs down. Meanwhile, German consumers were prudent. This meant that Germany had a persistent tendency towards running a large trade surplus. But the deutschmark tended to rise and this largely offset the effects of low increases in costs. While this attenuated the growth of exports, it ensured that consumers' real incomes, and hence consumers' expenditure, rose.

The facts speak for themselves. From 1970 to 1978 – that is, until the last year before the euro's formation – the average annual growth rate of German consumer spending was 2.5%. Under the euro, from 1999 to 2016, the annual average growth rate was 1%. From 1970 to 1978, the average current account surplus was 0.8% of GDP. From 1999 to 2016, the average surplus was 4.6% of GDP. From 1999 to Q1 2017, the total increase in real GDP in the US was 42%, against 40% in the UK and 27% in Germany. The equivalent figures for consumers' expenditure are even more striking: for the US, growth of 53%; for the UK, 44%; and for Germany, only 18%.

There should be no puzzlement about why German consumption growth has recently been so weak. The simple truth is that German workers have not been paid very much. The fruits of German export success have gone largely to their employers, who have then sat on the money. From the formation of the euro in 1999 to the end of 2016, real wages increased by about 18% in France and 30% in Finland, but in Germany by only 14%.

Has Germany benefited from the euro?

Nevertheless, there is a widespread belief that although the eurozone may not have been a success, at least Germany has done well out of it. It seems to follow from this that Germany would do badly from a euro break-up.

As the above discussion makes clear, I think this argument is basically right – as far as it goes, which is not very far. There are two serious flaws in it. First, it is true that German exports have been strong, but because Germany has not bought corresponding amounts from its trade partners, including its fellow members of the eurozone, it has amassed substantial net claims on other countries. Putting it crudely, Germany has sold umpteen BMWs and Mercedes to Greece and has lent it the money to pay for them (partly through the intermediation of the ECB). Greece is in no position to pay the money back, so Germany has effectively *given* the BMWs and Mercedes to Greece. That does not sound like good business to me.

Countries can get hung up on export success. Nevertheless, man cannot live by exports alone – not even German man. The ultimate end of economic activity is consumption. Producing things for others to consume does you no (direct) good at all. Exports are merely the price you pay for imports.

There is another country that suffers from export fetishism – China. It is even more absurd for a country as poor as China to run a huge current account surplus. The problem is not so much the exports themselves as the lack of corresponding spending on imports. The result is lower living standards for the Chinese people than would be possible under a different policy. The similarities between the policy approaches of Germany and China are so great that British economist Martin Wolf has coined the term 'Chermany'.

The second flaw is that although German exports have
been strong, as I pointed out above, German consumption
has not been. Accordingly, although the German economy
has bounced back well from the crisis of 2008–09, over the
whole period since the formation of the euro German GDP
growth has not been that wonderful. So, as argued above,
it is by no means clear that the German economy overall
is better off under the euro than it would have been under
the deutschmark. Meanwhile, the countries of the periphery
are unambiguously worse off.

Furthermore, as a result of the euro, German monetary
and financial management is mired in the most ghastly
mess: monetary transactions by the ECB, which according
to German monetary orthodoxy threaten an inflationary
disaster at some point, and continued fiscal transfers to the
south, which, in some form or other, imply a continuing
burden on the German taxpayer.

The end of the euro as the answer?

Therefore, the end of the euro could, in my view, improve
Europe's relative economic performance. Whether the EU
could survive the collapse of the euro is a subject I take up
in Chapter 8.

Let us put this into perspective. The EU was doing
badly before the introduction of the euro, as I made clear
in Chapter 3. Excessive regulation, the drive towards harmonization and the tendency towards ever-increasing
interference in more and more aspects of economic life
were tendencies of the EU before the advent of the euro.
Accordingly, unless something else changed radically, even
without the euro the EU would be likely to go on being a
relatively poor performer.

So, although the end of the euro would help the EU's

performance, in the absence of other changes it would not be a game changer. Yet there is something else that has got nothing whatever to do with the euro that is liable to make a big difference to the EU's performance: they just aren't making enough Europeans any more.

The demographic timebomb

Of all the problems besetting the European continent that cannot be laid at the door of the EU, surely Europe's dire demographic outlook is one of the most obvious. Indeed, European countries that are outside the EU, such as Switzerland and Norway, also have low birth rates.

Low birth rates mean that populations are ageing and, before long, the workforce will be falling. Soon after that, the absolute level of the population will be falling. I am not arguing that having a large population is necessarily better than having a small population, nor am I suggesting that there is an automatic link between the level of population and the level of GDP per head. The point is simply that the smaller the population is, other things being equal, the smaller will be the total size of GDP.

Of course, other things are not always equal. For a time it is possible for an economy to offset the effects of a falling population by increasing the so-called participation rate, the proportion of the population of working age that works, or by putting back the age of retirement. Nevertheless, in the end the scope for doing this will run out and a lower population will imply lower GDP; that is, a smaller economy.

In 2015, according to the World Bank, the number of births per woman was running at 1.6 for the EU as a whole and as low as 1.3 for Greece and Spain, and 1.2 for Portugal. According to the Population Division of the United Nations Secretariat, by about 2028 the EU's population should be starting to fall and it will carry on falling to 2050. Within the total, though, there should be some marked shifts. The UK's population is forecast to continue rising, but Germany's is projected to fall quite sharply. By 2050, Germany's population is forecast to be slightly below the UK's.

In the outside world, China's population is projected to fall from 2028 onwards, but in India and the US numbers are projected to carry on rising. For the world as a whole, there are projected to be about 2.8 billion more people in 2050 than there were in 2010. Accordingly, the EU's share of the world's population is projected to fall from 7.3% to 5.2%.

One way of avoiding the consequences of low European birth rates for the size of the population, and hence ultimately the size of the economy, is to allow this development to be offset by large-scale immigration. This might well happen and if it does it might be the way, or at least part of the way, in which the EU could avoid a sharp fall in its share of global GDP. However, since electorates have turned against this option just about everywhere in Europe, it seems unlikely to be taken. (I examine the issues raised by recent migration into the EU in Chapter 9.)

Medium-term GDP forecasts

So what does all of this imply for the prospects for the EU's GDP over the next few decades, compared to other countries? This is an area where angels should fear to tread. Forecasting long-term trends in population growth and the growth of output per head may well be worse than forecasting the weather or the macroeconomy. Still, here goes.

First, let me clarify a conceptual issue. The growth of output per head is influenced by more factors than simply the growth of productivity, including workforce participation rates and the level of unemployment. Nevertheless, over the long time periods considered here, the scope for these to vary is limited. So the growth of output per head comes down to the growth of productivity. Accordingly, hereafter I use the term 'productivity growth' to stand for the growth of output per head.

Despite the huge uncertainties, there are some useful things that can be said. On the basis of plausible assumptions about productivity growth in Europe and elsewhere in the world, given the population prospects that I discussed above, a possible future path for the share of the EU in the world's GDP can be suggested.

Rather than rely on a single-point forecast, though, I think the best way forward is to look at three scenarios. Under all three, the EU's share of world GDP is projected to decline quite sharply. This is due to a combination of slower population and productivity growth in the EU than in China, India and other emerging markets. However, the pace of these changes varies depending on the assumptions made about productivity and population growth. (In this instance, though, the assumptions about population growth are the same in all three scenarios.) For simplicity, the GDP projections for Japan, Brazil and Russia are also unchanged in all three scenarios.

Under the first scenario, productivity is assumed to grow by 1.7% in the EU, compared to a world average rate of 2.4% and a rate for China and India of 4.5%. Although the uncertainties about the future are so huge that it seems rash to say that any proposition appears reasonable, given recent experience this scenario can be described as a plausible central case. It is significant, then, that in this 'plausible central case' the EU's share of world GDP is projected to decline from 19.4% at present to 9.8% in 2060. Meanwhile, in 2060 India and China would together account for almost

40% of world GDP, compared to about 25% for the US and the EU combined.

The second scenario assumes marginally faster productivity growth in China and India, with both averaging 4.75% per annum. By contrast, productivity growth at 1% per annum in the EU and at 1.5% in the US is slower than in the base scenario. In this case, in 2060 India and China would represent 46% of world GDP, compared to less than 20% for the US and the EU combined.

While the third scenario is more favourable to the EU, it is also, for the reasons given in this book, the one that I judge to be the least likely. Here, the growth of productivity in the EU picks up to an average of 2.3% per annum; the same figure is assumed for the US. Both China and India experience slightly slower growth in productivity than in the other scenarios, at only 4% per annum. In this case, in 2060 India and China would represent 32.5% of world GDP, compared to about 30% for the US and the EU combined.

Let me make clear that no one should take these figures seriously as a forecast of what is actually going to happen. They represent an exercise in imaginative thinking that draws out the implications of current trends and the way in which they may develop in future.

What is striking is that even in the most unlikely, optimistic scenario, which includes markedly higher European productivity growth, perhaps linked to fundamental reform of the EU, in 2060 the EU's share of world GDP would be well below that of the US and China and only just a little bigger than India's.

In relation to the world that existed in the mid-1950s when what we now call the EU was conceived, the picture revealed by these projections is startling. The idea behind what was to become the EU was to strengthen Europe's economy through integration and to increase its influence in the world. It would have been incredible then to suggest that by 2060 the EU could end up as a smaller economy than India.

It is noticeable also from the scenarios discussed above that in the coming decades no country will enjoy the commanding preponderance that America once did. This also marks out the future as being significantly different from the early postwar world, dominated by America and the Soviet Union – the world in which the EU was conceived.

I am not trying to suggest that the EU's prospective fall in relative importance is all its own fault. Even if the EU were a paragon of virtue in relation to economic management and even if national governments were to act in ways most favourable to economic growth, with the result that European growth rates were higher, they would still, almost certainly, be lower than those enjoyed in the emerging markets, led by China and India.

Moreover, as the EU as a whole falls in relative size and importance compared to other parts of the global economy, the same will tend to happen to its member states. Indeed, they may be so small that they cease to matter to the Indias and Chinas of this world and accordingly lose the ability to negotiate satisfactory trade relationships with them. However, as I argue in Chapter 11, this seems unlikely. It may well be that most European countries would enjoy higher economic growth, and therefore slower relative decline, if they were outside the EU, and it should be possible for them to trade successfully across the world.

The importance of decline

There are three major factors operating against the EU's economic prospects:

♦ The workings of the euro, which impose a deflationary bias across the monetary union.
♦ The persistent tendency towards low productivity growth, allied to weak investment and excessive anti-business interference in markets.
♦ Severely adverse demographic trends, which will see the EU's population shrinking sharply as a share of the world total.

Of course, the biggest factor in the EU's prospective relative decline is something about which the Europeans can do nothing, namely the continuing rise of the emerging markets. Nevertheless, being a relatively slow growth area and losing share of world GDP is not necessarily a disaster. But while membership of the EU might still confer net benefits, each member state's relations with the rest of the world would grow in relative importance. If the EU were to set up barriers against interaction with the rest of the world as the rest of the world got bigger, the balance of advantages from being inside the union would shift towards the negative.

Moreover, a lower European share of world GDP would imply a weakening of Europe's influence in the world. It would also call into question the rationale for being a member of this bloc of countries and even whether the bloc of countries should exist at all. Putting it more provocatively, belonging to the EU would become less and less relevant. What would be most important for each and every European country would be to ensure that it derived maximum benefit from the opportunities afforded by the rapid growth of the emerging markets.

In fact, this development has already begun. The EU's economic growth rates have been low compared even to most other developed countries, but especially compared to the emerging markets, and European businesses have started to wake up to the implications.

Although the prospective relative decline of Europe seems inexorable, if Europeans want to slow this decline, short of creating more Europeans, the EU's economic performance needs to be radically improved. This means that the EU needs to be fundamentally reformed – or dissolved.

One way or another, the UK's vote to leave the EU has intensified the pressure to make a decision. And how well Brexit turns out will surely have a major bearing on which way is chosen.

Part III

Brexit: The Process and the Consequences

6

Negotiating Brexit –
The Principles and the Pitfalls

*If you open that Pandora's box, you never know what
Trojan 'orses will jump out.*
—Ernest Bevin, UK Foreign Secretary, referring to
the Council of Europe in 1949

Britain's exit from the EU is a momentous event. But just knowing that the UK is going to leave doesn't tell us that much. In particular, we don't know what sort of deal it will forge with the EU or, indeed, whether there will be any deal at all. It is perfectly possible that the UK could walk away during the negotiations without having secured one. Equally, it is possible that whatever deal is hammered out between the two sides before the two-year deadline is rejected by one or more of the EU's member states. (According to the Lisbon Treaty, each of the Union's 27 remaining members must approve the arrangements concerning the departure of one of the 28.) What then?

Focusing on the main issues

The negotiation process is going to be treacherous. Indeed, the former Greek Finance Minister, Yanis Varoufakis, who has extensive experience of negotiating with the EU, has warned the UK of the EU's way of using its mastery of agendas and deadlines to browbeat its adversaries.[14]

There was an early sign of what may lie ahead in the treatment of the tricky problem of the position of EU nationals resident in the UK, and UK nationals resident in the EU. The UK government had wanted to settle this straightaway with reciprocal guarantees agreed on both sides. But the EU was unwilling to do this and it now seems that this will be another of the things to be dealt with as part of the negotiation process.

Moreover, the EU's negotiating stance laid out in a published document made clear the difficult task that the UK faced. It said that it wanted a 'phased approach' to the UK's withdrawal and that the 27 nations must 'maintain unity and act as one'. It set out its 'red lines' – principles on which it will not budge. These include:

♦ The Brexit deal will be a single package. The whole deal must be agreed before anything is signed.
♦ The four freedoms are 'indivisible'. There can be no 'cherry-picking'.
♦ The European Court of Justice will remain the arbiter of disputes between the UK and the EU. Any trade deal with the UK cannot be as good as Single Market membership.

In truth, there is going to be much toing and froing during the negotiations and much changing of minds. But in a book such as this, it does not make sense to try to anticipate the twists and turns of the negotiation process. Rather, the purpose here should be to focus on the main issues at stake and the consequences of the various possible outcomes.

Before the point of exit is reached, though, the UK economy has to negotiate some very difficult waters of a different sort. Is the UK set for some sort of Brexit misery even before it formally leaves the Union as the economy plunges? This might well influence the attitude the UK's negotiators, and thereby affect the eventual outcome. Accordingly, I address this question first, followed by a discussion of the attitudes of big business to leaving the

EU, and of the differences between a 'hard Brexit' and a 'soft Brexit'.

Then, I analyse six key issues:

♦ The view from across the Channel;
♦ The possibility of an interim arrangement;
♦ What it will mean if the UK has to rely on World Trade Organization (WTO) rules;
♦ Could the UK fearlessly walk away without a deal?
♦ The importance of Mutual Recognition Agreements (MRAs);
♦ The EU membership bill and the 'divorce settlement'.

This sets the scene for an analysis in the next chapter of the two key elements of the EU that the UK will be leaving – the Single Market and the Customs Union – and a discussion of the merits and feasibility of Free Trade Agreements with the EU and other countries. After that, Chapter 8 looks at the effect on particular industries and then tries to bring all this together with an assessment of the likely effect of Brexit on the UK economy as a whole.

Imminent disaster?

Most analysis of the effects of Brexit on the UK economy has rightly focused on the medium and long term, considering the balance of all the factors mentioned above, as well as some others that will emerge in the next two chapters. I will turn to this issue in Chapter 8. But there is also the pressing matter of the possible short-term impact.

After all, before the referendum in June 2016, the international forecasting community was pretty much united in asserting that a vote to leave would produce an immediate sharp downturn in the UK economy. This august group included HM Treasury, the Bank of England, the IMF, the OECD and umpteen private sector organizations. Only a doughty few, including the group of economists called Economists for Brexit (now renamed Economists for Free Trade), of which I am a member and, dare I say it, my firm, Capital Economics, stood out against this steam-roller consensus.

Up to the point of writing (in August 2017), apart from a slowdown in the first three months of the year (which might have happened anyway), there has been hardly any sign of economic damage. Indeed, after the Brexit vote the UK economy pretty much bowled along as though nothing had happened. We have to ask how the overwhelming consensus could have apparently got this so wrong. And, relatedly, could their error be merely one of timing, such that the UK's economy will yet turn out to be weak during the period of EU negotiations, and perhaps beyond?

The fact that so many forecasting bodies came to broadly similar conclusions gives us a clue. Some commentators have suggested that there was collusion between them. But this is unconvincing and, as I will argue in a moment, collusion was unnecessary to produce the same result. Admittedly, the then UK government, headed by David Cameron, was committed to a 'Remain' vote and orchestrated what became known as 'Project Fear'. The then UK Chancellor of the Exchequer, George Osborne, commissioned two Treasury studies, one on the long-term impact and the other on the short-term.[15] He clearly wanted these studies to come out with conclusions that heavily favoured 'Remain'. This will have had some influence on those who were conducting the studies.

Moreover, Osborne threatened that in the event of a vote for Brexit there would be a 'punishment budget' that tightened fiscal policy, and he said that interest rates would have to rise. Both this public stance and the outcome of the Treasury deliberations helped to create a climate of Brexit pessimism among private sector forecasters. This was doubtless intensified by the institutional bias in favour of 'Remain' of nearly all those organizations that employed economic forecasters.

The two Treasury studies subsequently came in for intense criticism with regard to both their methodology and the assumptions they made.[16] Most other organizations that had forecast sharp pain ahead were forced by the economy's resilience to substantially upgrade their forecasts.

Chronicle of a death postponed?

But is the pain foreseen by so many eminent bodies still lying in wait in the future, ready to surprise us? There has been little attempt by the forecasting establishment to disown the gloomy forecasts of the Treasury and other bodies.

Admittedly, Andy Haldane, Chief Economist of the Bank of England, is an honourable exception. He described the Bank's forecast of imminent economic slowdown as 'a Michael Fish moment'. But Sir Nicholas Macpherson, who was head of the Treasury until just before its Brexit reports were published, said in April 2017 that the analysis 'still looks rigorous and remarkably prescient'.[17] Yet once you realize how flawed the various attempts were to predict the short-term outlook for the economy after the referendum, then the presumption that there *must* be trouble ahead melts away.

It is still possible, though, that the economy will suffer a sharp slowdown. After all, at the time of writing, and perhaps at the time of reading, the UK has not yet left the EU. Moreover, the lower pound has precipitated a rise in inflation that is eating into real incomes. Consumers may yet rein in their spending considerably. So it is still too early for Brexit supporters to be crowing. Everyone should be prepared for turbulent times ahead – even if the long-term impact of Brexit is positive.

In particular, there are bound to be times when the UK's negotiations with the EU seem to be going badly and there will inevitably be several bouts of bad news concerning foreign firms not coming to the UK, or reducing or closing their existing UK operations. Doubtless, there will also be a string of stories about various banks relocating some or all of their business to the continent or Dublin. (More on this in Chapter 8.) It is not difficult to imagine a bunching of various bits of bad news, with the result that business and household confidence take a knock.

But I am more than hopeful that the economy will sail through all this. The rise in inflation will be temporary but the boost to competitiveness from the lower pound will be permanent (as long as the pound stays down). Admittedly, devaluations do not always work – but they often do, with 1931 and 1992 being key examples. Given that the overall inflationary climate is benign and overseas demand is strong, the conditions are in place for 2016's fall of the pound to have a major beneficial effect. I suspect that the benefits will be gradually building up just as uncertainty over the Brexit negotiations is gathering. And the jobs market is likely to stay strong.

It may seem surprising to some readers that the over-whelming consensus of economic experts could turn out to be so wrong. It doesn't surprise me. Indeed, there is a long record of the consensus of experts being proved completely wrong. When the UK left the Gold Standard in 1931, this was widely believed to be a disaster. On the contrary, it ushered in the fastest period of sustained economic growth in our history.

In 1992, when sterling was forced out of the European Exchange Rate Mechanism (ERM), the forerunner of the euro, this was again widely believed to be a disaster. Before the exit, the Treasury had proclaimed that if we left the ERM, inflation and interest rates would rise and the economy would fall back. In fact, interest rates and inflation fell and the economy surged ahead.

In the late 1990s, it was widely believed by the economic establishment that if the UK did not join the euro, its economy, and especially the City of London, would suffer seriously. In fact, outside the euro, the UK grew strongly, considerably outperforming the eurozone, and the City thrived as never before. These were all errors in forecasting the effects of known events. But the consensus has been just as bad in not foreseeing major changes. It did not expect the collapse of Communism, and it did not foresee what I called 'The Death of Inflation'. Nor did it anticipate the financial crisis of 2007–9.

So, in putting forward a positive view of the UK's future after Brexit, I am not at all perturbed by the weight of 'expert' opinion that takes the opposite view. As I argue below, despite the probable flow of adverse news items, the dominant story, I think, is likely to be 'business as usual'. Yet, to some extent, of course, the performance of the UK economy is bound up with what sort of Brexit we are going to have, which I will turn to in a moment.

Why big business inclines towards pessimism about Brexit

But economic experts are not the only group with a questionable record on major economic issues. By no means all British business leaders supported staying in the EU, but a preponderance of the leaders of big business, and their lobbying organizations, such as the CBI, did (just as they had favoured joining the euro). Accordingly, after the Brexit vote there was widespread apprehension in the business community. As regards the likely consequences of Brexit, what weight should be given to business views?

On the surface, the answer is 'quite a lot'. After all, these business leaders have some ability to influence the result that they are being asked to anticipate and assess, since their decisions on investment and employment will have a crucial bearing on economic performance. Mind you, the prominence and apparent eminence of so many of the key individuals involved may give a misleading impression of their ability to judge the economy. Typically some grand, lavishly paid, corporate panjandrum, often bedecked with some gong or other and speaking as the chairman of this, that or some other business organization, opines to the effect that EU membership has been vital to their business and, by extension, to the whole of the UK economy. Accordingly, the UK should seek the softest of soft Brexits.

We should beware of such wisdom. There they are, having been throughout their life immersed in widgets, insurance or water management, and now in their fifties or sixties, given a position of power and prestige, newly able to pronounce on the state of the world beyond the widget. With a few honourable exceptions, such corporate wizards should go back to their widgets, insurance, water management or whatever and leave the issues of national economic and political management alone.

The essential problem is that insofar as they can accurately assess the interests of the current widget-making industry, or their own part of it, they cannot judge how that industry will change, whether or not there will be any need for widgets in five years' time, or whether, if there is, widgets will all come from China. Nor can they speak for the widget manufacturers, still less the manufacturers of widget substitutes, as yet unborn.

Most importantly, they cannot speak for the huge part of the economy, the dominant part, which has nothing whatever to do with making widgets and yet is still profoundly affected by the EU and its various interferences. The essence of economics is substitution and uncertainty. The essence of successful economic policymaking is to fully recognize the latter and to give full rein to the former. This has little relevance to the widget-making processes so well known by Sir Thingummy Whatnot.

In fact, when interpreting what business leaders say, there are some key structural features of the economic case that need careful attention. Even if the net balance of advantages and disadvantages from Brexit were exactly zero for the country as a whole, there would be distinct gainers and losers. It is quite understandable that the losers should make it plain that they would rather stay in. The potential losers from Brexit tend to be those companies with substantial exports to the EU, minimal imports from the rest of the world and comparatively little UK business. Businesses that fall into this category are predominantly large – and well represented in the CBI.

Moreover, such businesses tend to be able to cope well with the burden of EU regulation, since they are able to lobby Brussels successfully and have sufficient scale to bear the burden of complying with regulation without suffering damaging costs. Indeed, they may even welcome intrusive EU regulation as this favours large incumbents and deters potential competitors. By contrast, because of the UK's new-found freedom to drop tariffs and other restrictions on imports from the rest of the world, the gains from Brexit will be felt disproportionately by consumers, in the form of lower prices, including for food, and perhaps also lower taxes. Consumers, of course, have no representation in business groups.

Meanwhile, those companies that are net gainers from Brexit will tend to be those who suffer from excessive EU regulation but don't export much to the EU. These will tend to be small and not heavily represented in the CBI. Indeed, many representatives of small and medium-sized businesses did come out in favour of Brexit. John Longworth resigned as Director General of the British Chambers of Commerce (BCC), in order to be able to speak out freely against EU membership.

Also, there is a category of gain that will not appear directly in the calculations of any business leaders, namely the benefit from the end of the EU regulatory juggernaut in the public and non-profit sectors. Although this does not figure in any profit-and-loss reports, this is a serious and substantial factor. For example, Britain's most prolific cancer researcher, Professor Angus Dalgleish, told the journalist Dominic Lawson that the EU's Clinical Trials Directive had increased the cost of experiments more than tenfold. This, and other considerations like it, will not figure at all in the prognostications of business leaders.

The upshot is that although it is important for the voice of business leaders to be heard, and we should be conscious that pessimism on their part could become a self-fulfilling prophecy, we should beware of thinking that they have some special insight into the balance of economic advantages – still less into the all-important political and constitutional issues. (I expand on this matter in the discussion of the Single Market and the Customs Union in the next chapter.)

Hard or soft Brexit?

Once the Brexit referendum had taken place, much discussion centred on the question of whether the UK should seek a 'hard' or 'soft' Brexit. It was widely accepted that a soft Brexit would be preferred by those who had voted 'Remain' and a hard Brexit by those who had voted 'Leave'.

The softest of soft Brexits is to join the European Economic Area (EEA), which includes membership of the Single Market for everything except agriculture and fisheries. This is widely known as the 'Norwegian option'. Compared with full EU membership, its EEA status does give Norway a few advantages, including the freedom to set its own tariffs and to negotiate trade agreements with other countries. Moreover, being outside the Common Fisheries Policy is particularly important to it, and, on a proportionate basis, it pays somewhat less into EU central funds than a full EU member would. Doubtless some equivalent modification might be available to the UK if it were to go for this EEA/Norwegian model.

But this option would come so close to staying in the EU that you could call it a non-Brexit. For it would imply:

- Having to accept most EU laws and regulations;
- Indirectly, having to accept the jurisdiction of the European Court of Justice (ECJ);
- Continuing to have no control over migration from EU countries;
- Continuing to pay into the EU budget.

It would surely be a betrayal of those who campaigned and voted for Brexit to accept such an arrangement. And it would be a bad bargain to have gone through the referendum and the subsequent tortuous negotiations to end up with this, having gained next to no sovereignty but having lost a considerable amount of influence over the decisions that critically affect the UK, for the UK would have no vote in the EU. This would be particularly relevant for the UK's financial services industry. Over the years the UK has managed to use its power and influence within the EU to deflect it from several initiatives that would have caused the City of London considerable damage. If the UK were in the EEA and not in the EU then it would lose this power. Interestingly, there is growing dissatisfaction in Norway with its EEA arrangement and a considerable number of Norwegians now want a referendum on Norway's continued membership.

In her Lancaster House speech on 17 January 2017, Theresa May sought to make it crystal clear that the UK would definitely be leaving the Single Market. I will argue below that this is absolutely the right course for the UK to take. But, after Mrs May's failure to secure an overall majority in the General Election in June 2017, it was not certain that the UK would leave the Single Market. The election put two groups of MPs that favour a 'softer' Brexit in a position of great power – the Scottish Conservatives and the DUP in Northern Ireland. Given the precarious political position of the government, it seems unlikely that it could pass the necessary legislation to take a contentious Brexit through the House of Commons in accordance with the two-year time limit for negotiations.

Furthermore, it will be extremely difficult to get legislation through to enact a radical programme of deregulation, tax-cutting and tariff reductions that would be needed to make the most of Brexit. So, even though the EEA option is, in my view, decidedly second-best, it is now a possibility, particularly as a short-term, temporary solution.

After all, it would allow the UK to negotiate trade deals with countries around the world and it would give more time than the two years allotted by the Lisbon Treaty to negotiate a trade agreement with the EU. What is more, this EEA option could end up securing the support of formerly Brexit-supporting Conservative MPs if it prevented a Labour government. For the latter would deliver an exit from the EU accompanied by more regulation and higher taxes, which is exactly the opposite of what is needed to make a success of Brexit.

It has been widely assumed that a so-called 'hard' Brexit is bound to be more economically challenging, if not downright economically disadvantageous. The implication must be that those who would embrace such an outcome must be emphasizing non-economic matters such as control over immigration, or overall national sovereignty, above purely economic matters. Accordingly, if the UK is going to aim for, and presumably secure, a hard Brexit then this does threaten a marked economic slowdown, if not a recession.

But this conclusion does not follow at all. The terms 'hard' and 'soft' are unhelpful. It would be clearer if we used the terms 'partial' and 'full'. I also quite like the term 'clean' to replace 'hard'. Unfortunately, though, the corollary is that 'soft' should be replaced with 'dirty'. And I suppose that not even the most ardent of Remainers would say that they were in favour of a *dirty* Brexit!

Enough of 'soft' or 'hard' Brexits. Rather than bandying around such unhelpful terms, it is best to focus on precise questions concerning the negotiation process, starting with how the EU sees what future relationship with the UK is in its best interests, before turning to the concrete questions about Single Market membership and belonging to the Customs Union in the next chapter.

The view from across the Channel

The EU has a strong economic self-interest in maintaining the closest possible trading relationship with the UK, post exit, subject to an important qualification that I will come to in a moment. After all, the UK is the largest single export market for the other 27 EU members, larger even than the US. Moreover, many of Europe's largest businesses operate complex and interwoven supply chains between the UK and the continent. This scale of the trading relationship suggests that the EU will be keen to do a deal.

Moreover, Brexit supporters sometimes comfort themselves with the thought that because the UK runs a large trade deficit with the EU this will give it the whip hand in negotiations. It won't. For a start, the underlying assumption behind the supposed importance of the UK's deficit seems to be that economies don't benefit from imports. Or, if they do, the consumer interest cannot organize itself sufficiently to bring weight to bear in trade negotiations, and governments more or less ignore it.

Of course they shouldn't. Trade brings benefits from both exports and imports. (More on this in the next chapter.) But let us assume that this cynical presumption is justified and the consumer interest carries no weight. This still does not give the country with the trade deficit – in this case, the UK – the whip hand.

No one negotiates about deficits – even if they are aware of what they are. They negotiate about exports. The UK's exports to the EU-27 are much larger as a share of the UK's GDP than the EU-27's exports to the UK are as a share of the EU-27's GDP. Nevertheless, many Irish and continental businesses – including German car manufacturers and French cheese-makers – have an enormous amount at stake,.

Now comes the qualification. In order to ensure its own survival, the EU has to make sure that whatever is offered to the UK is worse than what is available to members. Otherwise other countries may seek to leave the EU. After all, as I made clear in Chapter 2, the EU is pretty unpopular across much of Europe and the various petty annoyances that it gives rise to grate far more than a sober assessment of their importance would justify. If people could be shot of these things while simultaneously enjoying the benefits of the EU, surely this would be an appealing prospect. If that is what the UK has managed to achieve, then the electorates of several countries might think they want that outcome for themselves.

Nicholas Véron, an economist and senior fellow at Bruegel, the Brussels-based research institution, has put it pithily: 'You don't allow someone who leaves the club to have better terms than someone who's in the club, or otherwise the club doesn't mean anything.' Moreover, most EU leaders and officials are convinced that the UK has made a major mistake and, unless it secures a trade deal with the EU, will face a bleak future. Accordingly, they believe that the EU has a much stronger negotiating hand and will not need to make many, or indeed any, concessions to the UK, which will have to accept what it is offered or get nothing at all.

I think this continental perception of the UK's situation and its options is misguided, as I will argue in a moment. But as long as EU negotiators think this way it makes a deal between the EU and the UK less likely.

An interim arrangement

Many people on both sides of the negotiation fear that it will be extremely difficult to conclude a deal within the two-year period laid down by the Lisbon Treaty. In that case, they fear a 'cliff-edge' as the UK 'crashes out' of the Single Market and the Customs Union, and worry that trade barriers, including tariffs, would go up on both sides.

A number of analysts and commentators have suggested that, even if EEA membership is not an option for the long-term, it offers a convenient way of minimizing the short-term disruption for the UK's businesses. There is something in this, of course, but remaining in the EU temporarily would also prolong the agony, delay adjustment and might even be thought to imply that the UK would never properly leave the EU. In any case, whatever the merits or demerits of the idea of temporary EEA membership as a safe harbour, initially at least, the UK government effectively dismissed it.[18]

Another possible way of avoiding a 'cliff-edge' is for the two parties to agree a ten-year interim arrangement. Under the little-known Article 24 of the WTO's General Agreement on Tariffs and Trade, the UK and the EU could be allowed a 'reasonable length of time' after Brexit to agree a free trade deal before having to impose the same tariffs on each other as they do on everyone else. WTO rules state that an interim agreement should 'exceed 10 years only in exceptional cases'. So this seems to suggest that an interim agreement of ten-years would be acceptable to the WTO. A more likely stumbling block would be the other 27 members of the EU who, under the Lisbon Treaty, would have to unanimously agree such an arrangement.

But would this be in the UK's interests? It all depends upon what the conditions of the agreement are. If the EU lays down that during this period the UK must maintain the Common External Tariff (CET) on imports from the rest of the world (ROW) and must not conclude FTAs with third countries then, for all the reasons I will discuss in the next chapter, this would not be in the UK's interests. The UK would be better off facing the EU's CET and agreeing FTAs with as many countries as possible as quickly as possible.

But suppose that the EU did not impose these conditions. In that case, the UK could continue tariff-free trade with the EU while also dropping the CET immediately if it so chose (although this would require the implementation of the Rules of Origin arrangements with the EU to prevent the circumvention of the EU's tariffs by non-EU members) and/or sign FTAs with as many countries as possible, as quickly as possible. This could mean that at the end of ten years (or sooner if agreement could be reached) the UK would enjoy tariff-free trade with just about the whole world, including the EU. What's not to like about that? But would the EU agree to such arrangements? I very much doubt it.

Relying on WTO rules

In her Lancaster House speech, Theresa May said that 'no deal is better than a bad deal'. This was widely interpreted as meaning that the UK would be prepared to walk away from the negotiations before an agreement was reached, or to reject a proposed agreement that was deemed unsatisfactory, and to rely on WTO rules as a framework under which to conduct trade. This was supposed to strengthen the UK's negotiating hand because it implied that if the EU did not play ball with the UK there was a perfectly acceptable fall-back position that did not rely at all on an EU agreement.

But this 'WTO option' was then widely decried by erstwhile Remain supporters as being a thoroughly disastrous outcome for the UK and was widely referred to as 'crashing out' of the EU. It is important, therefore, to establish just how attractive a proposition it might be, both because this will influence the outcome of the negotiations and because, after all, there is a real chance that the UK *will* fail to reach an agreement and therefore will have to rely on trading under WTO rules.

In October 2016, the heads of four industrial lobby groups, the CBI, the EEF, the ICC and techUK, published an open letter to the Prime Minister saying:

> *... every credible study that has been conducted has shown that this WTO option would do serious and lasting damage to the UK economy and those of our trading partners. The Government should give certainty to business by immediately ruling this option out under any circumstances.*

Unfortunately, they did not identify the credible studies they had in mind.

In some accounts the WTO option is referred to as 'falling off a cliff' or 'falling into the clutches of the WTO', as though the WTO is some sort of monster organization that consumes its members – especially juicy new ones like the UK. In fact, the UK was a founder member of the WTO and has retained its seat throughout – although not being able to act as a full member while belonging to the EU. When it leaves the EU it will simply take up its seat that has been there all along.

In some versions, the outcome of relying on WTO rules is referred to as 'WTO Only', which seems to convey more clearly the supposed unattractiveness of this option. In a previous edition of this book, sensing that with or without the 'Only', this WTO option would sound rather Spartan and unattractive, I suggested another name for it – 'the American option' – because America trades with the EU, including the UK, under WTO rules. In fact, umpteen countries do. Suddenly it doesn't sound so disastrous.

Indeed, when you examine the facts about different trading relationships, as collated by the redoubtable Michael Burrage,[19] 'WTO Only' does not sound unappealing at all. Trading on a 'WTO Only' basis simply means that the countries trading with each other do not have a trade agreement, and rely on the rules of the WTO for their trading arrangements and to settle any disputes. The WTO rules dictate only the maximum tariffs that may be applied. It is perfectly possible for a member country to reduce these tariffs or, indeed, to abolish them altogether. But, except where a country has an FTA, whatever the tariff rates that are chosen they must be applied to all other countries without discrimination.

Critics have painted the WTO option as 'stepping into the unknown'. Yet the UK currently trades with 111 countries around the world under WTO rules, including China (and Hong Kong), India, Russia, Brazil, Indonesia, Singapore, Canada and the United States. Moreover, since the formation of the Single Market in 1993, the growth rate of UK exports to these 'WTO Only' countries has been four times faster than the growth of UK exports to the EU. Meanwhile, over this same period, the growth rate of exports from the 14 top 'WTO Only' countries to the EU has been 27% higher than exports to the EU from the UK. Of course, this reflects the faster growth of these countries rather than the inherent superiority of a 'WTO only' model. But it does at least show that 'the clutches' are not at all clutch-like.

Walking away without a deal

None of this means that the 'WTO Only' option is first-best for the UK. First-best is surely the 'deep and special relationship', securing free trade between the UK and the EU, that has been openly sought by Theresa May – but only on reasonable terms. If this proves impossible to secure, the prospect of trading with the EU under WTO rules should hold no terrors for the UK.

Some critics might argue that if the UK government openly regards trading under WTO rules as a perfectly viable option this would make the chances of securing a deal even slimmer. I disagree. If it is plain that the UK has a perfectly viable Plan B this weakens the position of those on the EU side pressing for a really tough deal with the UK. So, having a fully worked-out Plan B both makes not having a deal less frightening and makes it more likely that a deal will in fact be secured.

Indeed, you could reasonably say that the only really robust strategy for the UK government to pursue is one that requires absolutely no approval whatsoever from the EU. In that way, the UK would completely escape from the position of supplicant, which is likely to bolster the EU's intransigence. Moreover, if the UK walked away from negotiations without an agreement, this would sow dissension among the EU's other 27 members, many of whom would be anxious about the impact on their countries across a range of issues:

♦ Who would plug the financing gap created by the loss of the UK's budget contributions? (This may be especially tricky if 'no deal' implies no divorce bill either. See below.)
♦ How would their exports to the UK be affected?
♦ How would the UK's departure without a deal affect future defence and security relationships?

According to some analysts and commentators, the prospect of the UK walking away without a deal may be enough to scare the EU into making an attractive offer to the UK. This is the view of the former Conservative Cabinet Minister John Redwood. He envisages that if the EU will not allow the UK tariff-free access to its market then the UK should impose the CET on EU exports to the UK (and, under WTO rules, this implies continuing to impose it on imports from the rest of the world) while negotiating FTAs with many other countries as quickly as possible.

Once the FTAs have been agreed, then non-EU countries

would sell manufactured goods and food to UK consumers at lower prices than currently apply. The result would be a large drop in the prices that continental suppliers could get for *their* produce in the UK market. Hence the conclusion that continental suppliers should fear the 'no deal' outcome. (I analyse this effect in more detail in the next chapter.)

Some commentators have suggested that the UK has a very tough position vis-à-vis the EU because it employs hardly any experienced trade negotiators, having long since transferred this 'competence' to the EU. But this is a red herring. Having recently appointed a Canadian as Governor of the Bank of England, the UK is surely capable of securing the services of experienced trade negotiators from around the world.

Much more concerning, in my view, is the inherent tendency of British senior civil servants towards defeatism and inherent enthusiasm for all things 'E'. They are used to trying to reach consensus with their European 'partners' rather than fighting tooth and nail for the UK interest. They will need to acquire some backbone. But I rather hope (you might say immodestly) that the arguments deployed in this book may help them.

Mutual Recognition Agreements (MRAs)

There is a further aspect to this matter that seems to be extremely arcane but has proved to be important in the debates about Brexit, and could turn out to be important in practice after the UK leaves the EU.

For manufactured goods to be allowed to enter the EU market, and indeed other markets, they have to meet certain requirements, confirming that they have undergone conformity assessment procedures certified by the appropriate bodies. EU recognition of other countries' conformity assessments is normally built into Free Trade Agreements. Where an FTA is not in place, conformity is acknowledged through so-called Mutual Recognition Agreements (MRAs). Umpteen countries that do not have FTAs with the EU have such MRAs – including Australia, Canada, Japan and the United States.

Anti-Brexit campaigners paint a picture in which, if the UK does not secure an FTA with the EU, then it will not have such MRAs in place after Brexit. And, without them, UK goods exports would grind to a halt under a huge burden of testing and inspection. So, suddenly, it seems that, after all, it is not possible to trade with whoever you like without trade agreements.

Yet the need for MRAs hardly seems an insuperable barrier to overcome. All it means is that the UK should negotiate MRAs with the EU before it leaves. This should be a simple matter since it just involves continuing with the status quo. Similarly with regard to other countries, such as the US, with which the EU has MRAs. Again, this simply means each side agreeing to continue with the MRAs that they currently have. Where's the problem?

Some commentators, including the author and commentator Richard North, have suggested that the EU might decide deliberately to withhold MRAs from the UK even though it has them with other countries. Yet this would be a blatant case of discrimination and as such would be justiciable in the WTO courts and the UK would be bound to win. Nevertheless, it is not clear how long this process might take and in the meantime much damage could be done to UK trade. It would undoubtedly be better if the UK could secure EU agreement to issue the required MRAs.

A variant of this argument – that the absence of MRAs threatens a devastating blow to UK trade – has been advanced strongly by Christopher Booker in the *Sunday*

Telegraph. To avoid crippling delays, even where MRAs are in place, cross-border traders register as Authorised Economic Operators (AEOs). Inter alia, this enables them to file all necessary documentation electronically in advance. By now you will surely have guessed the problem: the UK is only a member of the AEO system by dint of its membership of the EU. Booker suggests that when the UK leaves the EU, membership of this AEO system will lapse, with dire results.

Yet membership of the AEO system is not in the EU's gift. It is organized under the auspices of the World Customs Organization (WCO) and is administered in the UK by HM Revenue and Customs (HMRC). It should be relatively easy to agree with the WCO the continuation of the current arrangements after Brexit. Indeed, following the coming into force of the Trade Facilitation Agreement (under the auspices of the WTO) providing facilities for electronic pre-submission of documents for customs clearance is now a legal obligation for the EU.[20]

This discussion of MRAs and AEOs links up with the important issue of what we mean by 'walking away from negotiations with the EU without a trade deal'. In the extreme, that could be taken to include leaving without having any MRAs in place. I suppose that there may be some hardest of hard Brexit supporters who would favour such an outcome or, at the very least, would say that they would not fear it. But this would surely be a small minority.

When I write here about leaving the EU without a trade deal I do not include MRAs. That is to say, I am assuming that the EU will agree to the required MRAs. I am also assuming that it will be easy for the UK to conclude MRAs with third parties. The groundwork for this needs to be done during the two-year negotiating period such that, from day one of the post-Brexit world, there are no unnecessary problems or delays at borders.

Similarly, 'walking away' without a trade deal does not mean walking away without an agreement on the rights of EU nationals living in Britain and British nationals living in the EU, or without an agreement on a host of important non-trade issues, such as aviation.

The EU membership fee

How these factors stack up and what the likely impact will be on the UK's industries and the overall economy is the subject of the next two chapters. But before we leave the subject of the negotiations we need to discuss a factor that will both affect the UK's eventual net benefit (or loss) from leaving and have a major influence on the negotiations themselves – namely the EU membership fee.

You would think that it must be easy to assess the gains to the UK from not having to make an annual contribution to the EU's budget and I suppose, compared to some other aspects, this is more readily quantifiable. But even here we are not dealing with one hard-and-fast figure. For a start, the amounts paid vary from year to year. In 2015/16, the UK government made a gross contribution to the EU budget of £17.6 billion but received a rebate (the fruit of Mrs Thatcher's 'handbagging' many years earlier) of £4 billion, giving a figure of £13.6 billion for the gross contribution. But the public sector also received £2.8 billion, giving a figure for the net public sector contribution of £10.8 billion.

Over and above this, though, the private sector also receives some payments directly from the EU without passing through the UK public sector, which are not, therefore, included in the figures quoted above. Data on these payments are less timely but over recent years they have been running at between £1 billion and £1.5 billion per annum. Taking the upper end of this range would give a figure for the UK's net national contribution in 2015/16 of £9.3 billion, or just under 0.5% of GDP.[21]

For some purposes it is appropriate to look at the gross cost to the government; in some cases the net cost to the government; in others, the gross or net cost to the UK as a whole. The key point is that, whichever definition you take, the sums are not tiny (and they have been tending to rise). But neither are they gargantuan. Moreover, depending on the exact nature of the UK's arrangements, the UK may well discover that, rather like Norway and Switzerland, both of which are outside the EU, it might feel obliged to make some continuing contribution to EU funds.

Leaving the club

Assuming that the UK does not have an arrangement like those applying to Norway or Switzerland, most British people will naturally assume that once the UK leaves the EU that is the end of their financial obligations to it, so they will save about 0.5% of GDP per annum. But that is not the way things may turn out.

A word of warning is in order. This is the EU. Therefore this issue is horrendously complicated. If anyone wanted a reason to leave the EU and has not yet ploughed through the arrangements governing the so-called Common External Tariff, then I suggest they take on the various documents surrounding the UK's supposedly continuing financial obligations. What follows here is the briefest of thumbnail sketches designed to lay out the main issues.

When thinking about the questions facing the EU and the UK over the financial implications of the UK's impending departure, it might help to consider two competing analogies. Is leaving the EU to be thought of as rather like resigning your membership of a club, or is it more like divorcing your spouse?

When you leave a club you will normally have paid your subscription in advance up to a certain date and you continue to be able to use the club's facilities up to that point. But, assuming that, if notice is required, you gave the necessary amount of notice, then at the due date you cease to be able to use the club and you make no more financial contributions to it. When you became a member of the club you were not asked to make any contribution towards the cost of the assets built up before you joined. Similarly, when you leave you do not have any claim on the assets that exist at the point of your departure.

This is implicitly the model that most British people, and perhaps the British government, have in mind when they think of the EU. Accordingly, suppose that UK membership ceases in March 2019, then they tend to assume that the UK must continue to make budget contributions up to that date but not after. Since whatever the date is, departure is unlikely to coincide exactly with the end of the EU's financial year, then some adjustment will need to be made, one way or the other, depending upon when payments are made. But that is the end of it.

Or a divorce settlement?

A rather different analogy is to think of EU membership as a marriage. When a couple decides to split there may well be continuing financial obligations from one party to the other and a division of assets and liabilities between the couple. If this model is accepted as describing EU membership then the UK may well be liable to make payments after it leaves the EU, rather like 'maintenance' payments, known as 'alimony' in America. Or, mirroring the clean-break option in divorce settlements, when the UK leaves it could choose, or be obliged, to transfer a substantial capital sum to the EU in settlement of any continuing 'obligations'.

What are these obligations? First there is the matter of the EU budget. This is planned in blocs of seven years. The current period runs from 2014 to 2020, and therefore includes a period of almost two years after the UK will have left, assuming that is in March 2019, two years after the triggering of Article 50 in March 2017. Clearly the UK may leave earlier than this, in which case the part of the budget planning period that falls after the UK has left will be longer. Now the UK signed up to this EU budget, albeit with considerable reluctance and indeed resistance. But it signed up to it. Accordingly, it could be said to be liable for its contribution until the end of 2020.

However, although the UK is a substantial contributor to the EU budget it also receives considerable funds from it. Arguably, in computing the UK's liabilities, these prospective receipts from the EU should be deducted from the amounts that the UK supposedly owes to the EU. In assessing what these amounts are, regard has to be paid to the matter of the UK's contribution rebate, won by Mrs Thatcher. Should this be applied to its planned contributions up to the end of 2020 or should it be disregarded?

Second, there are legal commitments to certain forms of spending, including on European Structural and Investment Funds, that stretch beyond the period of the UK's departure from the Union, as well as various contingent liabilities, whose outcome will not be known until after the UK has left.

Third, there is the question of the EU's pension obligations. The EU has not operated a funded pension fund.

Rather, about a third of the cost of pensions has been funded by contributions from existing employees, while the remaining two-thirds has come from the member states through the EU budget. Arguably, the UK has an obligation to contribute its due share of future pension liabilities beyond even the end of the current budgeting period up to 2020.

The British might reasonably counter that the cost of contributing to the pensions of EU employees cannot be separated from the benefits provided by EU membership. Indeed, they should be regarded as both essential parts of the whole. Accordingly, when the UK ceases to be a member of the EU, and therefore ceases to enjoy its benefits, then it should cease to be liable for continuing pension payments.

Fourth, there is the matter of the EU's assets. If the UK has to contribute to the EU's future financial commitments, and perhaps even if it doesn't, then arguably the UK should be entitled to a share of the EU's assets, including property, which have been built up mostly during the period of its membership and which its substantial net contributions have helped to finance.

So how much will the UK have to pay? EU officials have suggested that the 'divorce settlement' will have to be as high as €100 billion. But this should be interpreted as an opening gambit. According to the Brussels-based think tank Bruegel,[22] the net Brexit bill, as a one-off amount, ranges from some €25 billion to €65 billion, that is to say from about 1% of the UK's annual GDP to about 2.5%. If we assume that the UK's annual net contribution to the EU is about €10 billion, on this basis it would take between two and a half and six and a half years before the UK saw any overall fiscal gain from leaving the EU. Needless to say, the prospect of paying anything like this sum to the EU would be greeted in Britain with outrage.

One factor to be traded off against others?

In this regard, it is noteworthy that in March 2017 the British House of Lords said that, legally speaking, all the UK's financial commitments to the EU are linked to membership. Accordingly, they cease when membership ceases. So you pays your money, and you takes your choice. All I can say is that this has the makings of an almighty row. Despite the EU's attempts to settle this matter upfront, before getting into nitty-gritty issues concerning trade, in practice the eventual financial settlement is likely to form part of the overall negotiations with the EU.

You might reasonably argue that the fact that the EU wants money from the UK strengthens the UK's hand. More than this, the EU *needs* money from the UK. If the UK left without any agreement and ceased to make any continuing payments to the EU this would unleash vicious disputes among continuing EU members over who should pick up the tab.

Perhaps you can see here the outline shape of a deal, namely the UK agrees some level of payment in return for access to the EU's market. But how much should it be prepared to pay? Should it be prepared to pay anything at all? That depends upon how important 'access' is. This is the subject of the next chapter.

7

The Single Market, the Customs Union and Free Trade Agreements

---

... if you look at the trend of EU-wide productivity, the single market leaves no trace ... It has been downhill ever since the official start date of the single market in 1992 ... the data are telling us ... that the single market is a giant economic non-event, for both the EU and the UK.

—Wolfgang Munchau, columnist
on the *Financial Times*, June 2015

We came to the conclusion that the less we attempted to persuade foreigners to adopt our trade principles, the better ... we avowed our total indifference to whether other nations became free-traders or not; but we should abolish Protection for our own selves, and leave other countries to take whatever course they like best.

—Richard Cobden, free trade campaigner,
looking back on the UK's abolition
of the Corn Laws in 1846[23]

Now that we have discussed the key underlying factors behind the Brexit negotiations we can direct attention to the two key economic features of the EU – the Single Market and the Customs Union – that the UK will be leaving. In particular, we need to ask if being outside these twin pillars of the EU would inflict major damage on the UK such that it may need to make an arrangement that mimics continued membership even if, in formal terms, it stands outside.

This then leads on to a discussion of Free Trade Agreements (FTAs) with both the EU and other countries around the world and, via a brief excursion into economic theory, to an analysis of the unilateral option – that is to say, unilateral free trade (UFT). The chapter concludes with an analysis of the 'EFTA option', and a discussion of whether FTAs are really that important anyway.

Single Market delusions

Ironically, it was a British Commissioner who, with the active support of Prime Minister Margaret Thatcher, developed and pushed through the Single Market idea. The driving force was the desire to reduce regulatory obstructions to trade. In some ways this has been a great success. The Single Market now unites 28 countries in the world's largest integrated trading bloc, with a combined GDP of some €12 trillion. But in other respects, it has been a disappointment, and some would even say a disaster.

The Cecchini Report published in 1988, before the Single Market came into being, was supremely optimistic about what gains it would achieve. The Report predicted increases of up to 6.5 or 7% in GDP over five or six years after the Single Market's inception. Even its supporters now admit, though, that this was a gross overestimate. Indeed as I shall soon argue, membership of the Single Market – and the Customs Union – have brought the United Kingdom a net loss. Yet wise heads and craggy diplomats, lofty businessmen and grizzled politicians all nod sagely in agreement when someone suggests that it is vital that the UK remains part of the Single Market, although it is clear that usually they don't understand what the Single Market actually is.

I mentioned in Chapter 1 that belief in, and adherence to, the EU has many of the characteristics of a religion. This is perhaps best illustrated by prevailing attitudes towards the Single Market. It is widely held to be the EU's 'crown jewel' and the importance of belonging to it, or of preserving 'access' to it, is widely asserted by all and sundry. Belief in it has a sort of talismanic quality that transcends rational thought and argument. As I will show in a moment, however, the reality bears scant relation to the hype.

Several leading Remain politicians are in the habit of waxing lyrical about the Single Market without adducing a shred of evidence that it has in fact been extremely beneficial. This group includes Nick Clegg, Kenneth Clarke, Sir John Major and Tony Blair. Nicola Sturgeon, Scotland's First Minister, even seems to be prepared to break up the United Kingdom on the basis of the Single Market's supposedly overwhelming importance to Scotland's economy – again without evidence.

Meanwhile, leading British businessmen, and especially the trade associations that are supposedly there to represent the business interest, have virtually all lined up in support of the importance of the Single Market, again without mustering a shred of evidence. Muttering support for the Single Market has become rather like, during the dying years of the Soviet Union, mouthing ritualistic quotes from Marx about the inevitable triumph of Communism – things you just repeat because that's what you have always done and it's what everybody else does, without ever questioning their relation to reality.

What many businesspeople seem to mean when they extol the importance of the Single Market is that 'we sell an awful lot of exports there'. But of course that is not the same thing as saying that they sell these exports there *because* of the Single Market, or that they would cease to sell these things there if the UK withdrew from the Single Market. To conclude that would require a detailed and sophisticated study, and even that would leave the outcome to some extent up in the air. Needless to say, the politicians, businesspeople and lobbying organizations that opine so confidently on this issue have not conducted any such a study.

Single Market realities

What is the Single Market? Professor Patrick Minford has provided a pithy definition:

> *The Single Market is simply the geographic area within which EU regulation creates ease of doing business and around which the EU creates a protective trade barrier as well as mandating free migration. Thus to be 'in' it requires that one submits to the regulation, the protection and the free migration.*[24]

Being within the Single Market and meeting all its regulatory requirements and standards means that British exports enter continental markets on an equal footing with goods produced there. If Britain were outside the Single Market and thereby able to apply different regulations and standards, the danger is that manufacturers would have to use two sets of labelling and packaging – or, in the worst case, two manufacturing processes.

The downside of belonging, though, is that its regulations are applied across the whole economy, including those parts of it that have no connection whatever with exporting to the EU. (More on this below.) How could Mrs Thatcher have supported such a thing? She didn't. The original vision was of a group of countries with a common, minimal level of regulation. Since then, however, regulation has grown like Topsy.

When supporters of the EU speak of the possibility that the UK will leave the EU, they often talk about it 'turning its back on', or even 'being shut out of', the Single Market. This sounds, and is meant to sound, apocalyptic. With such a large share (probably between 40% and 45%) of British exports going to the EU, it holds out the threat of some sort of economic disaster.

The image seems to be of some internal space where the Single Market is located and within which it does its business. Perhaps we can imagine a hall that is the centre for the trading of financial securities, just like stock exchanges past and present – or perhaps one of those grand buildings in old market towns that served as the Corn Exchange. Entry to this trading space is secured by a door, closely guarded by Jean-Claude Juncker, who carefully checks membership cards before allowing entry. Leaving the EU amounts to having the door slammed shut and your membership card taken away – thereby losing access to the market.

Admittedly, some commentators seem to envisage the possibility of a halfway house because they talk of departure from the EU as removing or closing 'full access' to the Single Market. The image seems to be one in which non-members are allowed into part of the space, but not all of it, or perhaps allowed into all of it but only for some of the time, perhaps Mondays and Tuesdays only, or every day but only between the hours of 11 a.m. and 3 p.m.

This analogy is completely misleading. Every country in the world has access to this room. Indeed, every country in the world has 'full access' to it. The United States, China, Japan, India and a host of other countries manage to export successfully to the EU without being part of the Single Market. They are all trying to get a Free Trade Agreement (FTA) with the EU, so far without success, but this does not involve belonging to the Single Market. So why is it so essential for the UK to be part of it?

Admittedly, non-members may have to pay some sort of entrance fee at the door (the common external tariff), which I discuss below, and in order to offer goods for sale inside this trading hall they have to comply with all the conditions and standards laid down under the rules of the exchange. But that is all: no locked doors, no limited hours of access.

Having to obey all the rules and standards of the Single Market is exactly what exporters have to do when they sell into any other market around the world. When Britain exports to America, it has to obey American rules and meet American standards, and similarly if it exports to China or Australia. The difference is that the UK does not have to apply American, Chinese or Australian rules and standards to the whole UK economy whereas, while it is in the EU, it does have to apply European rules and standards throughout the UK.

Interestingly, in so far as the formation of the Single Market has brought advantages by standardizing regulations and certifications and thereby lowering business costs across the Union, this has benefited every country that trades with the Single Market, rather than just the members. So, with regard to the UK you could say that the most important thing for British advantage is that *they* should have joined the Single Market.

This mirrors the situation with regard to the formation of the euro. Whatever else this did, it reduced transaction costs for British businesses and households since, for the bulk of their European activities, they now had only one exchange rate, namely the pound–euro rate, to worry about. But the fact that *they* had brought us some advantage by forming the euro did not mean that we should join it.

Confronting the evidence

Although it is perfectly possible to sell into the Single
Market from outside it, it is understandable that people
might presume that this would nevertheless put a country
at a disadvantage compared with being inside it. But the
evidence referred to below does not offer much support for
this presumption. In fact, while the share of the UK's goods
exports going to the EU rose sharply during the Common
Market years, from 1973 to 1992, under the Single Market
it has declined from about 54% to just below 44% now.

Moreover, the evidence suggests that many countries
outside the Single Market have done better at exporting to
it than the UK has, even though the UK is inside it. During
the existence of the Single Market, in a league table of the
40 fastest-growing exporters of goods to the 11 (other)
founder members of the Single Market, from 1993 to 2015,
the UK comes in at number 36. What is more, 14 countries
that traded with the EU under WTO rules, including the
United States, India and Japan, increased their exports to
the Single Market (excluding the UK) by 52%, compared
with 25% for the UK.

None of the above numerical comparisons makes a
conclusive case. In particular, any analysis suffers from
the bane of the economist's life, namely the absence of a
'counterfactual'. That is to say, we do not know what these
figures for the UK would have been like if it had been
outside the Single Market. It is possible that UK exports to
the Single Market countries would have been even weaker
than they turned out to be in practice. But at the very least,
these figures cast serious doubt on the thesis that for the
UK membership of the Single Market is absolutely vital.

Indeed, they suggest that the benefits of Single Market
membership are probably rather small. The really important

factor appears to be the overall health of an economy and its growth rate. And whatever benefits there have been must be set against the costs, including the UK's annual payment to the EU and the burden of EU laws and regulations.

Damage to the wider economy

As I mentioned above, while it is a member the UK has to impose EU laws and regulations on all parts of the economy, including those that are not involved in trade with Europe. Even for an open economy like the UK, these parts of the economy overwhelm the parts involved in all trade, never mind trade with Europe.

Roughly 12% of the UK's GDP is directly accounted for by exports to the EU. That means, of course, that some 88% is not accounted for by exports to the EU. (If one makes a reasonable allowance for the Rotterdam/Antwerp effect,[25] the proportion of GDP not involved in exports to the EU might be as high as 90%.) In almost all western countries, the bulk of GDP and employment concerns the satisfaction of consumer wants and these are supplied within the domestic economy: health and welfare services, the retail trade, utilities, entertainment, bars and restaurants, services such as dry cleaning and home repairs and maintenance.

Under current arrangements, such purely domestic activities are severely affected by various sorts of EU regulation. For instance, the number of hours doctors can work in the British National Health Service (along with all other workers in the economy) is limited by the European Working Time Directive, which came into force in the UK in 2009. It limits working hours to an average of 48 per week, measured over a reference period of 26 weeks, as well as imposing other obligations and limitations concerning rest and breaks.

The results for the NHS have been disastrous, since it

has been customary for junior doctors to work very long hours and in the process to build up substantial experience quite quickly. The restrictions now imposed by the EU mean that there is a shortage of experienced doctors and accordingly a shortage of would-be consultants.

Moreover, when thinking about losses from being outside the Single Market, due recognition must be made of the fact that as regards exports, across much of the service sector the Single Market does not work at all. Yet still the regulations apply. This is particularly pertinent to the UK, as it is in the traded services sector that much of its comparative advantage lies. (I will consider the particular circumstances of the City in the next chapter.) When you examine the evidence, it becomes clear that, as Michael Burrage puts it:

> *The benefits of EU and Single Market membership have been illusory, while its costs are real, onerous and unacceptable to the majority of the British people.*[26]

The Customs Union

Leaving the Single Market does not necessarily imply that the UK must be outside the so-called Customs Union, although it goes right to the heart of what the EU is about – or at least the economic side of it. The Customs Union was there from the start, whereas the Single Market only began in 1993. There are three related elements to the Customs Union and to all such arrangements between countries:

1. The members may not impose tariffs or non-tariff barriers on imports from other member states;

2. They do, however, impose the centrally agreed tariff rates on imports from the rest of the world, the so-called Common External Tariff (CET);
3. They give up the ability to negotiate trade relationships with other countries. This power is transferred to the EU.

What Theresa May appears to want for the UK is for it to have its cake and eat it. She wants to have tariff-free trade between the UK and the EU. But she also wants the UK to be able to drop the CET on imports from non-EU countries and to have freedom to negotiate FTAs with them.

As I indicated in the last chapter, this was going to be tough to achieve even before the weakening of the UK's negotiating position caused by the result of the June 2017 General Election. In particular, if the UK enjoys tariff-free access to the EU while not imposing tariffs on imports from third parties, then there is a massive incentive for other countries to divert their exports to the EU through the UK, thereby circumventing the CET. This would completely undermine the CET and cause a massive loss of customs revenue to the EU.

In order to prevent this, complex and onerous Rules of Origin arrangements, such as those that are currently operated by Norway, would need to be put in place. These assess goods' domestic content and treat them differently for tariffs depending upon what the answer is. Given goodwill on both sides – and sufficient time – it should be possible to make arrangements that are not too onerous. Nevertheless, we cannot be confident about either the goodwill or the time.

It would be open to the UK, I suppose, to agree to continue to impose the CET on imports from the rest of the world. It is even conceivable – just about – that it would give up (at least for a time) the ability to strike FTAs on its own. But this would be a bad bargain and it seems unlikely that the UK would agree to it. Accordingly, we need to analyse the UK's position assuming that a 'bold and ambitious free trade deal' is not reached with the EU and that the UK faces the CET. What then?

The Common External Tariff (CET)

The word 'common', as in the 'Common External Tariff', gives a wholly misleading impression of simplicity. I am frequently asked what rate the CET is set at. Unfortunately there is no simple answer. The word 'Common' refers to the fact that tariffs are imposed by all Union members alike, and not to the rate of tariff applied. Indeed, there is a multiplicity of tariff rates, and the mind-boggling detail of the different categories of goods to which different tariffs are applied, all painfully discussed and negotiated by the panjandrums of the trade negotiating bodies, is itself an indictment of the EU's trading arrangements. For instance, there are seven different tariff rates applicable to various sorts of coffee. Tariffs on metals are only 2% but on transport equipment they average just over 4%. And there is considerable variation within categories. Tariffs on imports of unicycles are set at 15% but suborbital spacecraft incur just 4.2%.

Tariffs on food and agricultural products are generally much higher. The tariffs on imports of confectionery average just under 30% while some dairy products attract tariffs of over 50%. The tariff regime is also constantly changing. Since the UK's referendum, the duty on grapes has increased from 14.4% to 17.6%, and some 266 new tariffs have been introduced, including a 20% impost on frozen prawns.[27]

The really interesting, and indeed revelatory, thing about this tariff regime is that no one seems able to say why a particular tariff is what it is and why it is so different from tariffs on other goods. We don't know whether the reason is because the industry producing the good in question is deemed to be strategically important, whether the workers employed in it are deemed to need special protection or whether the industry was just particularly effective at lobbying in its own self-interest. Or was the tariff imposed just to raise revenue?

Perhaps somewhere deep in some Brussels building there exists an official who negotiated the tariff on frozen prawns and can tell us – provided that he hasn't retired or forgotten – just why the tariff is 20%. But whatever he thinks the reason is, who else concurred with this judgement when the tariff was imposed, and who disagreed? What account was taken of the consumer interest? On all these questions we are left in the dark.

Facing the tariff wall

If the EU imposed the CET on British exports, the overall extent of damage is unlikely to be large. Since the UK's accession in 1973, the EU's tariffs have been coming down, in common with experience around the world. The average tariff on manufactured goods is about 4%. If British exporters to the EU had to face such tariffs the impact on their businesses would not be large. If they passed the full costs onto consumers, that would only increase prices by about 4% on average. If they instead opted to absorb the tariff, the hit to their profits would be approximately £4 billion per annum, a not unbearable sum. Most exporters would probably opt for some combination of these two options.

The size of possible CET tariffs does not fairly represent the overall extent of the burden that may need to be borne.

Between December 2015 and May 2017, the pound fell by about 17% against the euro, thereby easily offsetting the average EU tariff, if it were to be applied. Indeed, this depreciation even exceeds the 10% tariff that could potentially be imposed on UK car exports to the EU. Tariffs are really largely a non-issue – although there are particular concerns for particular sectors, including the car industry, which I discuss in the next chapter.

Perhaps the biggest concern about the UK leaving the Customs Union is the possible effect on cross-border supply chains. It is impossible to be sure how large the impact will be. It would surely be smaller if, whatever the EU decided to do about tariffs on British exports to it, the UK imposed no tariffs on imports from the EU, or elsewhere (more on this below).

But it is quite wrong to suppose that you have to be in the Single Market or the Customs Union in order to operate cross-border supply chains. Car makers operate them across North America even though NAFTA isn't a customs union (although it is, of course, a free trade area). Indeed, a large number of countries around the world operate complex supply chains involving countries that do not have trade agreements with each other.[28]

Non-tariff barriers

It is now widely acknowledged that in today's world, non-tariff barriers (NTBs) are more significant than tariffs. NTBs are varied and non-standard. Accordingly, they can be difficult to pin down and to evaluate. Examples include regulatory requirements concerning health and safety and product standards.

They certainly seem to constitute an important part of the EU's protective wall against the rest of the world. One way of assessing their impact is to compare domestic prices with world prices. Comparing the prices of manufactures solely between OECD member countries comes up with a price discrepancy at the factory or border level between the EU and the rest of the world of about 20%. Since the average tariff rate on manufactures is between 2% and 4% (depending upon how you weight different goods with widely differing applicable tariffs), this implies that the impact of non-tariff barriers on EU prices is between 16% and 18%.[29]

When the UK leaves the EU, removing these various non-tariff barriers will constitute an important part of its opening up to free trade with the world. In practice, even as an EU member, the UK faces considerable non-tariff barriers in exporting to the EU, particularly in the service sector (see below). In the goods market too, market segmentation and national preference remain key features, for example in the market for wine.

There may be some tendency for such non-tariff barriers against the UK to increase after exit. But the continuation of MRAs, as discussed in Chapter 6, deals with the most important issues affecting goods.

As with everything else in this debate, it must be remembered that Brexit simply puts the UK in the same position vis-à-vis the EU as the rest of the world, including the United States, China, India and Japan. It is difficult to see how the UK would face any extra non-tariff barriers than they face, unless it is as a result of some sense of pique over the UK leaving the club.

Most EU purchasers of UK goods and services will be too conscious of their own advantage to be much influenced by such emotional factors. The lower pound, which has made UK goods and services more competitive, will reinforce a hard-nosed assessment of continuing to buy British on normal commercial grounds. Moreover, the really important factor to bear in mind when considering both tariffs and NTBs is that the proportion of the UK's exports going to the EU has been steadily falling. For overall exports (including services) it is now down to about 44%, from 55% as recently as 1999.

The gains from trade

If the UK left the Customs Union, regardless of what the EU decided to do with regard to imposing tariffs on imports from the UK, the UK would have to decide what to do with its own tariffs. By WTO rules, unless there were a Free Trade Agreement (FTA) with the EU or other countries, the UK would have to impose the same tariff regime on imports from the EU and the rest of the world. What should the UK do? Getting the answer to this right involves an excursion into economic theory – which I will endeavour to keep both brief and (relatively) painless.

Many discussions about these issues are bedevilled by a fundamental economic illiteracy. Most importantly, the balance of trade is often viewed as a sort of profit and loss account. Exports are good (revenues) and imports are bad (costs). But this is nonsense. If this were a true reflection of reality then the world as a whole could not gain from trade since one country's exports are another country's imports and therefore 'profits' and 'losses' must sum to zero.

In reality, the world as a whole benefits substantially from trade. The gains from trade derive not specifically from exports but rather from the exchange of exports for imports. In this exchange, imports are just as important as exports. The point is that trade allows you to concentrate on producing the things that you are relatively efficient at producing and importing those that you are relatively inefficient at producing.

What is more, the gains from trade do not depend upon a country being absolutely more efficient than its trading partners at producing anything. Rather, the gains derive from each country specializing in what it does best in relative terms. This is known as comparative advantage. This point has been proclaimed by economists since the time of Adam Smith in the eighteenth century and has been spectacularly vindicated by the improvements in real incomes enjoyed as a result of globalization over the last 30 years.

There is a similar confusion about the importance of tariffs. It is widely believed that putting tariffs on your imports is 'good' because it raises revenue, as well as discouraging those pesky foreigners from selling their goods in your market. But there are umpteen ways for a government to raise revenue. Our focus on tariffs should not be about their revenue raising role but rather about the efficient allocation of resources and the maximization of income and welfare. That can include those pesky foreigners selling their goods in your market.

Another form of illiteracy concerns the ultimate objective of economic activity. According to all the great economists, the ultimate objective is consumption. We can argue about whose consumption, and of what, and when the consumption is to be enjoyed, but consumption is the end goal. Investment and production are to be regarded as merely means to reaching this end.

Yet this is not widely understood by politicians, businesspeople or the public at large. Indeed, there is another tradition in economic thinking – and in politics – that values production for its own sake. According to this viewpoint, exports are good and imports bad and countries should actively seek to achieve trade surpluses.

Economists call this belief system 'mercantilism'. Adherence to it is more prevalent than most economists would like to think. This is the philosophy that seems to underlie the economic policies of China, Germany, the Netherlands and Switzerland, which all appear content to run huge current account surpluses without end.

This is important because many of the gains that derive from free trade accrue to consumers in the form of lower prices. Moreover, these occur, at least to some extent, to the cost of some producers. So if you adopt the mercantilist view, you are bound to underestimate – or even miss altogether – the gains from free, or freer, trade.

Long spoons and the devil

In an ideal world, all countries would recognize that it was in their interests to abandon restrictions on imports in order to maximise the gains from trade. In that case there would be no need to do trade deals as each country would abandon import restrictions unilaterally.

But suppose that even if you believe that this would be in your country's interests and in other countries' interests, you know that the leaders of those other countries do *not* believe this. In other words, they are willing to drop restrictions on their imports from you (or in the case of the UK and the EU desist from imposing the CET on imports from the UK) only if this is in exchange for you dropping restrictions on your imports from them (or agreeing not to impose them). In these conditions, freer trade can be achieved by 'deals' in which one side 'concedes' entry for the other side's exports in exchange for the equivalent concession from them. This is known in the trade as 'tit for tat'.

Declaring a tariff-free policy without a trade deal is known as unilateral free trade (UFT). In a world in which the other side believes that imports are bad, if you proceed to drop your tariffs unilaterally then you make their abandonment of tariffs (or their non-adoption) *less* likely. They can just sit there and enjoy you reducing/abolishing/ not imposing tariffs without reciprocating.

In that case, if you pursue UFT you will reduce your move to free trade to about half of what it could be. Accordingly, even if you know that if you don't secure a deal you will still not impose tariffs on them, then arguably you had better keep quiet about it.

Encouraging good behaviour

There has been a suggestion from the Conservative MP and former Cabinet Minister Peter Lilley that, as the UK exits the Union, it could say that it will not impose tariffs on EU exports, hoping that the EU won't impose tariffs on the UK, but the UK will (or might) if they do. This does not make sense in a purist world. But it might be good politics and a good negotiating ploy. This would maximise pressure from European industry on EU governments and the European Commission.

Nevertheless, there are four related factors that should constrain the UK's willingness to play this 'game' and may make it better simply to declare UFT:

◆ The EU may be determined not to allow the UK tariff-free and hassle-free access to its market come what may, and certainly not within the two-year negotiating window laid down in Article 50 of the Lisbon Treaty. In that case, the UK would be wasting its time. More than that, it would be putting up with the losses implied by continuing to impose tariffs on imports from the rest of the world, and operating the CAP, and not signing FTAs with other countries, in the hope of realizing the first best option which, *ex hypothesi*, is unattainable.

- The delay and the associated uncertainty is itself economically debilitating. If businesses have to wait up to two years, or more, to know the regime they will eventually be operating under, they are likely to delay investing.
- Having to suffer EU tariffs on British exports only imposes a burden on the UK to the extent that these exports cannot be costlessly diverted elsewhere. If they could be so diverted, then there would be no loss from EU tariffs and the UK might as well unilaterally abandon its own tariffs immediately because there is nothing whatever to be gained from negotiating a 'deal' even though this means that the EU will impose tariffs on imports from the UK. (More on this below.)
- The EU is fading in relative importance and the UK's future prosperity will depend upon trade with the rest of the world. If the imposition of the CET by the EU persuades British exporters to pay more attention to boosting their markets in the rest of the world this could be all to the UK's long-term good.

The attractions of unilateral free trade (UFT)

To anyone who has not been schooled in economics – and even to quite a few who have been – unilateral free trade can seem heroic to the point of naivety and absurdity. (The world 'unilateral' has unfortunate connotations.) Yet UFT has a distinguished pedigree. It was advocated, among others, by Richard Cobden, John Bright and John Stuart Mill in the nineteenth century, and embraced by Sir Robert Peel, who abolished the Corn Laws in 1846. Speaking in the House of Commons in that year he said:

> *I trust the government ... will not resume the policy which they and we have found most inconvenient, namely the haggling with foreign countries about reciprocal concessions, instead of taking that independent course which we believe to be conducive to our own interests ... (L)et us trust that our example, with the proof of practical benefits we derive from it, will at no remote period insure the adoption of the principles on which we have acted ... Let, therefore, our commerce be as free as our institutions. Let us proclaim commerce free, and nation after nation will follow our example.*[30]

After the repeal of the Corn Laws, a number of countries entered into bilateral trade treaties with Britain, although it is a matter of dispute between economic historians just how successful Britain was in persuading other countries to liberalize trade in their own interest and indeed whether UFT was the optimal policy for the UK at the time. What we do know, though, is that under UFT during the nineteenth century, the UK economy flourished and was dominant in international trade.

In today's world, if the UK declared UFT, even though the EU would surely remain protectionist initially, it might subsequently be persuaded to move towards free trade itself, as it acknowledged, and European consumers recognized, the benefits that the UK had reaped from the policy.

Strikingly, in the twentieth century, UFT was advocated by the left-wing Cambridge firebrand Joan Robinson. Despite her profound misgivings about neo-classical economics, she remained a free-trader. She once said: '... just because your neighbours throw rocks in their harbours doesn't mean you have to throw rocks in yours'.[31]

UFT is also the policy adopted by Hong Kong and Singapore today. Although Hong Kong does limit market access in some service sectors, as far as goods are concerned it has not imposed duties or quantitative restrictions on exports and imports since 1841. Over the last half-century, Singapore has been the most open economy in the world. Although it imposes tariffs on some goods, e.g. alcohol and cars, according to the WTO, the average tariff on imports of manufactured goods is zero. What is more, Singapore moved to this state of more or less completely free trade unilaterally.

New Zealand is another interesting case. Up to 1984, according to the OECD, New Zealand had probably the highest tariffs on manufactured goods of any OECD country, and it was the only developed country to maintain a comprehensive system of quantitative controls. Subsequently, although it has signed many FTAs, New Zealand has transformed itself from a highly protected economy into a highly open one, largely unilaterally.

China has not exactly followed UFT but it did reduce tariffs substantially in order to qualify for admittance to the WTO. Today, its tariff rates are roughly the same as those imposed in most emerging markets. Clearly, China is not a paragon of free market virtue, and over and above tariffs it operates some significant non-tariff barriers. But the large trade surplus that China still runs is mainly the result of the interaction between high savings rates and unhelpful macroeconomic policy, rather than a deliberate policy of discouraging imports.

The macroeconomic impact of UFT

If the UK unilaterally dropped tariffs on its imports from the rest of the world this would undoubtedly pose a competitive challenge to UK producers. This challenge would be all the stronger if, simultaneously, the EU imposed the CET on UK exports to it. One's natural response is to imagine that this would be bound to exert a depressing effect on the UK economy, as imports rose at the expense of domestic production, resulting in diminished incomes and reduced employment.

To some degree this effect would undoubtedly occur. But it is not the end of the story. For a start, if this were the sum total of the macroeconomic effects then the declaration of UFT would probably result in a further drop of the pound that would serve to boost exports and retard imports in order to counter the loss of competitiveness caused by the tariff changes. (In fact, the fall of the pound registered so far may reflect the widespread assumption in the markets that something like UFT will indeed emerge. In that case, as and when the declaration comes, there would be no need for the pound to fall any further.)

But, in any case, other factors mean that in the UK's current circumstances, the macroeconomic effects of UFT may not work out in quite the orthodox way. For a start, if the UK goes down the UFT route, it would be lowering its tariffs on only some of its imports, namely the proportion that comes from the rest of the world, which is just over a half. The resultant fall in prices in the UK market would put competitive pressure, not only on UK producers, but also on the suppliers of the other half of the UK's imports, namely the EU. They would probably react by dropping their prices in the UK market in order to compete. These price cuts would affect a wide swathe of goods from German cars to French wine. The result would be that the UK's terms of trade (the ratio of export prices to import prices) would improve.

Putting it simply, there would be a source of gain to UK consumers that would exceed any losses to UK producers because it would come out of the prices charged by EU suppliers to the UK. The extra spending power created for consumers would enable them to spend more, thus creating a boost to aggregate demand to set against any depressive effect caused by the substitution of goods produced in the rest of the world for domestic production.

Of course, there would be some loss of tariff revenues. But under the current EU arrangements, of the customs revenues collected from tariffs on the UK's imports from the rest of the world, amounting to just over £3 billion per annum, about £2.3 billion is passed to the EU. In other words, if the UK dropped the CET on imports from the rest of the world, the gain to consumers from lower prices is only offset by a corresponding loss to the exchequer at the rate of 20%. There is a net gain to UK purchasing power equivalent to 80% of the value of the tariffs.

Note how different this situation is from the case normally assumed in most models of the economic impact of tariffs imposed or removed, where all the tariff revenues go to the domestic government and hence the removal of tariffs creates a substantial revenue loss for the exchequer. In that case, the loss of revenue has to be compensated by an equivalent increase in some other tax, which will withdraw purchasing power from the economy, exactly offsetting the increase in purchasing power created by the removal of the tariffs.

There will still be the prospect of damage to UK producers if the EU imposed the CET on British exports. But, because the UK is now a relatively small part of the world economy, once the initial shock of tariffs imposed by the EU had passed, UK exporters should be able to shift some of their exports from the EU to other markets with little or no loss of net revenue.

The upshot is that the net effect of a policy of UFT on the level of aggregate demand is ambiguous. Everything depends upon the relative responsiveness of domestic and foreign producers and consumers. But, in principle, there is a chance that a declaration of UFT might even improve the current account of the balance of payments and boost the level of aggregate demand. At the very least, the size of any hit to net exports and aggregate demand will be less than would have occurred in the past, e.g. in the 1930s, and less than would be implied by most macroeconomic models that assume an across-the-board reduction in tariffs, with all tariff revenue going to the domestic government.

The implication is that a declaration of UFT might not require any fall of the pound in order to maintain UK competitiveness, or at least a much smaller one than is widely believed. Since this point is not generally appreciated, and certainly not in the foreign exchange markets, if the announcement of a policy of UFT caused the pound to fall, it is quite possible that this movement would subsequently be wholly or partially reversed.

Compensating the losers

Under UFT the UK would be able to find a way of protecting some industries that were suffering, if it wanted to. But directly compensating exporters who would have to suffer tariffs on their exports to the EU, or would suffer from tariff-free competition from the rest of the world, is not allowed by WTO rules. It would be possible, however, to devise ways of indirectly compensating them.

Of course, this might not be thought necessary or desirable. After all, on average, the fall of the pound has more than compensated for any tariffs the EU might impose, or the loss of protection from competition from the rest of the world caused by dropping the CET. Even so, the UK government would need to pay particular regard to industries (including farming), where the tariffs have been particularly high and which might be adversely affected by UFT.

Nor is this only a matter of equity and fairness. It is all very well for theoretical models to assume that resources (including people) move smoothly between different occupations and areas but in practice they do not. The result can easily be large-scale unemployment and blighted towns and communities that can then impose heavy fiscal costs on the exchequer. The best approach is surely to provide transitional support that does not stand in the way of eventual adjustment but smooths the path and gives time for businesses and individuals to react with the minimum degree of disruption and suffering.

Negotiating Free Trade Agreements (FTAs)

During the referendum campaign, it was widely argued that one of the major economic advantages of the UK remaining in the EU was the ability to benefit from the EU's superiority in negotiating trade deals. Supposedly this emanates from the EU's far greater 'clout'. The EU economy, ex the UK, is about five times the size of the UK economy. Accordingly, it stands to reason, doesn't it, that outside the EU the UK will find it more difficult to negotiate beneficial trade deals than the EU does?

As regards clout, this must be true. But clout isn't the only factor involved. Because it is a union of 28 (soon to be 27) countries, each with their own different interests, in fact the EU finds it extremely difficult to conclude trade deals. Indeed, just how difficult was demonstrated in 2016 when an FTA with Canada, negotiations over which had been dragging on for seven years, was almost derailed, not by a single member country, but by the Belgian region of Wallonia.

This explains why, despite its clout, the EU's record in

agreeing FTAs is actually very poor. Admittedly, it has a fairly large number of FTAs in place. But these are over-whelmingly with small countries, many of them former colonies of EU members. In 2014, the mean size of the annual GDP of states with which the EU has made agreements was only $191 billion, which is approximately the size of Peru's GDP. By contrast, the equivalent figures for FTAs secured by Chile and Peru were $2,965 billion and $4,396 billion respectively. Meanwhile, the EU has no FTAs with the United States, India, China, Japan, Brazil, Russia, Mexico and Indonesia – in other words, with just about all of the economically significant outside world.

Moreover, the EU's trade deals rarely cover Commonwealth countries, with which the UK could be expected to conclude good agreements, and only two-thirds of them include services, while 90% or more of the agreements of Chile, Korea, Singapore and Switzerland include services.[32]

It is often suggested that the task for the UK of renegotiating the EU's existing FTAs is immensely complex and onerous. In fact, because the EU's performance at securing trade deals is so poor, the EU's FTAs cover only 14% of the UK's goods exports and 9% of its service exports. Indeed, if the UK renegotiated the two largest of these it would secure more than 60% of the market value of all the agreements concluded by the EU in 43 years. For services, more than 80% of the value of the markets covered are accounted for by exports to Norway and Switzerland.

Furthermore, some of the EU's FTAs are so-called 'mixed competence' agreements, meaning that member countries as well as the EU are parties to them. With the Korean agreement, for instance, all that would be required for this to continue post-Brexit would be a statement by the UK that it intended to continue to operate the terms of the FTA with Korea, and a corresponding statement by Korea that it would do likewise. Not exactly an overwhelming burden.

Even with the EU's 'non-mixed competence' FTAs it surely cannot be that difficult to negotiate a straightforward carry-over of the existing EU agreement with country X into a UK agreement with country X. Both simply agree to carry on with the deal that existed beforehand. Accordingly, shorn of the need to reach agreement with 27 EU partners, there is every reason to believe that the UK could easily, quickly and advantageously conclude FTAs with umpteen countries around the world.

This is confirmed by Australia's experience. When he was Prime Minister of Australia, Tony Abbott noticed that Australian trade negotiators had spent years not reaching trade deals with a host of countries, including China and Japan. So he set them deadlines. It then took Australia's negotiators just six months to sign a deal with South Korea, eight months to sign one with Japan and thirteen months to sign one with China.

In fact, signing trade deals need not be that difficult or lengthy as long as you restrict the negotiations to matters of trade, rather than getting bogged down in things to do with regulations, standards, legal disputes or environmental matters, as the EU is prone to do. The EU has spent 27 years negotiating a trade agreement with America, culminating in the much-vaunted Transatlantic Trade and Investment Partnership (TTIP) – which looks as though it is not going to get off the ground.

The attitude of other countries to Free Trade Agreements (FTAs) with the UK

Many countries around the world seem to want to do trade deals with the UK and it is likely that these could be concluded relatively easily and quickly. This includes China, India, Canada, Australia, New Zealand, Japan and, post-Trump, the United States, plus umpteen smaller countries. This group would account for a huge proportion of world GDP and trade.

A deal with the US would, of course, be the most important because of its size alone. But it also might set the tone for deals to be agreed with other countries. The election of Donald Trump as President may well have brightened the prospects for the UK. First, he seems genuinely well disposed towards the UK – unlike his predecessor. Second, he is apparently not at all well disposed towards the EU in general and Germany in particular. For good economic and political reasons he would probably see it as helpful if a successful US–UK deal could be finalised quickly.

Mind you, with regard to FTAs in general, the same tactical issue arises here as with a possible UK/EU deal that we discussed earlier. Should the UK engage in tit-for-tat negotiations or should it simply declare UFT? If it is known that the UK intends not to impose any tariffs on imports from the rest of the world, i.e. to declare UFT, then arguably it has no bargaining chips with this wide group of countries. Of course, they may decide to allow the UK tariff-free access to their markets for the same reasons that the UK might declare UFT but if they did this it would not be 'a deal' as such. After all, there would be nothing to negotiate. And they might not decide to give the UK tariff-free access, for all the usual mercantilist reasons.

The UK could therefore end up in the awkward position of trying to get both the EU and the rest of the world to give it free access to their markets as part of a quid pro quo while its intention, all along, is to give them what they want, namely free access to the UK's markets, come what may. If they know this then they may well feel little incentive to give the UK what it wants, and indeed there may be nothing worth negotiating in an FTA.

In practice, however, there are other things that could be part of FTAs with the rest of the world, even after the UK has declared UFT, including intellectual property rights, Foreign Direct Investment (FDI) and trade in services. These aspects are coming to be increasingly important compared to tariffs. Accordingly, the UK could declare UFT and still conclude mutually advantageous FTAs with a range of countries.

The European Free Trade Association (EFTA) possibility

In Chapter 11, I will argue that the European Free Trade Association (EFTA) provides a template, if and when the EU breaks up, for a wide European association of states. But, quite apart from that, could it be advantageous for the UK to rejoin EFTA as part of a strategy for building up trading relationships after Brexit? The answer, I am afraid, is that it all depends.

Currently, EFTA membership comprises only Norway, Iceland, Switzerland and Liechtenstein, but EFTA has 27 FTAs covering 38 countries. For the UK to rejoin EFTA would not involve it having to join the EEA, or to construct a Swiss-style bilateral trading relationship with the EU (both of which have been rejected by the UK government). Nor would it constrain the UK government's ability to negotiate FTAs with other countries.

The advantage of joining EFTA would be not so much the securing of tariff-free trade with EFTA members, although Switzerland is a far from insignificant market, as the ability to be party to the FTAs that EFTA has in place.

As it stands, EFTA's FTAs cover countries to which the UK sends about 19% of its exports.

Provided that the UK's accession to EFTA would not require it to submit to the panoply of the EU's regulations or other aspects of pseudo-membership of the EU, and provided that it would not require renegotiation of EFTA's FTAs – and on this it is not yet completely clear what the legal position is – securing access through EFTA's FTAs to some of its target markets would allow the UK to concentrate its trade negotiators' time and energy on securing FTAs with other countries.

The importance of trade deals overdone

So, the possibility of the UK securing trade deals is not at all bad. But does this matter much anyway? Most discussions about trade policy and trade negotiations implicitly place high importance on securing trade agreements. And, perhaps unsurprisingly, most people involved in trade negotiations do likewise. But, at the very least, they are less important than they seem and some economists even argue that they are not important at all.

This is the view of Professor Patrick Minford. He argues that countries like the UK trade at a single world price for the goods and services that they sell. They are too small to influence this price. This is known in the trade theory literature as 'the importance of being unimportant'. If a country, or group of countries, imposes tariffs on your exports, thereby reducing the (ex tariff) price that you can receive on your goods, then you can simply divert your exports to other markets. Accordingly, all the tariffs – or the FTAs that abolish them – achieve is a redistribution of trade between different countries. It is pure trade diversion.

There is much in this argument. But it is not the last

word. The analysis is consciously directed at the long run. Yet we do have to pass through the short term first! In practice, although the UK is now only a medium-sized country, in many of the things that it exports – e.g. aerospace, pharmaceuticals, financial services – it is actually a large player.

Moreover, it takes time and money to build up the infrastructure and sales operations to be able to sell effectively into new markets. Although transport costs are much less significant than they used to be, they do still matter to some degree. Accordingly, it will not be completely costless to replace existing export markets with new markets somewhere else around the globe.

The implication is that FTAs do have a role to play in securing prosperity – albeit nothing like as large a one as most trade negotiators would have you believe. Accordingly, it would be to the UK's advantage to negotiate a close FTA with the EU, and as many FTAs with as many other countries as possible.

Beyond negotiation and into the unknown

Clearly, the process of negotiating Brexit could end up well or badly. This leaves a considerable margin of uncertainty for British businesses – and businesses elsewhere. Different sectors will be affected differently. This raises particular issues that may require a response from public policy. It is now time to analyse how the balance of advantage stacks up for both particular industries and the economy as a whole.

8

The Impact of Brexit on
Particular Industries and the UK Economy

For the EU, Britain's exit would be a heavy blow, but for the British it would be a real disaster ...
—Joschka Fischer, former German Foreign Minister, in January 2013

We have at last a free hand to do what is sensible ... I believe that the great events of the last week will open a new chapter in the world's monetary history.
—John Maynard Keynes, a week after the UK left the Gold Standard in 1931[33]

What the impact of Brexit on the UK economy proves to be, of course, depends upon what sort of arrangements exist between the UK and the EU post-exit, and on how UK policy is set. As indicated in the previous chapter, there are many possible outcomes. That said, the logic of the UK's situation as analysed in the previous two chapters, and the thrust of the Prime Minister's remarks in her Lancaster House Speech in January 2017, suggest that, with or without the 'bold and ambitious free trade deal' that the Prime Minister hopes to secure, we should assume a *full* Brexit, that is to say, exit from the Single Market and the Customs Union. On that assumption, how would the British economy be affected? The place to start is with the impact on particular industries.

I begin by looking at the car industry before moving on to manufacturing in general and considering the possible effects on Foreign Direct Investment (FDI). I then go on to discuss the outlook for agriculture and fisheries before turning my attention to the City and other service sectors. I follow this with a discussion of the wider options for post-Brexit Britain, including joining NAFTA and upgrading ties with the Commonwealth. I then discuss the implications of Brexit for the integrity of the United Kingdom itself. I round off with an attempt to assess the overall impact on the economy.

The car industry

The UK's car industry has been at the centre of concerns about how the UK would fare outside the EU. It employs over 800,000 people and accounts for about 12% of the UK's total goods exports, over half of which go to the EU.[34] Despite this the UK's car exports to the EU are heavily outweighed by its imports, whereas the reverse is true for trade with countries outside the EU. There are no British-owned volume car manufacturers. The bulk of UK production is accounted for by German, French, American and Japanese firms, so the possible effects of Brexit are closely connected with the attitude of foreign business owners, something I will turn to in a moment.

Although the UK's car industry is a success story, the overall industry trends are dominated by global over-capacity and the shift of car production to the emerging markets, where costs are lower. Contrary to most people's expectations, Germany is only the world's third-largest car manufacturer, after China and Japan, followed by Korea, India, the United States, Brazil, France, Spain, Russia, Mexico, Iran – and the UK, in thirteenth place.

There will clearly be massive industry pressure to forge an FTA with the EU. It has even been suggested that if a wide-ranging FTA proves to be out of reach then a specific deal for the automotive sector might be possible. If an FTA

– either general or sector specific – were not forthcoming, then exports from the UK to the EU would face the EU's external tariff, which is currently 10% on cars and 5% on imported components.

That is a significant barrier, although it would not be insurmountable. It would have the same effect as a 10% rise in the exchange rate and could be counteracted by a 10% fall in the exchange rate. Of course exchange rates bounce around but from the end of 2015 to May 2017 the pound fell against the euro by about 17%, thereby easily offsetting the tariff on finished cars, never mind components.

Of course, whatever the EU decided to do, it would be open to the UK to impose a tariff on car imports and car components into the UK from the EU, while maintaining it on imports from the rest of the world. For the reasons given in the previous two chapters, however, such tit-for-tat games are not to be recommended. Indeed, it would be better for the UK to refrain from imposing any sort of tariffs at all. That way, at least UK car manufacturers would not need to worry about having to pay the tariff on imports of components from the EU and, compared to now, would be able to import components more cheaply from the rest of the world.

This is particularly important because of the car industry's integrated supply chains. Unfortunately, though, the industry's concerns go beyond mere tariffs and concentrate on the various non-tariff barriers to which the UK could be subject once it leaves the EU, including delays and paperwork at borders, which I discussed in Chapter 6.

Mind you, every cloud has a silver lining. It has been suggested that in order to avoid these obstacles, Brexit might prompt UK-based car manufacturers to invest in building up their supply chains in the UK. This response would fit in perfectly with the lower value of the pound, which has made UK production much more cost-competitive.

The future of UK manufacturing

The automobile industry is a special case of a wider issue. It has been argued that once the UK leaves the EU, particularly if it follows a policy of zero tariffs on imports from the rest of the world as well as the EU, its manufacturing would be hit heavily. It has even been suggested that the UK's manufacturing sector could collapse. In fact, there are no reasons why UK manufacturing cannot thrive after Brexit, even after a declaration of unilateral free trade (UFT).

The fall of the pound has given UK manufacturers an enormous competitive advantage and, as argued above, on average, easily offsets any loss from tariffs, if the EU seeks to impose them. Similarly, the fall of the pound easily offsets the increase in price competition in the UK home market from outside the EU if the UK ceases to impose the EU's CET. Moreover, in that event, UK manufacturers would benefit from the lower cost of imports as a result of tariffs on imports being dropped. (Admittedly, though, costs will go up as a result of the weaker pound.)

Manufacturing also stands to gain from a relaxation of the regulatory regime imposed by the EU. Similarly, if the British government so chooses, it would be possible to operate a less rigorous green energy policy, implying lower energy costs. This would especially favour manufacturing, due to its high energy intensity. Because of these points, contrary to the widespread pessimism about the future of UK manufacturing, it is readily possible to imagine international firms relocating some manufacturing activity to the UK and/or investing more heavily in manufacturing facilities that they already have.

This may sound surprising, After all, it is often argued that the UK's comparative advantage lies in services. This is true. But this does not mean that it needs to accept a weak manufacturing sector as a necessary consequence of having a strong service sector. In particular, the financial services sector of London and the southeast hardly competes at all for labour, space or raw materials with the manufacturing sector in the Midlands and the North. After all, has the resurgence of car manufacturing in the UK reduced or inhibited the success of the City?

It is also often argued that the UK's small share of manufacturing in GDP – just under 10% – is the inevitable concomitant of the UK being a rich, successful country and that it cannot/should not aim to compete with countries in Asia that have extremely low labour costs. Yet in Germany the share of manufacturing in GDP is just over 20%. In Sweden it is about 17%. And both countries have a higher GDP per capita than the UK. Further afield, it is noteworthy that, as a share of GDP, manufacturing is higher in free trade Singapore than it is in EU-protected Britain. In fact, its share is almost double the UK's. Nor is this explained by Singapore being at a lower level of development than the UK. On the contrary, Singapore's GDP per capita is higher than the UK's.

As a successful developed economy, it is likely that those parts of manufacturing that will thrive in the UK post-Brexit are the high-tech parts. But this does not mean that low-tech manufacturing should and will be completely squeezed out. For one thing, the UK is a very diverse country with, at one end, high levels of skills, education, talent and motivation and, at the other end, the opposite. Employing large numbers of the latter group, albeit at relatively low wages, may require the continuation – perhaps even the expansion – of some low-tech manufacturing.

Moreover, the UK has been running a huge deficit on the current account of the balance of payments which has necessitated large-scale borrowing and the sale of assets to foreigners. This cannot continue. Since such a large part of the UK's trade involves manufactures, closing this gap without an expansion of the manufacturing sector is difficult to imagine.

In this regard, the recent fall of the pound is absolutely critical. It is noteworthy, for instance, that, after sterling's fall, the outlook for the UK's steel industry – and the many low-tech as well as high-tech jobs in it – looks better. So, provided that the pound remains competitive, there is every prospect that post-Brexit the share of manufacturing in the UK's GDP will rise – even if the UK declares UFT. This would be a good thing, not least because it would help to redress some of the UK's regional imbalances.

Admittedly, many analysts argue that the pound fell because Brexit implies a weaker prospect for UK exports, including manufactured goods. Provided that the market has correctly estimated the effects, then the lower pound is no reason to be more optimistic about manufacturing. Whatever advantage the lower pound gives merely compensates for what Brexit promises to take away.

In my view, however, things are not this simple. The pound has been overvalued for years. What the Brexit vote did was to act as a catalyst for a fall that needed to happen anyway. Nevertheless, if Brexit turns out to be as benign as I expect, then there is a danger that the pound could go back up again. In that case the authorities would need to deploy policies to keep it down.[35]

Foreign reaction and Foreign Direct Investment (FDI)

Given the predominance of foreign owners in UK car manufacturing, as well as in some other manufacturing industries and in financial services – which I will turn to in a moment

– foreigners' concerns deserve special consideration. Are we likely to see a substantial reduction in overseas investment in the UK?

In July 2013, the Japanese government sent a note to the UK Foreign Office warning that Japanese companies invest in the UK because they see it as a gateway to European markets and hinting that 130,000 British jobs could be at risk if the UK pulled out of the Union. The document said that there were about 1,300 Japanese firms with operations in Britain that could review their position if Britain did not continue to play a 'major role' in the EU.

As if to back up this view, in October 2013 Toshiyuki Shiya, Chief Operating Officer for Nissan, which employs 6,400 people at its plant in Sunderland in northeast England, said that it was 'very important' that the UK was a member of the EU. He also said that the threat of import tariffs imposed by the EU on British-made cars if the UK left the EU was an 'obstacle' for Nissan. Mind you, Nissan's concerns seem to have been put to rest by the Prime Minister, Theresa May, who met Carlos Ghosn, Nissan's CEO, in October 2016. We still don't know, though, quite what assurances, concrete or flimsy, she gave him.

It is possible that having withdrawn from the EU, the UK could lose some FDI, including Japanese FDI already in place. Nevertheless, this remains unlikely. The idea behind the fear is that such investment in the UK is made because the UK is a member of the EU. It is true that Japanese firms have invested in the UK not primarily to supply the UK market, which is comparatively small, but rather to use the UK to supply the EU market.

Yet the UK's attractiveness for FDI is not solely about membership of the EU. There are several reasons why Japanese and other foreign-owned firms choose to locate operations in the UK. Tariff-free, and interference-free, access to the rest of the EU is only one of them. The UK's advantages include the English language, a legal system that can be relied on and trusted, a flexible workforce, a favourable cost structure, a welcoming social and political culture and global links. And location in the UK has been made more attractive by the recent fall of the pound.

Interestingly, the Japanese government and Japanese firms are not well known for making astute judgements on major European matters. In fact, they made much the same negative noises in the late 1990s and early 2000s about the UK not being in the euro. They turned out to be completely wrong.

As if to prove that concerns about EU withdrawal are not a uniquely Japanese phenomenon, in January 2014 Steve Odell, Chief Executive of Ford's manufacturing operations in Europe, the Middle East and Africa, said that if the UK left it would be 'cutting off its nose to spite its face' and that it would be calamitous for British jobs and businesses. (Ford employs nearly 15,000 people in the UK.)

Yet, even if the UK did not secure tariff-free access to the EU, this need not present an insuperable barrier. After all, as I pointed out above, countries all round the world manage to export successfully into the EU without themselves being members of the EU. Incidentally, that includes a considerable volume of goods produced in Japan. These non-EU countries that manage to trade so successfully with the EU have no representatives on EU bodies, no seat at the Council of Ministers and no MEPs. Nor do they have to pay a penny towards the EU budget, nor impose EU regulations on the rest of their economies. (They do, of course, have to meet EU standards on those goods that are exported to the EU.)

Admittedly, it is conceivable that such rational considerations could prove wide of the mark. It is possible that, post exit, the EU could become extremely nasty in its dealings with the UK. And it is possible that, faced with such treatment, foreign operators in the UK might decide to downgrade their operations there. This danger must be weighed against other factors in the balance of considerations.

But by no means all foreign observers of the UK scene take such a negative view of Britain's prospects outside the EU. Notably, Mr Ueli Maurer, the Swiss Finance Minister, while welcoming the prospect of having the UK as a fellow European country outside the EU, warned in 2017 that Switzerland needs to beware of British competition. He said:

> *The UK has lots of advantages and if they are used cleverly to decouple from the EU, as well as the new freedom in a good bilateral relationship, then the UK could develop very positively – I'm convinced of that.*[36]

Moreover, once the initial shock of the Brexit vote had subsided, there was an impressive flow of announcements by foreign firms that indicated continued confidence in the UK. In early 2017, the Qatar Investment Authority announced that it intends to invest another £5bn in UK infrastructure over the next three to five years. Meanwhile, Siemens reaffirmed its commitment to London and Deutsche Bank, Google, Facebook, Apple and Snap all announced investments in the capital.

The exaggerated importance of Foreign Direct Investment (FDI)

That all sounds good. But there is a more fundamental point. Is FDI that important? Yet again, the British establishment's typical assessment of the extreme importance of the FDI factor is at odds with the evidence. The level of

FDI a country receives is not an accurate indicator of the amount of benefit that accrues from it.

It is possible to secure more FDI by offering more generous grants and other inducements for firms to locate operations in your country. But in that case, taxpayers' money is being used to subsidize such activity and resources are being drawn away from other sorts of activity. In general, economists think that such interference with the market is not a good idea. Why should FDI be any different? Only if the FDI makes a contribution to the economy over and above what can be captured by the participants in normal market dealings might such interference be justified. There may well be such benefits through the spillover of enhanced skills and management practices into other parts of the host economy. But this is not inevitable. The case needs to be argued and assessed against the costs, not merely taken for granted.

Given that the UK pays for Single Market membership, directly through the UK budget contribution and indirectly through the cost of the EU's regulations imposed throughout the UK economy, if FDI comes to the UK only because of the UK's Single Market membership, then this FDI has indeed been heavily subsidized. Moreover, to the extent that such subsidy is justified by the benefits that FDI brings, then it might be possible to secure the FDI more cheaply by offering direct subsidies to attract it, funded out of the money saved by not being part of the Single Market.

The bias towards the filmable

FDI is an example of a well-known phenomenon in economics, namely the concentration of the losses and hence their easy identification versus the diffusion and opacity of the gains. Suppose that withdrawal of the UK from the

EU caused a Japanese car manufacturer to close down operations in the UK. It would be easy to identify the losers, most notably all those workers in the Japanese company's UK plants. Television crews could be easily despatched to film the now deserted buildings and the closed-down or boarded-up local shops. Interviews could be held with the now redundant car workers, and all those local businesses and their employees that were dependent on the now defunct plant.

Yet that only deals with a fraction of the issue. Workers let go by this car operation will be employed elsewhere. The land and buildings formerly occupied by this plant can be used by another enterprise. And the money saved by the UK's withdrawal could be used to bring benefits elsewhere.

But where exactly is this observable? How do you film substitution effects rippling through the economy? Who do you interview? Because of the impossibility of knowing exactly how an economy will adapt to the new opportunities and challenges presented by a business failure or withdrawal, there is a natural tendency to overestimate the importance of the business's survival.

FDI is a serious issue in the debate about EU membership, but I feel sure that its importance tends to be overestimated compared to other factors.

The Common Agricultural Policy (CAP) and the outlook for British agriculture

Another topic that figures large in the UK media is the cost of the Common Agricultural Policy (CAP). The CAP provides subsidies to European farmers and keeps the prices of agricultural products artificially high through tariffs and other barriers. On dairy products, the EU's tariffs average

36%, on sugar 25% and on cereals 15%. As a net importer of such goods, the UK ends up as a net loser and its consumers pay more for food than they would if the UK were able to buy food freely on world markets.

Estimates of the cost of the CAP have varied widely over the years, with the figures generally falling over time, at least when expressed as a share of GDP. Estimates by the OECD in 1993 seemed to imply a total cost to the UK from the CAP of 4% of GDP, including government transfers. A more up-to-date study by Open Europe, published in 2012, put the cost at about 1.1% of GDP, again including the fiscal costs.

Compared to the years immediately before and after the UK's entry to the EU in 1973, when food prices figured large in the debate, the CAP has faded in relative importance. Even so, this is still a big issue. Owen Paterson, formerly Secretary of State for Environment, Food and Rural Affairs, has estimated that when the UK withdraws from the CAP, the price of food to UK consumers will drop by about 7%, thereby adding to their real incomes.[37]

But what will happen to British farmers? Following the removal of tariffs and the complex web of restrictions on imports, we could expect a major increase in food imports from outside the EU and a substantial reduction in the UK's price of food and food products. This would be bound to deliver an immediate hit to the incomes of UK farmers, who would have to slash their prices to compete. Some would be threatened with going out of business altogether.

In truth, the UK needs a national debate about land use and how to pay for farmers to provide benefits to tourists and the environment that would not be provided without some form of public subsidy. Moreover, quite apart from this, some farmers will need some sort of income support, probably mirroring the system used before the UK joined the EU.

But this is not the same thing as saying that the UK needs something like the current blanket subsidies to farmers regardless of the size and profitability of operations. This issue will no doubt generate a lot of noise. But it should be remembered that, important though agriculture is, it represents only about 1% of the UK's GDP, compared to just under 10% for manufacturing and 8–10% for financial services. (See below.)

Moreover, the experience of New Zealand, which abandoned all agricultural subsidies from 1985, suggests that the sector could be galvanized by exit from the CAP. Before 1985, the New Zealand wine industry had been protected by a tariff. It was not profitable to import cheap wine, so New Zealand produced it. In the words of Sir Lockwood Smith, former New Zealand High Commissioner to the UK, '... it was battery acid.'[38] And, of course, it was next to impossible to export the stuff. Now, just over thirty years after the abolition of the tariff, New Zealand produces some wonderful wine, which is exported across the world.

As with so much else to do with the EU, some of the greatest gains from Brexit may come from the relaxation of excessive EU regulation, especially concerning perceived risks to health, safety and the environment. The EU's embrace of 'the precautionary principle' deters the development of technologies with even a very low probability of harm.[39]

One particularly important area is the development of genetically modified (GM) crops. Unsurprisingly, the EU has been extremely cautious in promoting or allowing GM. According to the Royal Society:

Since 1992, the EU has approved 2404 experimental GM field trials for research. In comparison, over the same time there have been 18,381 GM trials for research in the USA. In crops for commercial use, there

> *is only one GM crop, an insect resistant maize variety,*
> *that is grown commercially in the EU and no GM crops*
> *have yet been approved for human consumption as*
> *fresh fruit or vegetable. In comparison, there have been*
> *117 commercial releases in the USA since 1992 and*
> *in other countries outside Europe.*[40]

Clearly, GM food is a controversial subject. Some people will doubtless view the EU's foot-dragging over GM food as following in its best traditions of protecting the public interest against the depredations of the capitalist impulse towards profit. But others may see it rather as yet another example of policy directed towards the protection of a narrow group of established producers against the interest of consumers.

Admittedly for the UK's agricultural producers, after the abolition of tariffs there would need to be a considerable adjustment, which would be painful for some. But the end result could be positive for the UK as a whole – and even for quite a few producers themselves.

The Common Fisheries Policy (CFP)

Many people in the UK's fishing industry, as well as many in the communities in and around fishing ports, feel angry about what they see as a betrayal by the UK government when EEC entry was agreed in 1973. The reduction in the exclusive rights of UK fishing fleets and the incursion of large numbers of fishing boats from other EU countries, combined with declining fish stocks and various EU regulations directed at ensuring their sustainability, have resulted in smaller catches, smaller fishing fleets and fewer people working as fishermen. Since 1970, landings into UK ports of the more valuable demersal fish (that is to say, those that feed at or near the sea bottom), such as cod, have fallen by about 80%. Gallingly, under the CFP, a large proportion of the fish caught have been thrown back dead into the sea. For the period 2003–5, discard rates were 20–60% of the catch weight for fisheries specializing in demersal fish.

The UK would surely have done better to retain national control over fishing as Norway, Greenland and Iceland have done. When the UK leaves the EU, though, we must presume that it will leave the EU's Common Fisheries Policy (CFP) with the result that the waters of the UK's Exclusive Economic Zone (EEZ), which stretches up to 200 nautical miles from the coast, will return to national control and complete UK sovereignty will be regained over inshore waters.

Because of the need to preserve fish stocks, EU regulations would not give way to a fishing free-for-all. But at least fish quotas, and their allocation between competing UK fishermen, will be decided by the UK authorities. This will surely result in benefits to UK fishermen and their communities.[41]

The EU and the City of London

At the opposite end of the spectrum from car manufacturing, agriculture and fishing, businesses operating predominantly with tangibles, and clearly, therefore, very much affected by tariffs and other arrangements concerning the movement of goods, lies the financial services industry. It deals in intangibles, for which the tariff question is irrelevant. The industry is nevertheless heavily affected by EU regulations and ways of access to European markets. Moreover, just like the car manufacturers, many of the big businesses providing Britain's output in this sector are foreign-owned.

The UK's financial services industry is often referred to as the City of London, or simply 'the City', even though not all British financial activity takes place there. It is probably the UK's greatest global success story. The latest Global Financial Centres Index (GFCI) ranks London first, as it has done consistently since 2007, followed by New York, Hong Kong and Singapore. Indeed, London ranks first in all five key areas of competitiveness: people, business environment, market access, infrastructure and general competitiveness.

As with so much else that forms the subject matter of this book, however, there is no certainty about magnitudes. It is not uncommon to hear estimates of the financial services industry's contribution to UK GDP as high as 8–10%, and sometimes much higher once account is taken of legal and other ancillary services. But even without the ancillaries, these figures exaggerate the size of the internationally mobile part of financial services. They include things like mortgages and domestic insurance, as well as the wholesale and international activities that are more normally regarded as 'the City', and which would be potentially at risk from Brexit.

According to the City of London Corporation, the contribution of the City proper, that is, excluding the domestic part of financial services, to the UK's total national income is between 3.5% and 4%, compared to just under 10% for manufacturing. Still, that is plenty large enough to mean that how the City fares outside the EU will have a crucial bearing on how Brexit affects the UK economy overall.

The EU's ambitions

There is no doubt that the EU would love it if large amounts of financial business transferred from London to some continental city and/or Dublin. Actually, the EU's dislike of

London's role and its ambitions to take London's euro business are not much changed by Brexit. Even when the UK
was looking likely to remain in the EU it was outside the
euro, and looking likely to remain so, the EU authorities
wanted much of London's financial business – especially
in euros – to be transferred to Paris or Frankfurt. Writing
in the *Financial Times* in March 2017, Christian Noyer, the
former Governor of the Banque de France, said: 'No other
sovereign or monetary zone would allow itself to rely on
an offshore centre.'

In fact, there are only a handful of global financial hubs
in the world and so most countries do not have one within
their borders. So it is not uncommon to have large amounts
of trade denominated in your currency taking place in
another jurisdiction. That is even true of the United States,
even though it has its own global hub, namely New York.

And although much euro-denominated financial business takes place in London, euro monetary policy is, of
course, set in Frankfurt by the European Central Bank, and
the eurozone authorities have full control over their banks,
being able to set their capital requirements and regulate
their activities.

What the location in London does prevent is the eurozone's ability to stifle or suppress financial markets. But it
is the suspicion of financial market participants that this
is exactly what the eurozone authorities would want if the
markets were located in their jurisdiction. This ensures that
the financial businesses would be strongly disinclined to
relocate to Frankfurt, Paris or anywhere else in the eurozone.

The loss of 'passporting rights'

Probably the most serious issue arising from Brexit concerns
so-called 'passporting rights'. These enable a financial

institution with operations in one EU country to sell into all other EU members without having to have separate operations there.[42] At present, a bank can sell from London throughout the EU. By contrast, Swiss financial institutions cannot sell directly into the EU. They have to set up a subsidiary in an EU member country. In practice, foreign banks, both Swiss, American and from just about everywhere else, overwhelmingly choose to run their EU operations from London. But when the UK leaves the EU, under existing rules they would have to set up subsidiaries in a member country, with dedicated capital – as would British banks wanting to do business in the EU.

At the very least, British banks and foreign banks with operations in the UK would face a substantial increase in costs as they would have to transfer a significant volume of business, together with the attendant jobs, from London to some other European city. In the extreme, they might think that it wasn't worth having two European centres, one inside and the other outside the EU. Given that they would have to have one inside the EU, they might plausibly move all their business out of London and close their London operations altogether, or maintain just a token presence.

How serious is this threat? In 2015, even though the US was the biggest single country destination, the EU accounted for 33% of UK exports of financial services. A recent report by Oliver Wyman put the percentage of the City's international and wholesale banking business that is EU-related at between 20% and 25% of the total.[43]

But would the loss of business be even as great as these numbers might seem to imply? There is a spectrum of possible outcomes ranging from complete relocation from London at one end, to setting up a token operation on the continent at the other. Where the outcome turns out to be along this spectrum will probably differ as between different parts of the financial sector, and will also depend upon the result of negotiations between the UK and the EU.

One possible way round the passporting problem lies in the so-called 'equivalence' provisions for non-EU countries, which allow them to export financial services to the EU without passports. Under such arrangements, UK regulations would not need to be the same as the EU's but rather they would need to be 'equivalent'.

Unfortunately, though, equivalence does not provide a real substitute for passports, not least because it is the European Commission that determines whether regulation is equivalent. And the Commission could change its mind. In any case, the UK should not be trying to regulate financial services as is done in the EU. It should surely be aiming for a better regulatory regime. In some aspects that might imply tighter regulation but in others it would surely imply looser regulation.

There has been a suggestion that a looser but more attractive solution than equivalence might be what is described as 'voluntarism'. That is to say, individual financial businesses undertake voluntarily to abide by all EU standards, laws and regulations in relation to their business and even to submit to the jurisdiction of the European Court of Justice.

This may be worth exploring but it is difficult to resist the conclusion that it would leave those firms affected in a worse position than if they had an EU passport. One concern is enforceability. As Barney Reynolds of Shearman Sterling put it: 'The idea of signing a contract to submit to EU jurisdiction does raise questions about how EU rules would actually be enforced if there were a breach.'[44]

In practice, the loss of passporting rights is of significant concern only for business banking and parts of investment banking. By contrast, it seems likely that the fund management industry would not be greatly inconvenienced by the loss of passporting rights. Passports are less useful for asset managers because the marketing of funds is still subject to many national regulations. Accordingly, asset managers often prefer to use subsidiaries for their European clients. And most big fund managers already have established legal entities in other parts of the EU, usually Dublin or Luxembourg.

For insurance, about 87% of business is handled by subsidiaries and only 13% by passports and branches. The CEO of Aviva has said: 'In the EU there is not one single market. It's no easier for me to do business in France than Singapore or China.' In total, it is likely that less than 10% of total financial services revenue is potentially at risk from the UK's exit from the EU. And the share of revenues that is likely to be lost is much smaller than this.

London's strengths

In practice, even for banks, several factors will encourage them to keep as much as possible of their business in London. For a start, London has a huge network of support facilities, including legal and accountancy services, which no other European city can match.

Equally, it has been easy to lure European bankers and other professionals to work in London, not only because of the entertainment and life-style attractions of this great global city, but also because of a relatively favourable personal tax regime – particularly compared to France. Accordingly, the efforts of several continental cities, including Frankfurt, Paris and Luxembourg, as well as Dublin, to lure bankers and other professionals into relocating to them have so far met with limited success.

Not only that, but the EU potentially has a lot to lose

from the impairment of London as a global financial centre since the EU – both its governments and its businesses – are heavy users of the financial services that it provides. Of course, such rational considerations are not necessarily going to cut much ice in Brussels.

The Clearing House problem

This is relevant to a particular area of financial activity widely believed to be especially at risk of relocation – namely the clearing of euro-denominated financial instruments, which the EU authorities have long wanted to be conducted in the euro area. Indeed, they have tried before to get this activity 'repatriated' from London but lost the case in the European Court of Justice. But with the UK out of the EU they will surely try hard to secure this objective. Former French President François Hollande recently said:

> *The City, which thanks to the EU, was able to handle clearing operations for the Eurozone, will not be able to do them ... It can serve as an example for those who seek the end of Europe ...? It can serve as a lesson.*[45]

But a lesson to whom? The EU authorities are, yet again, seriously misunderstanding financial markets if they believe that they can simply command financial activity to take place in chosen places. Clearing in various foreign currencies takes place in several overseas locations – not just London. If the EU prohibits the clearing of euro-denominated instruments anywhere except in the eurozone it will demonstrate to the world that it is a protectionist bloc.

It is noteworthy that in April 2017, Sharon Bowen, the head of America's Commodity and Futures Trading

Commission (CFTC), said that it doesn't matter where Clearing Houses are based. She added that the CFTC does not need dollar-denominated transactions to be cleared in the US.

The advantages of leaving

Even for the UK banking industry, leaving the EU is not all bad. There are some potential advantages that need to be given due weight. Over the years, a running battle has been fought between the British government and the EU over various attempts to influence or control the City's practices and institutions. Recently this battle has intensified, as major changes to EU financial-sector regulation have been proposed in response to the global financial crisis.

In particular, four measures are likely to have a large impact on the City: restrictions on the over-the-counter derivatives market; the EU's implementation of the so-called Basel 3 agreement, which imposes tougher requirements for capital and liquidity; caps on bankers' bonuses; and the proposed financial transactions (Tobin) tax.[46] From the UK perspective, the danger of such measures is that they might lead to an exodus of business, key personnel and/or financial firms to other financial centres in the world, such as New York, Dubai, Singapore and Hong Kong. If that were to happen, of course, far from strengthening Paris or Frankfurt, there would be a net loss for Europe as a whole.

In fact, although these changes may seem troublesome enough to many in the City, what should concern them more is what measures might be forthcoming in the future. After all, the story of the EU from the beginning has been that you accept one set of arrangements and then, bit by bit, you are bludgeoned into accepting something much more draconian – something that if you had been presented with in the beginning you would have found unacceptable. It is death by a thousand cuts – or, more accurately, increases.

It is widely recognized that financial services are not highly regarded in the EU. The proposed Financial Services Tax (FTT) is currently stuck somewhere in the EU regulatory long grass. If it were to re-emerge it could potentially deal a serious blow to financial services businesses. Taking this into account, would any self-interested investment bank transfer activities wholesale to Paris or Frankfurt? It is more likely that their approach would be to transfer only the bare minimum to comply with European regulations.

Looking to the longer term, despite its peculiarities and particular interests, the argument about the City falls within the same scope as the discussion about other industries. That is to say, over the long run the EU is going to fall in relative importance. In an ideal world the UK in general and the City in particular would not have to choose between doing business with the EU and the rest of the world. But if it comes to a choice, the most important market for the UK's financial services industry is going to be the rest of the world, for which it can surely be *the* global financial hub. It is essential that nothing prevents London from seizing that prize.

Remaining in the EU, with growing regulatory burdens and a profound dislike of financial services, might well prevent it. Outside the EU, even if the City loses some European business, it can still fulfil that role.

The Single Market in services

Although the financial services industry makes the most noise, it is far from being the UK's only export success story in the services sector. We need to give due weight to the interests of these other service industries. In their submissions to the Balance of Competences Review, a wide variety of service providers said that for their businesses the Single Market effectively did not exist. Chemical engineers said that the Single Market was a no-go area, while art dealers complained that while not benefiting at all from the Single Market they had to conform to EU directives.

From 1999 to 2015, from outside the Single Market and relying on their bilateral agreements, Swiss exports of services to the EU grew by virtually the same amount as UK services exports to the EU. Moreover, in 2015 Swiss service exports per capita were almost five times larger than those of the UK.

The only sector to identify the Single Market as a great benefit is aviation. The European Common Aviation Area (ECAA) enables any EU airline to fly between any two points in Europe, though it is not linked to EU membership. The ECAA has 36 members who must be prepared to accept EU aviation laws. Despite periodic scare stories about the impact of Brexit, it should be perfectly possible for the UK to be a part of this body and for intra-European aviation to be unaffected.

The British options

Having briefly reviewed the issues surrounding specific industries, it is now time to raise our sights and consider how post-Brexit Britain will relate to the world. What is the vision for the UK after it has left the EU? I have made it clear that the UK might secure a favourable and close trading relationship with the EU. I have recognized the risk, however, that this might not be achieved. This raises the fear in many people that the UK would be 'all alone' in the world. The above discussion points to factors that should allay some of those fears. In particular, I have explained that the UK would be able to negotiate FTAs with many countries around the world.

Indeed, the British government has indicated that it would like the UK to be a global champion of free trade. Nor is this just a piece of nationalistic tub-thumping. In 2017, John Bolton, the former US ambassador to the United Nations, suggested that alongside the US, the UK has the chance to forge a new 'special relationship', creating a force for trade and diplomacy.[47]

However well this vision translates into reality, there are two particular organizations that could provide the advantages of belonging to a club. The first of these is NAFTA. Unsurprisingly, though, the former Chancellor of the Exchequer, Kenneth Clarke, went out of his way to rubbish this idea, saying:

> *There has always been something of the romantic in the British soul. We can't fail to be stirred by Charge of the Light Brigade visions of Britain standing alone against the odds. It is the same sentiment behind the idea of exchanging the EU for NAFTA.*

In fact, joining NAFTA is a far from fanciful idea. The UK cannot join it while it is a member of the EU, but when it leaves the EU it could. This presents a favourable scenario for the UK because if it did join, it would have free trade with North America without any imposed restrictions on its economy, while still being able to negotiate FTAs with the EU and other countries or blocs around the world.

Senator Phil Gramm of Texas has floated the idea of the UK being invited to join NAFTA and it would undoubtedly enjoy considerable support in the US and Canada, as well as in the UK. Mind you, the relevance of this possibility has not been strengthened by President Trump's critical stance on NAFTA and his threat to renegotiate it.

Of course, if the UK had secured an FTA with the US this would replicate a large part of the benefit of belonging to NAFTA. Still, there would be some residual benefits, including securing free trade with Canada and Mexico.

The Commonwealth connection

There is another intriguing vista, which does not necessarily cut across the various other forms of association that may be available, including NAFTA. For the UK is at the centre of a remarkable group of nations called the Commonwealth.

Although this grouping has faded in the British national consciousness, the relative size of its collective GDP has been rising rapidly. The possibilities that it affords to the UK have recently been championed by the former Conservative Cabinet Minister David Howell in his book *Old Links and New Ties*.[48] In it he emphasizes that the Commonwealth is a 'network stretching across 54 independent nations, embracing 16 realms and 38 republics or other monarchies and somewhere above 2 billion people, just about a third of the human race – and on paper at least an economic colossus with 20 per cent of the world's trade and growth prospects that would make European eyes green with envy'.

It cannot be stressed enough how attractive the growth prospects of the Commonwealth now are – and they are not restricted to its Asian members, including India, good though prospects there are. The group includes several African countries that have recently been growing strongly. Indeed, many good judges think that the African economy may be about to take off in just the way the Asian Tigers did a few decades ago.

This is deeply ironic because when the UK joined the EU in 1973, and in the process downgraded its Commonwealth connections, this was largely because of the perception that the Commonwealth was old-fashioned and the EU represented the bright future – particularly as regards the prospects for economic growth. How wrong can you be?

Mind you, it is important not to overdo the possibilities of the Commonwealth. It is not an economic bloc in the way the EU is. It is not even a free trade area or a Customs Union. However, that does not make it irrelevant. David Howell emphasizes that in the new digital, networked world, the idea of blocs of countries looks increasingly passé. What the Commonwealth offers its members is a set of connections and linkages that facilitate trade. At the heart of it lies the English language and similar institutional and legal structures based on the British model.

There has even been a suggestion of creating a Commonwealth investment bank, a Commonwealth business visa and a Commonwealth airport queue. Even though these do not sound like game-changers, the possibilities from increased Commonwealth trade should not be lightly dismissed. After all, the EU began with the humble-sounding European Coal and Steel Community.

Too small to matter?

When contemplating such a vision, many British people (and some people elsewhere) imagine that the UK will not be able to negotiate Free Trade Agreements because it is such a small and insignificant country. This is not true. In fact, the UK is still a rather large country, the fifth- or sixth-biggest economy in the world, larger than Russia, Brazil or India. So why shouldn't it be able to negotiate satisfactory trading arrangements? After all, America does.

The reply is that America is extra-large. But then what about Singapore? Then the reply, of course, is that Singapore is especially small. It seems that the uber-pessimistic believe that you either have to be very large or very small and that the UK falls between two stools. It is a sort of reverse Goldilocks scenario: too big to be small, but too small to be big. This is nonsense. The truth is that as a still significant economy and a large market for others' exports, the UK is well placed to negotiate favourable trading relationships with many countries around the world, just as Switzerland has.

What is more, far from inexorably fading in global importance, as most people assume, the UK's position in the world's GDP rankings is set to hold its own, or even to rise somewhat. The demographic factors that I discussed in Chapter 5 will have a huge impact. Unless substantial immigration completely transforms matters, it looks as though the populations of Germany, Italy and Spain are set to fall, while France's population rises a little and then stabilizes. Meanwhile, even with tighter immigration controls in place, the UK's population is going to rise quite sharply. As I mentioned in Chapter 5, after 2050 it is quite likely that the UK's population will exceed Germany's.

Accordingly, the UK could easily be the largest economy in Europe. Although it is probable, by that point, that it would have been overtaken by Brazil and India, its overtaking of France and Germany would mean that the UK would in all likelihood still rank sixth in the world. (These comparisons are made in relation to GDP at market prices. At purchasing power parity the exact rankings are somewhat different, but the substantive point stands. What is more, when gauging importance in world markets, it is market exchange rates that matter.)

The Scottish question

So far I have considered the impact of Brexit on only economic issues. But potentially it could have the effect of shattering the United Kingdom. That would be an event of enormous significance, not just in the UK, but globally. It is possible that once the UK has left the EU, there will be a second referendum on Scotland's membership of the UK, probably to be held in 2021 or later, even though the first one, in September 2014, was supposed to settle the matter 'for a generation'. Following the Scottish National Party's disappointing showing in the UK General Election in June 2017, this prospect has receded. But it has not disappeared altogether and is still worthy of close consideration.

In the UK's Brexit referendum in 2016, a clear majority of Scots voted to stay in the EU. Accordingly, piqued by the UK's vote to leave the EU, a majority could readily vote to leave the UK. This should give many eurosceptics pause for thought. They may not like one union, namely the EU, but they tend to approve strongly of the other one, namely the UK. There is a tension, if not a contradiction, between these two positions, that reveals much about both the UK and the EU.

Clearly, not all unions are bad. Some work tolerably, or more than tolerably, well. I think there is a strong case to be made that the United Kingdom is a union that has worked well – and it promises still to do so in future. What makes the United Kingdom worth preserving (and the EU worth leaving) is the depth of British fellow feeling, a shared language, shared institutions, such as the monarchy, centuries of shared endeavours, shared suffering and shared success in war and peace.

Perhaps the EU could itself some day come close to these conditions. But it certainly isn't there at the moment. In spite of the appearance of possible contradiction between wanting to leave the EU while upholding the UK, the position is rational. In fact, the prospect of Scottish secession is less threatening than it looks. The UK government holds the cards with regard to when the referendum will be held, the question to be asked and the eligibility to vote. Moreover, although the opinion polls do not presently dance wholeheartedly to this beat, since the last referendum in September 2014 economic circumstances have moved sharply against independence. The economic arguments were always tenuous at best, particularly given the tricky question of what currency an independent Scotland would use.

But that was in the days of oil prices at $120 per barrel. Now that the oil price is nearer $50 a barrel, an independent Scotland would immediately have to levy huge increases in taxes and/or impose swingeing cuts in public spending. It is estimated that, as things stand, the non-Scottish UK taxpayer subsidizes his Scottish equivalent to the tune of about £1,000 a head per year.

Even so, many Scottish voters may feel that they would prefer membership of the EU to membership of the UK. Yet, assuming that the EU survives, it would not be bound to invite Scotland to rejoin. Indeed, various EU leaders have made it clear that after Scotland left it would not simply be able to stay in the EU. It would leave the EU when the UK left and then, after departure from the UK, would have to take its place in the queue of other countries wanting to join.

Spain in particular, with its concern over a possible secession by Catalonia, would be likely to veto any move to admit Scotland – despite its suggestion in April 2017 that it would not do so. So Scotland could easily find itself on its own for several years at least, excluded from not one union but two.

And in any case, if Scotland did eventually secure EU membership this would be far from a panacea. With the UK out of the EU, if Scotland were inside it, this would make for a very tricky border situation between England and Scotland. Even if the initial intention on both sides was to maintain a soft border, potential future difficulties over movements across the border would probably cause a substantial exodus of businesses and people from Scotland. Importantly, Scotland exports roughly four times as much to the UK Single Market as it does to the European Single Market. So which Single Market should Scotland seek to remain part of?

The upshot is that the economic losses for Scotland from leaving the UK are probably greater with the UK out of the EU. Meanwhile, as the EU's problems mount, and indeed the chances of an EU break-up rise, the wider case for Scotland to leave the UK looks weaker still. Suppose Scotland left the UK, believing that the EU would give it shelter, only to find that the EU had broken up. What a fate that would be. So, in contrast to the prevailing conventional wisdom, I believe that a Scottish secession from the UK is now much *less* likely than it was a few years ago.

The Irish question

From Scotland to Ireland, where the UK's exit from the EU is undoubtedly going to make life more difficult. Post-Brexit, Northern Ireland will still be part of the UK and therefore outside the EU, and the Irish Republic will still be in the EU. This raises the prospect of a 'hard border' being set up between the two, which could both inflame feelings and diminish trade flows, and hence damage the economies on both sides.

Partly because these issues come at a time of relative

peace, following the signing of the Good Friday Agreement that put an end to decades of sectarian violence, a clear majority of those Northern Irish people who voted in the Brexit referendum voted to remain in the EU. That being the case, some people believe that Brexit will set off a process that will lead to the departure of Northern Ireland from the United Kingdom and the reunification of Ireland.

This is a distinct possibility but I think that, just as with Scottish independence, it also remains unlikely. The British government seems determined not to impose a hard border between Northern Ireland and the Republic. In any case, there has been free movement of people between the Republic and the UK (including Northern Ireland) ever since Irish independence in the 1920s, well before the EU was even dreamed of. So free movement has in no way depended upon EU membership by both the UK and Ireland. Once the UK has left the EU it is surely set to continue.

A number of analysts have highlighted the precarious economic position that Ireland will be in after Brexit, whether or not Northern Ireland stays in the UK. A huge proportion of Irish trade is done with the UK. And Ireland has a strong self-interest in continued close ties after Brexit. So much so, in fact, that it has even been suggested that Ireland could also end up leaving the EU. This is not completely impossible. The EU is now much less popular in Ireland than it used to be. The twin drivers of disillusionment have been the EU's tough stance on Ireland after the financial crisis forced her into near collapse, and the transition, as a result of much increased prosperity, from being a net recipient of EU funds into a net contributor.

Clearly, much will depend on how well the EU fares in coming years and how well the UK gets on outside the club. If the UK does relatively well, and especially if it forges a strong trade relationship with the United States,

Ireland's other major trade partner, then an Irish exit from the EU is a distinct possibility. And that would surely make a closer association between Ireland and the UK more likely.

Weighing up costs and benefits

And so to an overall assessment. How do economists see the net costs and benefits stacking up? As you might imagine, there are umpteen possible answers. Anyone who comes up with a hard-and-fast figure, unhedged about with cavils, quibbles and ranges, just doesn't understand the complexity – and uncertainty – of the issues involved.

I briefly discussed the matter of the UK's contributions to the EU budget in Chapter 6. Not having to make these contributions – once the UK has fully extricated itself – would save the UK about 0.5% of GDP annually. A potentially more important saving, although tricky to assess, is the cost of EU regulations. A study by the think tank Open Europe, published in October 2013, estimated the cost to the UK economy of the top 100 EU regulations at £27.4 billion a year, or roughly 2% of GDP. Some analysts consider this to be way too high and others too low.

Quite apart from the difficulty of assessing the cost of EU regulations, we do not know which EU regulations, if any, will actually be rescinded. The UK government has announced (very sensibly) that a Great Repeal Bill will repeal the European Communities Act of 1972 but simultaneously will 'convert EU law as it applies to the UK into domestic law on the day we leave – so that wherever practical and sensible, the same laws and rules will apply immediately before and immediately after our departure'.[49]

It will then be up to the UK's Parliament to decide how much EU law, built up over decades and now embodied in UK law, to repeal or amend. There will have to be an intense national debate on just about all aspects of public policy, governing everything from fishing to financial services, and from GM foods to energy supply. Clearly, this is going to be spread over a long time. Accordingly, it is likely to be decades before we can begin to make a serious assessment of the impact of EU withdrawal.

As far as short-term economic factors are concerned, it is possible that the net balance of advantage or disadvantage from leaving the EU will be comparatively small. Interestingly, this is what many studies concluded immediately before and after the UK's accession in 1973. It is also the conclusion reached by Martin Howe and Brian Hindley in their pamphlet *Better Off Out?*, first published in 1996 and revised in 2001. This contrasts with the fulminations on both sides of the debate to the effect that membership of the EU is either absolutely vital, or completely ruinous.

Yet that is most assuredly not the conclusion reached by HM Treasury's study 'The long-term impact of EU membership and the alternatives', published before the referendum in April, 2016.[50] As noted in Chapter 6, it estimated that, compared to the option of staying in the EU, by 2030 on a central view Brexit would reduce the level of the UK's GDP by 7.5%. But the effect could be as large as 9.5%. Such spurious precision frequently invokes both scepticism and derision. In this case it justifiably met with both.

At the other end of the spectrum, Professor Patrick Minford has used his World Trade Model to estimate the effects of a 'full Brexit'. He puts the impact as a fall in consumer prices of about 8%, and an increase in overall GDP of about 4%. Moreover, on top of that, there would be further gains from the replacement of EU regulation with UK regulation and the introduction of something like a Green Card immigration system that stopped unskilled migration that does not pay for itself in higher tax receipts.

By now you will surely know that I am more sympathetic to Minford's view. But I cannot claim that there is an area where it is possible to be either confident or precise. I am highly sceptical of the conventional approach to such issues through the use of macroeconomic models. As with everything else in life, a judgement needs to be made about a series of uncertain elements.

The Singapore factor

One clear difficulty in making such a judgement is that we don't know what will happen to the thrust of UK economic policy, including with regard to regulation. Yet this is surely of great importance. Put the models to one side. On its own, Brexit represents neither the road to perdition nor the road to riches. Rather, it presents the UK with a series of options and a set of choices. In principle, the UK could do Brexit well or badly.

In the pre-negotiations with EU leaders, Mr Philip Hammond, the UK's Chancellor of the Exchequer, held out the prospect that if the EU did not play ball with the UK, including agreeing an ambitious free trade deal, then the UK might resort to a programme of radical tax cuts and deregulation, a strategy dubbed 'Singapore on steroids'. This reference to the tiny island state of Singapore, of which I am a great admirer, was extremely telling. When Singapore left the Malaysian Federation in 1965, few observers would have given it much chance of survival, never mind stellar success. Yet today it has a higher per capita GDP than the UK, its former colonial master.

How has this been achieved? Its taxes are low but it is wrong to think of Singapore as a capitalist nirvana where the state has shrunk back and business is left to 'just get on with it'. In fact, the truth is quite the opposite.

The state is highly interventionist and doing business there encounters a considerable degree of bureaucracy. But the government is intensely focused on the long-term growth of the Singapore economy and it has proved to be extremely successful at making major decisions in Singapore's long-term interest.

Could the UK seek to emulate this success? Its political culture is very different from Singapore's and it normally finds it difficult to make radical long-term decisions – even when they are clearly in the national interest – partly because the normal workings of the democratic political process prevent it. The prolonged indecision over the location of expanded airport capacity in the southeast of England amply demonstrates this.

The puzzling thing about Mr Hammond's remarks about 'Singapore on steroids' is that he appeared to think this is an attractive strategy only if the EU does not agree to an ambitious free trade deal. But if this strategy makes sense, why wouldn't the UK choose it anyway? Is the UK going to forswear lower taxes and deregulation as part of the price of securing a free trade deal with the EU? For the UK this would be a suicidal arrangement and I cannot believe that the British government would accept it.

Even so, it is unrealistic to imagine the UK abolishing all regulations and slashing tax rates. But it is possible to imagine it substantially reducing the regulatory burden on business and embarking on a programme of containing government spending so as to be able to reduce marginal tax rates substantially over time – for both businesses and individuals.

Actually, these are things, I think, that the UK should have done even without the Brexit shock. But it would probably not have done so, or at least would not have done so on a significant scale. By contrast, the post-Brexit reality of feeling left out in the cold – and just a bit worried – may be enough to persuade the British government and the British people to follow such a path. If this happens, it would not be the first time – in either personal or national life – that it took an outside shock, even one that some see as a disaster, to persuade someone to do what they should have done anyway.

So the impact of Brexit is not set in stone. Much will depend upon how well the UK reacts to it. Will it manage Brexit well or badly? I think that the main thrust of British history and the strengths of its institutions should lead you to believe that the UK will manage Brexit well. Indeed, on top of the recovery of national sovereignty and the re-invigoration of democracy, I suspect that in 20 or 30 years' time, the British people will wonder why they ever doubted the wisdom of leaving the EU. It might even be difficult to find people who will admit to having been Remainers in 2016.

But will the remaining 27 members of the EU be as successful in meeting *their* challenges?

Part IV

The EU's Future:
Reform, Integration or Break-Up

9

Could the EU Successfully Reform Itself?

Now in the Eurozone we are in the middle of nowhere.
We do not know if we should go further or take some
steps backwards.

—Luis de Guindos,
Spain's Economy Minister, 2017

By common consent, particularly after the Brexit vote, the EU will find it difficult to carry on as it is. One way or another, it has to change. And on past form it probably will. After all, as I explained in Chapter 1, what we now call the EU began modestly with some fairly narrow forms of economic association. Right from the beginning, though, the founding fathers envisaged that it would develop into some form of state. Since then it has made enormous strides, but it has not reached the final objective.

Moreover, several of the problems that bedevil it today are associated with the EU's current halfway-house status. Move on with the integrationist project (or perhaps even move back from it) and these problems might disappear. So change is in the air. But change into what?

The European Commission's view

There is no better place to start the discussion than the European Commission's view. In advance of the summit in Rome in March 2017, marking the sixtieth anniversary of the signing of the Treaty of Rome, Jean-Claude Juncker, the President of the Commission, produced a paper discussing the Union's future.[51] Whereas, in not so distant, more confident, times, Mr Juncker might have laid out a plan for another bold integrationist leap, on this occasion he put forward five different paths:

1. Carrying on (i.e. muddling through);
2. Nothing but the Single Market (i.e. focus on improving its workings but don't attempt any further reforms or radical integration);
3. Those who want more do more (i.e. an inner and outer ring, or a variable geometry arrangement);
4. Doing less more efficiently (i.e. some reversion of competences to national governments while the EU does more in certain chosen priority areas);
5. Doing much more together (i.e. pressing on towards full integration in foreign affairs and defence and, within the eurozone, greater coordination in fiscal, social and taxation matters, as well as European supervision of financial services).

The first and second of these options are largely variants on the status quo. You would have to be optimistic to believe that either or both of these would ensure the EU's survival, let alone its success. Indeed, the central thrust of Parts I and II of this book is that the EU cannot just soldier on as it is.

The fifth option is indeed a bold integrationist leap. It represents 'more Europe', which has been the European elites' classic remedy for problems encountered in the past. And I will turn to this 'more Europe' option in the next chapter.

But it is on options (iii) and (iv) that I wish to concentrate here. The essential question is whether there is a path that would involve reforms bold enough to ensure the EU's survival and yet be reasonably feasible. I start by discussing some of the housekeeping and tidying-up that could make the EU more attractive to its members. I then go on to discuss the possibility of more fundamental reform, including the variable-geometry option, put forward by the European Commission, and the issue of subsidiarity. I then discuss the barriers to reform. But the biggest challenge for would-be EU reformers is surely how to deal with the problem of migration. That takes up the later part of the chapter.

Ending petty annoyances

The EU has considerable scope to end the umpteen petty annoyances that diminish support for it. For instance, it could readily put a stop to the absurd duplication of the European Parliament's buildings and resources in Brussels and Strasbourg and the expensive shuttling of people between the two, simply by restricting itself to one site (presumably Brussels). It could also end the practice of employing umpteen translators by declaring that its institutions would work in only three languages – English, French and German.

As an example of the absurdity of current arrangements, at present, although just about everybody in Malta speaks English, the EU provides translations between Maltese and the EU's other languages. With an establishment of around 1,750 linguists and 600 support staff, the European Commission has one of the largest translation services in the world.

Furthermore, the EU could begin to address the issue of excessive regulation by declaring that for every new regulation that is brought in, an existing one (or even two) has to be dropped. As if to show that such a development is possible, in October 2013 the European Commission announced its intention to withdraw a series of proposed regulations covering everything from soil quality to occupational standards for hairdressers, which would have, among other things, prevented hairdressers from wearing high heels at work.

Equally, some of the EU's obvious failings that so annoy eurosceptics could simply fade away. As it is, as a percentage of the total EU budget, spending on the Common Agricultural Policy (CAP) has fallen from 73% in 1985 to 39% in 2015. Mind you, this is mainly because the overall budget has risen, rather than because the money spent on the CAP has fallen.

The possibility of reform

None of this, of course, addresses the fundamental failings of the EU. Fixing these problems would require radical reform that reshapes the roles of the Union and its member countries. Yet such a radical reform programme is far from impossible. After all, it isn't only the British who have been frustrated with the EU and out of sympathy with its aggrandizing tendencies. In June 2013, the Dutch government said: 'The Netherlands is convinced that the time of an "ever closer union" in every possible policy area is behind us.' The ruling party in the Netherlands said in the autumn of 2013 that it would like to see 'whole policy areas' returned to national governments and it has called for ways to overturn or challenge rulings by the European Court of Justice. Then there was a recent poll by the think tank Open Europe, which found that, by a majority of 2 to 1, German voters favour a decentralization of powers from Brussels. Furthermore, the Italian Prime Minister said that a return of powers 'could be possible and it could be useful for us too'.

In fact, in late 2013 a conference was held in Messina, Sicily, hosted by the former Italian Foreign Minister and eurosceptic Antonio Martino. The meeting, held under the banner of the Alliance of European Conservatives and Reformists (AECR), included representatives of parties from across Europe, gathered to discuss how a European Common Market might be formed. What made this meeting particularly poignant was the fact that it was held at the same hotel as the 1955 Messina Conference of the European Steel and Coal Community, the forerunner of the EEC. What is more, at the earlier conference, one of those present was Gaetano Martino, then Italian Foreign Minister, father of Antonio Martino.

The shift of popular opinion in Europe against the EU, which I analysed in Chapter 2, argues that across Europe political pressure for fundamental reform will be strong. Indeed, the UK's impending departure could act as the catalyst for reform. In 2017, Johan Van Overtveldt, the Belgian Finance Minister, said that Brexit had 'shattered' the principle of 'ever closer union' in the EU and he warned that it must now transform itself if it is to survive.

One could reasonably argue that, whereas a decade ago the integration fundamentalists were pressing for an EU army and justice department to build on the base of a successful monetary union, this is now widely regarded as *passé*. On this interpretation, the watershed moment was reached in 2005 when the French and Dutch rejected the EU constitution in referendums. After that, the dream of the European superstate was dead. Now, nation states are on the way back.

In any case, Germany has never been fully signed up to the 'statist' tradition that so dominates French thinking and it is well aware of the way so many EU laws and practices hold back EU economic performance. Now that Germany is stronger as a country, it is possible that it could throw its economic weight behind a programme of radical reform.

German policymakers understand that without the UK in the EU, Germany will become both more dominant and more resented, while France might seek to establish an informal grouping of Latin states against it. In addition, if Germany pressed strongly for reform, other countries would support it, including the Netherlands, Austria, Ireland, Finland, Sweden, Denmark and Poland.

Something that might strengthen the urge to reform is the need to unite against a common enemy. The most obvious candidate here is Russia, which has recently taken a more belligerent tone in its dealings with the outside world and appears to see itself as a rival to the EU with regard to association with former Soviet republics and satellites.

As I mentioned in Chapter 2, in late 2013, well before the seizure of Crimea, Russia managed to persuade Ukraine to back out of a planned trade deal with the EU, through a combination of financial inducements and veiled threats. Just before Latvia became the eighteenth member of the eurozone on 1 January 2014, its finance minister mentioned this fact and implicitly referred to Latvia's vulnerable position vis-à-vis Russia, when noting that Latvia would now be firmly tied into the institutions of the West: NATO, the EU and the euro.

If Russia continues in its current vein, then surely the countries of the EU will want to make sure they stick together. If reform is necessary to make them cooperate and to make them stronger, then they will have a clear motive to support it. Moreover, with regard to the *possibility* of reform, it must be remembered that the EU has changed dramatically in the last 50 years. When the Delors Commission came out in 1985 with a blueprint for the

Single Market, cynics were dismissive. Although it is not perfect, the Single Market now exists. Even the Common Agricultural Policy has been radically reformed, with the result that subsidies are no longer linked to production (which resulted in 'butter mountains' and 'wine lakes'), but are instead related to the area cultivated. So if the EU managed to make these radical changes in the past, why can't it reform itself now?

'Different rings' and 'variable geometry'

It is noteworthy that a few days before the Rome summit, the third, 'different-rings', or 'variable-geometry', vision of the Union's future was endorsed by the leaders of France, Germany, Italy and Spain. They envisaged an inner circle of integrated members and an outer ring of countries outside the euro and the obligation of maintaining free movement.

As a potential solution to many of the EU's problems it has much to commend it. After all, many of the EU's difficulties arise from its 'one size fits all' approach. This flies in the face of the fact that the EU's membership is extremely diverse, and many of the EU's voters do not want to be shoehorned into a common identity. Under a 'different-rings' approach, those countries that wanted to press on to full union could do so, while others that couldn't or didn't want to, could enjoy a looser form of association, but still be part of the 'European family'.

Ironically, this is a special case of the 'variable geometry' that British diplomats used to advocate as a way of squaring the UK's opposition to further integration with its continued membership of the Union. Indeed, a combination of the Commission's options (iii) and (iv), that is to say 'variable geometry', or inner and outer rings, and a return of some powers to national governments, matches the programme for reform laid down in the speech by David Cameron at Bloomberg, London, on 23 January 2013, that impressed so many people, myself included.

If such a prospect had been in view a few years ago then the UK would never have had a referendum in the first place, never mind voting to leave the EU. And there are those who believe that if and when such a prospect becomes a reality, the UK might yet decide to rejoin. Whether such a vision could feasibly be turned into reality, though, is a different matter. I will come to that in a moment.

Federalism and subsidiarity

Option (iv), that is returning some powers from Brussels while leaving the Union to concentrate on things that properly need to be done at Union level, amounts to something like the principle of subsidiarity, i.e. the idea that decisions in the Union should be taken at the lowest possible level, which I discussed in Chapter 2.

This principle can be interpreted as offering a combination of more Europe and less Europe. It would meet the aspirations of many of Europe's people for self-government while still sticking to the essential vision of the founding fathers, to develop a strong, integrated Europe. In principle, this option could be attractive with or without the simultaneous operation of option (iii).

Subsidiarity is usually presented as something that returns powers to nation states. This is feasible. But subsidiarity could also lead to the effective dissolution of nation states. The appropriate level for much decision-taking might be well below member states, that is regions or cities, while defence, foreign affairs and the environment could be transferred to the EU level. Under such a set-up, it is difficult to see what is left as the area of competence of national parliaments and governments. European nation states might as well dissolve altogether.

Under this regime, Italy would again come to resemble the patchwork of small states shown in Figure 4.2; the regions of Germany would separate, perhaps along lines similar to the various states that existed prior to German unification in 1870; the Spanish regions of Catalonia, Andalusia, Galicia and the Basque Country would separate from Castile; and Belgium would split between the Flemish-speaking north and the French-speaking south.

At first sight, France might seem likely to resist break-up as it has been a unified state for hundreds of years and, superficially at least, it seems united. But there are separatist movements in Corsica, Brittany and the French Basque Country. It might not be too fanciful to see Normandy as a separate mini-state under the European umbrella. Meanwhile, the Alpine country of the southeast might unite with northwest Italy, renewing ancient associations that existed under the Kingdom of Savoy.

Other countries might undergo similar separations. And perhaps there could even be the re-emergence of European city states. If the UK were going to remain in the EU then London would be an obvious candidate but there are others: Berlin, Munich, Paris, Madrid, Rome, Milan, Venice, and many more.

Whether this sounds like a nightmare or a dream come true, depends, I suppose, on where you stand on the great questions of identity that underlie the issues discussed in this book. For those who feel thoroughly European, it may sound like an appealing prospect. And for many people who feel primary allegiance to a region rather than a country, as is true in much of Italy, it could also seem appealing. It will be anathema, of course, to all those who believe in the nation state, or at least in *their* nation state or, in the case of the UK, in their *four*-nation state.

Like it or not, though, it is not a ridiculous vision. The prospect of regions and cities flourishing as autonomous entities within an overarching, common European umbrella, corresponds to the vision of so many of Europe's leaders, as discussed in Chapter 1. What it amounts to is a reversal of the last few hundred years of European history – or much less in the case of the new 'nation' states of Germany and Italy that were only formed in the second half of the nineteenth century.

Indeed, many of the countries of eastern Europe, including several states that are already in the EU, and a few that are in the queue to join, have had even shorter histories as independent nation states. For some, their heritage is as part of the Russian empire. For others it is as part of the polyglot Austro-Hungarian Empire – including, of course, Austria and Hungary themselves. So a federal Europe without nation states is not completely out of the question.

Barriers to reform

Is any of these radical options feasible? The fact that the Netherlands might oppose ever closer union sounds encouraging, but in practice, getting an agreement on the future shape of the EU will be fraught with difficulty. In particular, different countries have different requirements for fundamental EU reform. That may be an argument in favour of 'variable geometry' but whether that itself is going to be feasible is a matter that I will turn to in a moment. The very fact that Jean-Claude Juncker presented five options for the future of the EU underlines the central difficulty in pursuing any one of them – except, perhaps, the 'muddling through' one.

The EU has more chance of achieving reforms that do not need treaty change, not least because such changes have to be ratified by national parliaments and in some cases by referendums. Several countries, most notably France, are fearful that the EU is now so unpopular that they would not get a new treaty approved in a referendum. After all, in the first round of the French presidential election in 2017, the combined share of the vote of the two anti-EU candidates, Marine Le Pen and Jean-Luc Mélenchon, was 41%.

The trouble is that a reform package that did not require treaty changes would be unable to satisfy the demands of eurosceptics across the Union and make it fit to face the challenges that lie ahead.

Just to underline how difficult it would be to achieve fundamental reform of the EU, in October 2013 the then President of the European Commission, José Manuel Barroso, said that reform of the European Union could only be accomplished through review of the *acquis*; that is, the body of legislation, thought to comprise more than 150,000 pages, on a case-by-case basis. You can imagine what a tortuous process that would be, with different countries arguing the toss over each point.

And on the direction of radical reform, there is a fundamental cleavage between Germany and France. Whatever support Germany might glean for a liberalizing agenda from the Netherlands and the Nordic countries, it would be bound to encounter strong opposition from France. There, the tradition of an interventionist, protectionist state, going back to Jean-Baptiste Colbert in the seventeenth century, is deeply embedded. Plenty of people in Europe, particularly in France, want not to liberalize the EU but rather to consolidate it as the source of state power over markets. How on earth is it going to be possible to reach agreement between such widely differing objectives?

As to the notion that fear of a common enemy, Russia, might unite Europe, if it does, this is likely to push it in the direction of further integration rather than reform. In any case, it is interesting that some of the EU's greatest failings and weaknesses have been in the foreign policy/ defence arena. Perhaps this is because NATO provides an effective defence umbrella for Europe.

It is also worth noting that in the past, Russia has been adept at forging bilateral deals and relationships with individual EU members. It would be tempted to pursue this course again. It is not obvious that, faced with a combination of Russian bribes and threats (e.g. over energy supply), the members of the EU would be able to put up a united front. They barely managed it after Russia's seizure of Crimea in 2014. (More on this in Chapter 11.)

The feasibility of 'variable geometry'

If 'variable geometry', or inner and outer rings, seems the best way forward, it is also going to be extremely difficult to achieve – and difficult for the European elites to swallow. After all, the whole European project has been about moving forward together to a common goal. A variable Europe seems like a retreat from that vision.

Admittedly, to some extent such a multi-speed Europe already exists, with some EU members not being in either the single currency, or the Schengen area, or both. But, at least until recently, the EU's governing elites viewed this as a temporary phase. Eventually, the idea was that all countries would be in the euro and in Schengen. Indeed, all would be in everything. In the Brussels bureaucracy, those countries that had not joined the single currency were referred to, not as 'outs', but as 'pre-ins'. (I discuss the issues raised by the core countries pressing on to fiscal and polit-ical union in the next chapter.)

Accordingly, accepting a 'variable geometry' or inner and outer ring Europe as a vision for the future is a very diffi-cult thing. Indeed, such a Europe à la carte would seem, not so much a prelude to complete integration, as rather a stepping stone to break-up. The German Chancellor, in particular, has expressed fears that if countries are able to 'cherry-pick' which bits of the EU they would like and which they would not, the whole edifice could crumble.

Pushing power downwards

Nor does the subsidiarity agenda look feasible. As I pointed out in Chapter 3, this principle runs completely counter to the EU's ethos, which is all about the drive towards central control and harmonization. Accordingly, whatever EU leaders might say about subsidiarity, in practice the EU is run on principles that are directly counter to it. Moreover any move towards decentralization, especially if this pushes powers down to regions and cities, would be extremely difficult, as it involves a complete recasting of all EU arrangements and EU Treaties. And, after all, EU agreements and Treaties are between member *states*.

At the more prosaic level of their everyday lives, European people have to confront the reality of the EU's economic failure. This hardly seems to be the time to go about dissolving nation states, both ancient and modern.

Meeting the migration challenge

And now the greatest challenge that I mentioned at the beginning – mass migration. Whatever path the EU chooses

– whether it is some sort of reform agenda discussed in this chapter, or the 'more Europe' option that I discuss in the next chapter, it must address this question. There are two matters that need to be considered: admitting migrants from outside the Union and the free movement of people within the Union. The two are different but they are related.

The issue of free movement within the Union is another example of what has gone wrong with the EU since its original foundation. Free movement hardly caused any stir after the EEC was formed in 1957, not least because, as I pointed out in Chapter 2, the member states were at roughly the same level of GDP per head, and hence roughly the same incomes and living standards. Mass migrations of people from one part of the Union to another were unlikely. And they didn't happen.

But recent EU expansions have brought in countries with a much lower GDP per capita than the EU average. This has given a clear economic incentive for substantial numbers of people to move from these new EU members to the older ones. (And, of course, the attempted mass migrations of people into the EU from troubled and failed states in the Middle East and elsewhere, which I discuss next, is also a comparatively recent phenomenon.)

Migration from outside the EU

With the notable exception of the UK, you could say that in most EU member countries, movement of people from the former eastern Europe has not caused much problem at all. But this is not surprising since, with the exception of the UK, Germany and some of the smaller northern countries, the jobs market has been so weak that not that many workers from the former eastern Europe have wanted to settle there. But public attitudes to immigration from outside the EU are a very different matter. I will turn to the roots of public concern about this in a moment but first we need to recognize the links between migration from outside the Union and the free movement of people within it.

Once immigrants from outside the EU have entered an EU country, what is to stop them moving to another? Within the Schengen passport-free travel zone, nothing. This is the key reason why the Schengen system is close to collapse. Between the Schengen area and the non-Schengen UK there is a barrier and it showed up in the ramshackle refugee camp outside Calais. (Apparently, though, a considerable number of people who had found temporary refuge in this camp did manage to cross from northern France to the UK.)

The point is that, given free movement of people between EU members, each member state's border – and hence their population size and consumption – is effectively controlled, or not controlled, by every other member state. This is of key relevance to Angela Merkel's decision in 2015 to admit 1 million refugees to Germany. In what sense was it Germany to which she was admitting them rather than the EU? Granted, it was initially to Germany that they came and in Germany that they were given shelter, food and some money. Moreover, long-term residency is not enough to secure free movement rights. That would come after acquiring German citizenship. But surely that will come in time. After all, does Germany seriously imagine that it will accommodate 1 million Syrian refugees indefinitely without granting them full citizenship?

At the other end of the spectrum, Italy and Greece have unwillingly been in the front line of receiving refugees, simply because of their geographical location in relation to the flows of people. They have taken on a huge responsibility – and cost. In so doing, they have been acting for the EU as a whole but the burden remains mainly national, since other EU governments have not been in a hurry to take in migrants who have pitched up in Italy and Greece, or to share the cost.

Interestingly, while European elites are both keen to unite Europe and are relaxed about immigration, opposition to mass migration is an issue that really does seem to unite large numbers of people across Europe!

The result has been an increasing wedge between on the one hand, the majority of ordinary people who feel that they suffer from immigration economically and/or don't like its social consequences, and on the other hand, European elites, most of whom believe that mass migration is of economic benefit to the receiving countries. Are the elites right about this?

The economic principles of migration

The economic justification for the free movement of labour comes from the basic theory of resource allocation. Output and welfare are maximized if people are able to find jobs that they want to do anywhere inside the Union. After all, that is exactly what happens in any single country. Someone from Italy might want to live and work in Germany, while someone from Germany wants to live and work in France, and someone from France wants to live and work in Italy. When such movements are allowed to happen, employers can select from a deeper labour pool and employees can choose between a wider variety of jobs and conditions. The result is better businesses and richer and happier people. So no problem.

But this is not quite how things have turned out recently in Europe. Rather, there has been a tendency for large numbers of citizens from one group of countries to settle in one or more other countries. For instance, over the last ten years the UK has accepted up to 1 million immigrants from the former Eastern Europe, especially Poland, but hardly any British citizens have chosen to move to Poland. Accordingly, having lost control of their borders, individual countries have lost any control over the size of their population, which is at the mercy of these migrations of people. Nevertheless, you could argue that the mass immigration of people to countries in western Europe is advantageous. Certainly, the increased numbers of workers in a country will tend to increase the size of that country's GDP.

But, it might reasonably be interjected, why does the absolute size of a country's GDP matter if GDP per capita is unaffected? After all, no one eats GDP statistics. In fact, there are some respects in which it can be thought to matter. Other things being equal, the bigger a country's GDP is the weightier it will be in international affairs, including international negotiations. So admitting immigrants to your country can be the route to increased national power, prestige and influence. Moreover, in some circumstances, having a higher GDP because there are more workers, even when there is no effect on the per capita GDP of indigenous workers, could be advantageous in other ways. In particular, it may improve a country's fiscal position since having more workers may translate into more taxes paid.[52]

And there is a particular European circumstance that strengthens the case that immigration is in the economic self-interest of existing EU citizens even if their incomes are not immediately enhanced, namely the prospect, as things stand, of a major decline in population. With the exception of France and the UK, most European countries have very low birth rates. The result is that, without substantial immigration, their populations are set to shrink. This applies notably to Germany, Italy and Spain.

Naturally, this ties in with the issue, discussed above, of the relevance of the size of total GDP, but it also relates to GDP per capita. We can debate for ever the ideal size of population for a country, such as Germany or Italy, but population *contraction* is a different issue. In most western countries the population is ageing quite quickly. This raises the possibility of severe economic and financial problems, particularly with regard to pensions and public finances.

So, if a substantial amount of immigration could, by stabilizing the population and reducing the ratio of the retired to those still working, forestall or at least ameliorate these problems, then it could be doing the indigenous population a favour. Indeed, some economists would argue that the large, western members of the EU, and perhaps even the EU as a whole, should be actively pursuing a policy of mass immigration to head off what could otherwise become an economic and financial catastrophe.

Some analysts, and even some members of the public, thought that this was the decisive factor persuading the German Chancellor, Angela Merkel, to admit 1 million refugees into Germany. In practice, I suspect that humanitarian considerations and the abiding need of the German state to be seen as 'a good guy' in order to redress the events of the past, weighed more heavily.

The importance of per capita incomes

There is no doubt, though, that the effect of immigration on per capita GDP is of more importance than its effect on overall GDP – certainly in the mind of indigenous workers. And here the evidence is not at all conclusive in favour of allowing unlimited immigration.

Some studies have concluded, perhaps unsurprisingly, that much depends upon the type of immigration. A study by Ashton, MacKinnon and Minford on immigration into the UK found that while skilled immigration was beneficial, even to indigenous workers and to the public finances, the opposite was true for unskilled workers.[53] They estimated that each unskilled EU immigrant costs the UK taxpayer an average £3,500 per annum. It would be surprising if similar conclusions did not apply in other European countries.

Admittedly, even this is not an open and shut case since the issue is not solely about the impact on the real incomes of indigenous people now. Depending upon the type of people coming into the country, their skills, work ethic and culture, they may energize the receiving country. There is a good deal of evidence that immigrants tend to be more highly motivated and driven than the average in the societies that they have left.

Stolen jobs and/or depressed wages?

Clearly one of the most important channels through which immigration affects the welfare of indigenous workers is its impact on jobs. It is widely believed that immigrants take employment opportunities from indigenous workers. In the short term, this might be true. But for any length of time over which the economy can adjust, it is not true. This belief that immigrants take jobs corresponds to the 'lump of labour' fallacy, that is to say, the idea that there is only a fixed number of jobs to go round. But there isn't. In principle, the number of jobs is completely flexible, and can expand to take up all the labour that is available and willing to work.

Mind you, given the depressed state of the economies of most of the older EU member countries, the number of jobs available has *not* increased and this has intensified the resentment of the indigenous population toward immigrants. Indeed, in the eurozone, since the normal means of adjusting to an excess supply of labour, i.e. through the exercise of expansionary monetary or fiscal policy, are not available to individual countries, immigration into these countries actually *does* increase the rate of unemployment.

But this isn't necessarily how things will work out for all countries. As with most of economics, prices hold the key. An increase in labour supply brought about by immigration, without any corresponding increase in the supply of capital, can be expected to reduce the real wage at which people will be employed. By and large, this is how things have worked out in the UK, because the labour market is extremely flexible and macroeconomic policy is free to encourage the full take-up of all available labour. Accordingly, in the UK's case, immigration is more accurately described as reducing the real wages of indigenous workers rather than as taking their jobs.

There is an important flipside to the point that the labour market can adapt. The argument that mass immigration has been necessary as the immigrants do jobs that indigenous people don't want to do is also fallacious. If this immigration had not happened then the real wages earned in those activities would have risen and that would have brought adjustment. Some indigenous workers would have been incentivized to do these jobs, even though they didn't 'like them', and some of the activities that gave rise to this employment would have been reduced in extent because they would now have become 'too expensive' (e.g. 'designer' coffees and sandwiches).

There is a decided class issue at stake here. If it is true that immigration into western Europe has lowered the real wages of unskilled and lowly skilled people – and there is considerable evidence that it has – this has brought real benefit to many middle-class families who employ such people as builders and nannies. A cynic might say that the 'generosity and openness' of so many people on the well-heeled, liberal, left is merely thinly disguised self-interest.

Congestion, identity and security

But not all things that concern the public about immigration are readily brought down to measured real incomes. Many indigenous people are scared about being 'crowded out'. In Britain many people think that their country is simply 'full up'. Similar feelings are widespread in the Netherlands, Sweden and Austria. Mass immigration is widely perceived to lead to 'congestion' problems with regard to traffic, housing and access to public services – although, as they became aware of the prospect for a decline in the population of their countries, people might be less concerned about this issue.

If the said immigrants were carbon copies of the indigenous people, though, there would probably not be much of a problem. But they are not. In many European countries, the indigenous people feel that their culture and traditions, as well as their security, are under threat from people coming from other countries. This concern is most acute with regard to immigration from outside the EU. But, in theory at least, European countries are able to control this, whereas they have no such powers with regard to immigration from other EU members.

There is a widespread public perception that the EU has handled mass migration from outside its borders very badly, and that the Schengen passport-free travel zone which is, after all, the EU's baby, has greatly reduced the security of Europe's citizens.

For whose benefit?

The issue of the impact of immigration upon the income and welfare of pre-existing citizens has raised a fascinating issue of public policy that bears upon the judgement to be made about immigration but whose ramifications go far wider.

Suppose that the gains from immigration to the immigrants exceeded the losses to the original inhabitants. Does this mean that the said immigration should be allowed? Not under conventional concepts of what government should be about, which is, while adhering to international law and behaving with decency and humanity towards others outside the country, to promote the welfare of *existing* citizens. This is not the same thing as maximizing the welfare of all humanity. That is simply not the constituency to which national politicians are supposed to be responsible.

Interestingly, though, a former top British civil servant, Lord Gus O'Donnell, recently said that he thinks that public policy should be directed towards the maximization of global rather than national welfare. Mark Thompson, then Director General of the BBC, apparently concurred with this view.[54] One suspects that not many citizens of European countries would agree. And this probably serves to confirm what they had suspected all along, namely that their governing elites have not been governing in their interest.

Possible solutions

How could concerns about immigration be addressed? With regard to controlling immigration from outside the EU, it is reasonably clear what needs to be done. Firstly, EU leaders must agree on an EU-wide policy to deal with it. This will need to include an acceptance that an EU leader, such as Angela Merkel, cannot unilaterally decide to admit 1 million refugees without the agreement of other EU members.

As part of such an agreement, member states would have to be prepared to pay substantial amounts of money to significantly upgrade security at the EU's borders, including its sea frontiers, and provide financial help to countries like Italy and Greece that are in the front line. On intra-EU migration, the very least that needs to be done is to suspend the Schengen agreement for passport-free movement of persons. That would improve the security position although, of course, it would do nothing to limit legitimate movement of passport-holding EU citizens.

It might be possible, though, for the EU to reduce the demand for such movement by agreeing restrictions on the ability of EU migrants to claim benefits in their new country before the expiry of a certain amount of time, or until certain other conditions are fulfilled. Moreover, in the richer countries, a unilateral tightening up of the rules governing entitlement to certain benefits applying to all residents of a country, both indigenous people and recent immigrants, might deter some potential intra-EU migrants from relocating to those richer countries. Perhaps it would even be possible to apply temporary limits to the number of migrants from new EU member countries entering old EU member countries – or at least some of them. After all, that was done when Bulgaria and Romania joined the Union.

The most radical solution, of course, is to drop freedom of movement. But this would be a very bitter pill for the EU to swallow. For freedom of movement of people is included in the Treaty of Rome because it was intended that the Community, subsequently called the EU, should behave as a country. And in most normal countries, people can move about freely within them. The trouble is, though, that in most EU countries, many people, perhaps a majority, want to have control of their borders. This implies that the EU should *not* be constituted, or be regarded, as a country.

Reconsideration of the principle of free movement implies a complete recasting of the whole concept and vision of the EU. That would require a treaty change. And on this issue, if not on many others, it would probably be almost impossible to get agreement. Even if all 'western' members of the Union agreed, it would surely be very difficult to get agreement from 'eastern' members.

Reform to survive

So it is possible to imagine a way for the EU to recast itself to secure its survival. If a firm of management consultants were commissioned to construct a reform programme for survival it would probably contain five key elements:

1. Improve the EU's housekeeping, reduce regulation and stop the Union being such a busybody;
2. Allow countries to choose the level of integration that they want;
3. Push as much power and 'competence' as possible away from the centre;
4. Suspend the Schengen passport-free travel zone;
5. Significantly strengthen the external borders of whatever entity – either the EU as a whole or some inner core of it – that wants to maintain freedom of movement.

Nevertheless, such a package, and in particular the vision of Europe à la carte, goes against the grain of the integrationist tradition in the EU, and appears to be contrary to the intentions of the founding fathers. In any case, getting agreement on a radically different course for the EU is going to be extremely difficult – even if the agreement is that each country should be allowed to follow its own path.

So we come to option (v) in the European Commission's 2017 Strategy Review, i.e. to press on with more integration. In any case, as I argued in Chapter 4, that is going to be necessary for the eurozone to survive. But does 'more Europe' offer serious hope for the EU's future?

10

Is 'More Europe' the Answer?

Europe will be forged in crises, and will be the sum of the solutions adopted for those crises.
—Jean Monnet, *Memoirs*, 1978

Never let a good crisis go to waste.
—Attributed to Winston Churchill

The EU has always moved forward. Moreover, following Monnet's sage words, it has been envisaged by many of its leaders that the best way to carry on moving forward is through crises. So, with many threats in the world, shouldn't the EU's leaders seize the current opportunity, not to ease back on the integrationist push, but rather to intensify it? Indeed, this could be seen as the ideal opportunity to press forward to realize the dream of the founding fathers and create a United States of Europe.

Of course, this goes completely against the grain of the previous chapter where the case was made that the EU needs radical reform but it will find it difficult to achieve this. You could readily reach the conclusion from this analysis that the EU is heading, inevitably, towards the rocks. That is the outcome that I will consider in the next chapter. But here I examine the opposite possibility – that is, that the EU presses on to full union, in either the eurozone or the EU as a whole.

We've been here before

It would be wise not to write off the EU too easily. Adam Smith once said: 'There is a great deal of ruin in a nation.'

And the EU does have a habit of staggering on, not least because, to many of its members and their electorates, the alternatives seem too awful to contemplate.

British people in particular should be wary of pronouncing death prematurely. After all, the British stood aside from the early moves to form a common European association, haughtily asserting that the plane would never fly, only to find themselves later scrambling to get aboard. Subsequently, they stood aside from just about all further forms of closer integration, except the Single Market, which was their idea anyway, and again readily imagined some sort of disaster.

This was especially true of the plans to construct a common European currency, which many British analysts and politicians decried as pie in the sky. In this regard I too must plead guilty. From well before its inception, I argued that the euro was such a crackpot idea that it would not be adopted. I was surely right about the first part of this view, but manifestly wrong about the second.

This carries important lessons for the future. Just because you think that pressing on with more integration amounts to staying on the road to disaster does not necessarily mean that this won't happen. And, of course, it may not be a disaster. So the possibility of the EU integrating further needs to be taken seriously.

Is fiscal and political union feasible? And is it desirable? I start by discussing the specific issues raised by the eurozone forging a full union while the other EU member countries don't, before analysing the key issues raised by fiscal, political and other sorts of union. I then discuss whether the EU could withstand the break-up of the euro before going on to discuss the effects of Brexit on the EU.

The troubles of youth?

You could argue that the defects of policies and institutional arrangements that I discussed in Chapter 2 are a direct result of the fact that the EU is in an in-between position. It has assumed many of the roles usually taken by sovereign states, but it is not fully sovereign over its own territory. Most decisions are made as the result of a process of horse-trading between the EU's member countries, particularly its 'big two', France and Germany. So, once the process of integration is complete and nation states have sunk back in importance, if not actually disappeared, perhaps the quality of decision-making in the EU would improve.

After all, the United States did not emerge as the finished article in 1776. Indeed, it had to pass through a bloody and deeply traumatic civil war less than a century after its foundation. Its subsequent stellar success was far from obvious either before or immediately after that conflict. Why should we expect the United States of Europe to emerge perfectly formed?

In any case, why does the EU need to be *perfectly* formed? Even if the US, the UK, Germany, France or any of today's sovereign states are broadly well functioning, they are hardly paragons of good government. Each has its fair share of mistakes, problems and horror stories. So perfection is too high a standard. The more appropriate question to ask is whether it is reasonable to assume that, after its teething troubles had been overcome, the EU, or whatever it called itself then, would be likely to work tolerably well as a political entity.

The shape of the union

Most of the problems of fiscal and political union will be similar, whether it is the EU as a whole or just a subset of it, most probably the eurozone, that presses on to fiscal and political union – although the challenges and difficulties will probably be greater the wider the Union is cast. I will turn to those issues in a moment. But there is a series of questions posed for the Union if the eurozone presses on alone, and these need to be considered first.

As matters currently stand, given the split between those countries that use the euro and those that do not, of the 27 members of the EU (after the UK's departure), 19 would be inside such a union and 8 would be outside it, including Sweden and Denmark. Of course, it is possible that these outsiders would subsequently, one by one or together, join the eurozone. In that case, the problems of running the EU with these two different sorts of membership would be merely a transitional phase.

But this outcome does not look very likely. Sweden and Denmark will probably stay outside the single currency for the foreseeable future and perhaps for ever. Other 'outs' may stay out. In that case, the EU would have evolved into a two-tier membership. To some extent, of course, this has already happened, with various countries outside the euro and some outside various other arrangements. Nevertheless, while the euro is restricted to a currency union alone, the significance of this split is limited. Once the members of the eurozone press on to full fiscal and political union, though, the split would become more significant.

It would look as though non-euro members would be second-class, or at best 'country', members of the club. More importantly, unless some special arrangements were put in place, it might be possible for eurozone members to make laws and regulations applying to the whole EU without the 'country members' being able to prevent, or even influence, them.

That said, it might just be possible for these arrangements to evolve in a way that satisfies eurosceptics across the Union. Suppose that those countries that lie outside the integration occurring within the eurozone receive cast-iron protection against the core EU imposing its will on the fringe. Suppose, also, that they negotiate the repatriation of powers and competences from the EU that I discussed in the previous chapter. In that case, their links to the eurozone would be much closer to a free trade association, without any political baggage. (Even so, unless exemption from the Single Market was negotiated, the 'outs' would still be subject to EU regulations.)

Effectively, the eurozone would then have become an even more integrated EU, fulfilling the dreams of the founding fathers, and the outsiders would effectively, although not literally, have left it, but they would have retained the trade links that they wanted in the first place. This would be a simpler version of the 'variable geometry' discussed in the last chapter. From a sceptic's point of view, such a settlement seems quite attractive. Indeed, as noted in the previous chapter, if it had been on offer, such a set-up might well have kept the UK in the EU. Moreover, such a prospect does not seem that far-fetched.[55]

There are, however, three difficulties with this as a solution to the problem of bad governance and poor economic performance in the EU. Most importantly, although countries in the outer ring would get what they wanted, the majority of EU members would continue to be trapped in the existing EU, only with all the extra downsides of being within a full fiscal and political union. The factors I analysed in Chapters 2 and 3 making for poor governance would remain in place, but now magnified by the even closer union. Poor European economic performance would continue and the 'democratic deficit' would widen.

In any case, it is questionable whether, when push comes to shove, the leaders of the EU would countenance such an eventuality, not least because they would fear that other countries might favour the semi-detached status of the outer ring, thereby causing the whole structure to unravel. Also they would probably fear that the 'outs', now perhaps pursuing closer links with the UK, would launch just the sort of economic and tax competition that I referred to in Chapter 3. Worse, they might start to outperform the countries belonging to the inner core.

Such a two-tier Europe would effectively tear up the legal basis of the current EU and would require a new set of treaties, which would be a nightmare, if not downright impossible, to negotiate. In any case, there is a fundamental problem concerning which countries would choose to be in which tier. The easiest and least disruptive outcome would be if all countries chose to remain in their current places. But, as I argued in Chapter 4, the current make-up of the eurozone is far from ideal. It would be better if some of its members left, including Italy. Would the EU project be able to survive such a thing? This is a subject that I discuss later in this chapter.

And what about France? Suppose it chose to leave the euro, with or without Italy's earlier departure, what then? Despite the tensions, the close relationship with France remains the cornerstone of German foreign policy and the EU has depended upon the 'Franco-German motor'. If these two countries were to choose different tiers that would surely prove to be fatal to the whole project.

Is fiscal union possible?

The problems created by a two-tier Europe sound daunting but even if they were solved, or magicked away, achieving fiscal and political union would still be difficult for the members of the eurozone. In many ways it is much more demanding for disparate countries to form a fiscal union than a purely monetary one. Monetary union requires members to share an important part of their economic life, namely their currency, but it doesn't oblige them to share the same bank account. Fiscal union does.

Of course, it might be possible to approach fiscal union in stages, and at least some of the early ones might be achievable. This may well be the approach taken by France's new President Emmanuel Macron. But, as we saw with the euro, a halfway-house union can be extremely dangerous. To embark on the path to fiscal union you have to be sure of the ultimate objective. And it is on the feasibility and desirability of that ultimate objective that analysis must be concentrated.

For a true pooling of revenues and a mutual acceptance of spending obligations within the Union there has to be some sort of Union-wide agreement on tax rates, as well as on spending and benefit entitlements. That would require the mother and father of a negotiation. Moreover, once agreement has been reached, there needs to be Union-wide control. That is only possible democratically through the development of political union, which I will discuss in a moment.

The barriers facing fiscal union – never mind political union – are immense. Can you imagine the citizens of Germany, with its tradition and culture of fiscal discipline and probity, willingly entering into a fiscal union with Italy, whose tax system is famously leaky and which is characterized by high levels of tax evasion and corruption? As discussed in Chapter 4, in Italy there is intense strain between north and south over the perennial transfer of money from the prosperous north to the indigent south.

And if such a union were to be constructed, what about the details of policy? The large differences between economies would argue for continued differences between tax rates and even types and levels of expenditure. But everything about the EU's history tells you that this would not be accepted by the EU authorities. There would surely be a drive to harmonize tax rates and expenditures across the union. This would include VAT and other indirect taxes, as well as income and capital gains tax.

In due course, harmonized policy would also have to include pension entitlements. This would be not just horrendously complicated but also potentially dangerous. Different European countries have pension systems with different balances of public and private pension and different use of the contributory principle.

In order to operate such a fiscal union there would have to be a Union Finance Ministry, headed by a Union Finance Minister. Moreover, complementing such responsibilities, it would make sense for the Union to increase the financial resources available to it. This might be done by levying some new EU tax across the Union or, more likely, increasing the transmission of nationally raised taxes, such as VAT, to the EU's central budget.

Could political union work?

So fiscal union may be necessary to save the euro but doesn't sound like a good idea. In any case, good idea or not, it would need political union to make it work. Is political union viable – even for the members of the eurozone, never mind for the EU as a whole? At the very least, there are good grounds to think a European political union would not function well. So the quality of its governance would probably be low.

The population of the EU is about 500 million people, with an electorate of just over 400 million, compared with a population of 325 million and an electorate of 210 million for the United States. This would make the United States of Europe the world's second-largest democracy, behind India, which has a population of about 1.3 billion people and an electorate of over 800 million. The larger the polity, the more difficult it is to get genuine engagement from the electorate and the greater the danger of politics being enmeshed in webs of corruption and special-interest pleading.

Moreover, in contrast to the United States, the countries of the EU do not share a common language. Without this, people in different European countries cannot watch the same television shows, listen to the same radio programmes, read the same newspapers or blogs – or listen to the same party political broadcasts. Accordingly, it is extremely difficult to see how there could be fully functioning Europe-wide political parties. As the late Enoch Powell once put it, there cannot be a European democracy because there isn't a European *demos*.

Furthermore, EU members have very different institutions, political cultures and histories, encompassing everything from deeply ingrained democracy (as in the Netherlands and Sweden) to dictatorship (Germany and the former eastern bloc, as well as Greece, Portugal, Spain and Italy) and an extended period of dysfunctional democratic government (Italy again).

The political stresses and strains of keeping the EU family together are perhaps greatest with regard to Hungary. Its leader, Viktor Orban, is pursuing a radically different agenda from the liberal multiculturalism of the elites in western Europe. In March 2017 he laid out his vision of a Europe in which 'there is room for our Christian identity, our national pride'. Mr Orban has launched a campaign with billboards and newspaper advertisements screaming 'Let's stop Brussels!' These views are extremely popular – and not only in Hungary.

Of course, Hungary is not in the euro so the question of an early political union between it and the core of the EU is not on the agenda. But, with views like these shared by many Hungarians, it is difficult to see Hungary as a fully functioning member of the current EU, never mind as a candidate member of a fledging European political union.

Democracy and freedom

There is an important issue beyond the mechanics of the electoral process. In the West we have become obsessed with the idea of voting as the key to freedom. It is not. In Britain, universal suffrage was not granted until 1928, yet from the eighteenth century onwards it was widely recognized that the independence of the judiciary and the freedom of the press meant that Britain was a free country. Institutions really matter. The EU is being cavalier in the way that its elites create institutions and shoehorn states with different histories and characteristics into an artificial common identity.

It is ironic that the integrationist impulse is dominated by the noble objective of avoiding war, something that has been such a scarring part of Europe's history. For the proponents of full integration seem to have given little thought to the roots of Europe's most recent conflicts. The latest, and most terrible, of the European wars that we all so keenly want to avoid happened as a result of the institutional weakness of Weimar Germany and, through the democratic process, the collapse of democracy.

Moreover, Communism, whose icy embrace once stretched across half the European continent, arose out of the mixture of an enfeebled autocratic regime in Russia and its defeat in war. Going back further, could something like the Napoleonic wars have happened without the collapse of the ancien régime in France?

The rise of the Golden Dawn party in Greece has eerie parallels with the rise of the Nazis in Germany in the early 1930s. Meanwhile, populist right-wing parties have sprung up, or strengthened their position, more or less everywhere in Europe. If the EU's elites press on to full union without the endorsement and support of European electorates, they are risking the collapse of parliamentary democracy.

Without a clear vision of a united Europe's future political institutions, with several arguments as to why, whatever they are, they might not function well, and in view of Europe's history, to pursue the objective of full integration willy-nilly is surely an unprecedented gamble. The stakes could not be higher.

Other unions

Although people regularly talk of fiscal and political union being essential complements for the European Union to work well as a single entity, there are other unions that would need to take place. In particular, the EU edifice will not be complete without a full banking union. Across the Union it must be normal for banks to hold government debt of any EU member country rather than as now, whether pressured by national governments or acting voluntarily, to hold large amounts only of the debt of their own governments.

Similarly, regulation of banks, resolution of banking problems and the bail-out of banks – or the decision to let them go bust – would all have to take place at Union level. In such a set-up, it would be perfectly reasonable for the Union to be able to issue bonds in its own name.

As things stand, it is extremely difficult to imagine Germany – let alone other countries – agreeing to any of these proposals. In the best of all possible worlds they could only be acceptable – and workable – in the context of a fully functioning political union. Otherwise there is the prospect of complete alienation of the voters – and the tax-payers – from their governing institutions.

Two future challenges

There are two major issues coming up in the lift that would sorely test the EU's ability to make a success of fiscal union – the ageing of the population and the advent of artificial intelligence and robotics.

The first is economically important because of the hit it delivers to the sustainable rate of economic growth and the strain it places on the public finances. Everything in the EU's history suggests that it will try to 'harmonize' the approach to these challenges. Given the Union's disparate pension systems, that could be disastrous.

The second is important because of the *boost* it prom-ises to deliver to sustainable economic growth and the blow it delivers for particular forms of employment. Everything in the EU's history suggests that it will approach this issue by taxing and over-regulating the employment of AI and robotics, while in many other parts of the world it would be embraced, particularly in Asia. This could contribute to accentuating the EU's relative economic decline.

The danger is all the greater in a fully integrated EU because, as analysed earlier, EU leaders would be insulated from the full consequences of the bad decisions as the whole of Europe would be going down the same path. By contrast, without fiscal (and other) integration and harmonization, competition between different European jurisdictions would bring out clearly the cost of excessive taxation and regulation, and there would at least be the hope that European governments would be forced by this competition to embrace this most important technological revolution, rather than trying to suppress it.

The political consequences of euro break-up

If further integration poses serious challenges for the countries of Europe, so does its opposite – disintegration. This is most likely to happen as a result of one or other of two things – the possible future break-up of the euro, and the now certain and imminent departure of the UK from the EU. I will discuss the future of Europe – and the world – without the EU in the next chapter. But first we need to discuss how the EU is likely to withstand these two blows – one possible and the other certain.

If the euro breaks up would it still be possible to think in terms of further integration – i.e. 'more Europe'? Would the EU even manage to survive? European leaders have been saying that the continuation of the euro is vital to the survival of the EU. As a matter of economic logic, this is hogwash. The euro project was never necessary for the growth of European trade and prosperity. After all, several EU members, including the UK, have not been in the euro. Meanwhile, many countries in eastern Europe have continued to grow fast without being in the euro. Logically, the break-up of the euro should have no consequences for the EU. It should merely return it to the *status quo ante*, which should be perfectly viable. After all, a common currency is not needed to operate a free trade area, or even a single market.

What has been the secret of the success of the Asian Tigers? It has certainly not been the adoption of a single currency or the pursuit of harmonization. As I discuss in Chapter 11, while there has been some consideration of an Asian monetary union, the idea has never got off the ground. Meanwhile, these countries have concentrated on the real sources of economic growth, not some bureaucratic pipe dream. And, as we all know, they have continued to do extremely well – unlike their European equivalents, imprisoned by the supposed benefits of the single currency.

Politics over economics

However, that is just the logic. Clearly, politics is about something more than that – and sometimes everything but that. The departure of a single country from the euro might be bearable, depending upon which country it is. It has been widely believed that Greece is the most likely candidate for leaving the euro. Its economic plight is indeed the most serious. And it came perilously close to leaving in 2012. A Greek departure, whether from choice or because it is expelled by the other members, egged on by Germany, remains a distinct possibility. As it happens, I suspect that the euro could withstand a Greek departure, not least because Greece is a small country and it is widely believed – especially in Germany – that it should never have been admitted in the first place.

But Italy is an altogether different matter. If Italy left it would deliver a heavy blow to the integrity of the eurozone and hence to the EU itself. Italy is the EU's fourth-largest economy and a member of the G-7. Since it is such a significant country, an improvement in Italian competitiveness caused by the currency fall brought about by exit would unleash powerful pressures on other countries – including Spain, Portugal and Greece, not to mention France. Before too long, they could also choose to leave – or be forced out. And, quite apart from the economics of such a split, the optics would be terrible. After all, the Treaty set up for what was to become the EU was signed in 1957 in Rome.

If the euro broke up, even if it initially staggered on as two blocs, as discussed in Chapter 4, this would deal such a blow to the integrationist cause in Europe that the EU probably would not be able to survive in its current form. The sceptics would have been vindicated and disillusionment and anger against the European elites would spread widely.

As well as this, in the process of euro disintegration, national animosities would be fanned: the peripheral countries would be against the core for imposing such austere policies and not sharing in the burden of adjustment; the core would be against the peripheral countries for borrowing too much and perhaps not paying their debts; Germany would be against France for slipping towards the peripherals and failing to endorse austerity; and France against Germany for being so German.

Saving or dismantling the euro

Something like this seems to be the view of the European establishment. Addressing the Bundestag on 19 May 2010, the German Chancellor, Angela Merkel, said: 'It is a question of survival. The euro is in danger. If the euro fails, then Europe fails. If we succeed, Europe will be stronger.'

In 2013, the significance of the euro for the survival of the EU received support from a highly respected member of the French establishment, Professor François Heisbourg, chairman of the International Institute for Strategic Studies

(IISS). But he came to completely the opposite conclusion to Angela Merkel. In his book, *La fin du rêve européen* (The end of the European dream), he said:

> *The dream has given way to nightmare. We must face the reality that the EU itself is now threatened by the euro. The current efforts to save it are endangering the Union yet further ... You cannot create a federation to save a currency. Money has to be at the service of the political structure, not the other way round.*

He argues that European leaders have their priorities back to front and says that France and Germany should together plan a break-up of the euro in secret and implement it, with a return to national currencies, over a weekend, thereby saving the EU. Of course, merely ending the euro would not necessarily lead to fundamental reform and, as I argued in Chapter 5, would not be sufficient to end European economic under-performance. Moreover, for the reasons given above, it may not be possible to overcome the bad feeling created by a break-up of the euro.

Jacques Attali, former head of the European Bank for Reconstruction and Development, claimed in late 2013 that contractionary policies imposed in Europe by Germany were pushing France into a situation comparable with the position of Germany in 1933, when the National Socialists took over. While this may or may not be an exaggeration, Jean-Pierre Chevènement, who once stood for the French presidency, has compared the present mood in France to 1934 and 1935 before the Gold Standard blew up. He says that unless Germany changes course, the southern European countries will have to withdraw from the euro to prevent their industries from being irreversibly hollowed out.

On a different note, although it is impossible to be sure

what would come out of the chaos that would follow a break-up of the euro, as I have suggested in Chapter 4, I suspect that a complete return to national currencies would be unlikely (and undesirable). Germany could operate a successful monetary union with the Netherlands, Austria and Finland, and it might find this congenial. It is not impossible that Denmark and Sweden might join such a union and even, depending on the Union's conditions and its ambitions for statehood, perhaps Norway and Switzerland. It would be possible for France to lead a Latin monetary union consisting of itself, Spain, Italy and Portugal. Perhaps Greece would join such a group, although it might go its own way. (More on this in Chapter 11.)

How ironic it would be if this unnecessary and dangerous integration, namely the euro, designed to unite Europe, ends up by casting it asunder. But then, as the thrust of this book should have made clear, bad decisions are baked into the nature of the EU. If the failure of the euro does cause the break-up of the EU, perhaps we should regard this as happening, as Karl Marx would have said, as the inevitable result of the Union's internal contradictions.

The effect of the British departure on the EU

The threat to the EU from a break-up of the euro is there regardless of the UK's departure. Nevertheless, the two are related and Brexit introduces a whole new set of challenges for the EU to grapple with. Does the UK's departure advance or retard the forces of reform? Might it perhaps make further integration more feasible? Could it help to ensure the EU's survival? Or could it precipitate the EU's demise?

Jean-Claude Juncker, President of the European Commission, said in 2017: 'Brexit is a tragedy for the

European Union.' It certainly poses some serious challenges. The UK's withdrawal represents the loss to the EU of about 15% of its economy, nearly 12.5% of its population and almost 20% of its exports (excluding intra-EU trade). Moreover, at the very least, there will have to be extensive negotiations within the remaining EU about changing its institutions, quotas, budgets and voting procedures.

There will need to be an adjustment within the European Council to reflect the disappearance of the UK's 29 votes, and within the European Parliament as Britain's 73 seats disappear, or are reallocated. Similar issues arise in relation to the loss of Britain's European Commissioner, the depart-ure of British judges from the European Court of Justice and quotas regarding the employment of Britons or British representatives on various EU bodies. All of these changes can perhaps be accomplished easily, but they will be more likely to result in wrangling, which could easily lead on to calls for fundamental reform of the institutions.

As discussed in previous chapters, there is bound to be a wrangle about money, covering both the extent of the UK's continuing contribution to the EU budget and the size of any 'divorce settlement'. Nor will the rows be only between the UK and the EU. Different EU members are likely to be at loggerheads with each other over who should pick up the tab.

Admittedly, the UK's annual net contribution to the EU budget amounts to about £10 billion, or less than 0.1% of the Union's combined GDP. It should be possible for the EU to cope with the loss of such a comparatively small amount. In normal times, sharing out this burden among the other EU members might not be too difficult. But these are not normal times. Which country is going to line up to take its share of the burden? Germany – again? France? The result will be an unseemly row between members.

Indeed, this could precipitate a wholesale review of the EU's expenditure and funding arrangements.

The British departure will also affect the political balance and predispositions of the remaining members. Some fear that the withdrawal of one of the EU's most liberal members, and one of its strongest supporters of markets, will push the EU in the direction of greater regulation and protectionism. This is a fear most frequently expressed by businesspeople and politicians in countries that tend to agree with Britain on such issues, that is Germany, Denmark, Sweden and the Netherlands.

In April 2017 there appeared what may prove to be a harbinger of things to come. Brussels unveiled plans for a new European social policy agenda, the first major push on workers' rights for nearly ten years. This is the sort of programme that the British could be relied on to oppose, or at least to water down. It is likely to be warmly welcomed in France, despite the fact that the newly elected French President, Emmanuel Macron, is intent on liberalizing the French labour market.

Sweden's *Aftonbladet* newspaper made it clear that the British exit will be 'to Britain, Europe and Sweden's disadvantage'. It explained:

> *For the Swedish part, we would lose an important partner in the EU, we are close to the UK on many issues and it would be unfortunate for the Swedish political interests. The EU as a whole is losing a strong and important State. As the UK is one of the three heavy-weight countries in the EU, the whole Union would be hit hard by an exit. With Britain outside the EU would be a weaker Europe. It brings economic strength, military reach and credibility in international politics.*

On the other side of the account, some observers argue that since the UK is the EU's most awkward member, its departure will make the Union easier to manage and easier to drive towards closer integration.

In November 2013 Gerhard Schröder, Germany's Chancellor before Angela Merkel, blamed Britain for the eurozone financial crisis and for blocking EU measures designed to sort matters out. He said:

> *The problem has a name and that's Britain. As long as the British block these moves, nothing will happen ... We can be sure that Britain is no longer willing to join the euro area. Countries that are not in the euro area cannot prevent greater integration ... It's tough but you cannot say: 'I will not be there but I want a say.'*

Mind you, Britain's decision not to join the euro did not obviously allow the management of the single currency to be a major success. The problems of the eurozone did not emerge from, or because of, the UK. They were entirely home-grown. Indeed, had the UK joined the euro, the single currency's problems would probably have been even greater.

The demonstration effect

Far from making further EU integration more feasible, there is a clear risk that the UK's departure will make it more difficult to keep the rest of the EU together. This is particularly true if the UK appears to have obtained a good deal and seems to be doing well outside, while the remaining EU, now without British influence, moves in the direction of more regulation, integration and/or protectionism. The chances of this happening would be all the greater if, as discussed above, the financial and political forces unleashed by Britain's departure led to acrimonious disputes between remaining members.

In these circumstances, there would probably be a clamour for a new deal, or a referendum on membership, in several other countries. The leading candidates are the Czech Republic, Hungary, Poland and the Netherlands. As discussed in previous chapters, the danger of other countries taking the British route is an argument for the EU playing hardball with the UK. If the EU forces a tough deal on the UK and/or the UK leaves the negotiations without a deal, this may well lessen the dangers of an imminent departure of another country from the EU.

But, in practice, an imminent departure by another country is not on the cards whatever the deal the UK concludes. The greatest threat to the EU from the UK's departure will come a few years down the line. It will arise if, in contrast to the gloomy prognostications of the European establishment and others, the UK starts to do well outside the EU and Brexit is widely perceived to have been a success. As readers will by now know, I regard this as much the most likely scenario. Then other countries might well ask themselves whether they too might not be better off out.

The danger for the EU would be more acute if the perception of British success coincided with renewed problems in the eurozone, especially if these led to the exit of a major country. If the UK has made a real success of Brexit, Italy might end up leaving not just the euro, but the EU. And in these circumstances, the Netherlands might not be far behind. Then, surely, the writing would be on the wall for the EU as we know it. It would be deeply ironic if, having been a semi-detached member of the EU for some time, the UK's departure managed to prompt its dissolution.

Cause for regret?

Should this prospect give British eurosceptics pause for thought? Quite the reverse. I have argued in this book that whatever the EU achieved for Europe in earlier decades, it is now beyond its useful life. Indeed, with its elitism, self-aggrandizement, waste and focus on regulation, integration and harmonization, it has become the major factor holding Europe back. Accordingly, if the EU fails to enact radical reform, and if Brexit were to lead to the end of the EU, then Britain would have done the peoples of Europe a great service.

In the end, the impact of the UK's departure will depend partly on the terms of the UK's exit, its subsequent relationship with the EU and how it gets on once it has left the mothership. But the full and final assessment of Brexit and its impact will also depend on what might take the EU's place in Europe and on how the world adjusts to the end of what has, for good or ill, been a major part of its economic and political architecture.

11

The Consequences of an EU Break-Up

If the European Union collapses, you will have a new war in the western Balkans.

—Jean-Claude Juncker,
President of the European Commission, 2017[56]

You may have made yourself the Trustee for those in every country who seek to mend the evils of our condition by reasoned experiment within the framework of the existing social system. If you fail, rational change will be gravely prejudiced throughout the world, leaving orthodoxy and revolution to fight it out.

—John Maynard Keynes
in an open letter to US President
Franklin Roosevelt in December 1933

In the last chapter we reviewed the possibility of 'more Europe' being the solution to the EU's problems. Here we look at the opposite scenario. Suppose the EU breaks up altogether. What then?

I have already analysed the EU's economic performance in Chapter 5, where I argued that the EU has inhibited Europe – especially through the formation of the euro. Accordingly, I argued, the EU's demise – and the concomitant demise of the euro – could be good for Europe's future economic performance. But quite how things pan out economically will partly depend upon what, if anything, replaces the EU and on how the erstwhile members of the EU behave towards each other – and towards the world. What would Europe look like and what would its political future be? And what impact would the EU's demise have upon the shape of the world?

Together with its forerunners, the EU has been with us for 60 years and during this time it has been gradually taking over more functions from its member states. On the world stage, although its four largest members, France, Germany, Italy and the UK, have all retained individual membership of the G-7, the President of the European Commission, currently Jean-Claude Juncker, also attends its meetings. Meanwhile it has established an embryo foreign service. And it has clearly had ambitions to replace the permanent seats on the UN Security Council of Britain and France with a single seat in its own name. So it looks as though the end of the EU, if and when it comes, could be quite a spectacular event.

I start by asking whether, once it happens, the former members of the EU would be able and willing to preserve something like the Common Market from which their association began, or whether they would be likely to sink back into the bad old ways of trade restrictions. I then discuss whether there would be a serious risk of war in Europe, and what the implications of an EU break-up might be for defence and security. Then I consider what political associations might develop to take the EU's place, before turning the spotlight on how the world might look without the EU. Finally, I round off by putting the EU in an historical and intellectual perspective.

The need for a new vision

As I have argued throughout this book, if the euro manages to survive, it will be because some sort of fiscal and political union is cobbled together to save the currency union. This union would tax, harmonize and regulate until the (much subsidized) cows come home. All the indications are that without fundamental reform, such a union would make decisions profoundly inimical to the growth of the EU economy. The formation of the euro, with its awful economic effects, is a ghastly warning of what may be yet to come.

So if the EU breaks up, when thinking about future forms of association, the countries of Europe need to abandon all the thinking that led to the euro. That includes the pursuit of 'ever closer union'. In the economic sphere, they even have to abandon the idea of a Customs Union; that is, a union that imposes common tariffs on imports from outside itself. This model is becoming increasingly redundant.

The EU's Customs Union is a clear example of how the world in which the EU was established bears a diminishing resemblance to the world in which we live now. When the EU was conceived, trade flows were dominated by goods. Since then, trade in services has developed rapidly and it will surely continue to grow more in the future. This is particularly true of services that are delivered digitally – something that was, of course, unimaginable when the EEC was formed in 1957.

But if the EU were to end, there is no need for Europe to go back to a situation of atomistic states, at war with each other in all but name. As far as economic policy is concerned, the key requirement would be the development of a free trade area. This would not be beyond the wit of man to organize. The trading agreements NAFTA and ASEAN show the way forward.

The examples of NAFTA and ASEAN for the EU

President Trump is clearly not satisfied with the workings of the North American Free Trade Association (NAFTA) and is seeking a renegotiation of its terms. He may yet end up by undermining it. But for our purposes here the significant point is that the United States, Canada and Mexico successfully established NAFTA in 1994 without any of the political, legal or integrationist mumbo-jumbo that bedevils the European Union. These countries have maintained their own sovereign currencies, whose values have fluctuated considerably. And there has been no move towards forming a political union between these countries.

As a free trade area, NAFTA has some similarities with the present EU, but also some key differences. It allows free movement of goods and services, mutual access to government contracts, mutual respect for intellectual property rights and the free movement of capital. However, a key difference from the EU is that it does not involve the free movement of people. Three other key differences are that it does not force members' tariffs or other trade barriers to be the same, it allows members to negotiate trade agreements with countries outside NAFTA, and it does not have the equivalent of the EU's Single Market.

Similar points apply to the Asian trade association known as ASEAN (Association of Southeast Asian Nations), whose members are Brunei, Cambodia, Indonesia, Laos, Malaysia, Myanmar, the Philippines, Singapore, Thailand and Vietnam. In general, discussions about an ASEAN currency union have received much more publicity than those for a currency union for NAFTA, although they too have come to nothing.

Indeed, developments in the eurozone have prompted a number of high-profile officials to dismiss the possibility of an ASEAN currency union in the foreseeable future. Speaking at a press conference in early May 2012, the Chief Economist of the Asian Development Bank, Changyong Rhee, stated:

*The euro-zone should serve as a guide for Asia. Having
a single currency and a large union can create problems.
Let's see how they solve their problems and then let's
study whether it is still prudent to have a single currency.*

Overall, it is highly unlikely that an ASEAN currency union
will be formed in the foreseeable future. There are currently
no Asian policymakers pushing for further talks on this
matter. ASEAN leaders are thoroughly focused on the real
sources of prosperity: trade, investment, jobs, innovation,
education. Again, the lesson for Europe is that currency
union or political union is not required for close cooperation,
or even integration, on trade.

A model for Europe

Interestingly, the institutional structure is already in place
for Europe to do something similar to NAFTA or ASEAN.
It is called the European Free Trade Association (EFTA),
which has been in existence since 1960. Today, EFTA is
a poor relation of the EU, consisting of only Iceland,
Liechtenstein, Norway and Switzerland, but it used to be
much bigger. When it was established, its membership also
included Austria, Denmark, Portugal, Sweden and the UK.
The key change came in 1972 when the UK, accompanied
by Denmark, left EFTA to become a member of what
we now call the European Union. Portugal followed suit in
1985. Finland joined EFTA in 1986, but in 1995 it left to
join the EU, accompanied by Austria and Sweden.

The decision by the British government to leave EFTA
for the EU was a Category 1 strategic error. At the time,
the Economic Community, led by Germany and France, was
already a larger economic entity and was set to become
larger still. Being left out of the European Community

seemed like missing the only game in town. But this was before it became clear – in Britain at least – how far the Community's ambitions went to form a full political union, and before the full extent of the Community's interventions in national life became evident. Nevertheless, the EFTA structure offers a viable institutional model for Europe if the EU were to break up. There is no need to reinvent the wheel; just going back to EFTA would be an adequate starting point.

Possible political associations

Within such an arrangement, it would still be perfectly possible for various blocs, or political associations, to develop within Europe. Among the existing members of the eurozone there are two clear groupings of roughly equal numbers of people and one country that could belong to either.

Germany plus its like-minded fellow members Austria, Benelux and Finland form a group of about 120 million people. Club Med – that is, Spain, Portugal, Italy and Greece – also amounts to about 120 million people. The remaining country – the pivotal country – is France, with about 60 million people. It could join either group or it could go it alone. If the euro and the EU persist, it could hold the balance of power.

France could easily form a loose association of Latin states with Italy, Spain and Portugal. Nevertheless, it is highly unlikely that it would want a full political union with them – or they with it, or with each other. But why would France need to? Once the objective of 'ever closer union' is discarded, then it is open for countries to make their own individual choices based on different criteria.

Assuming that an EU-wide free trade area exists, there

would be no compelling economic reason to make a close association with other particular countries. If there is a rationale for such groupings it would rather be political, or to do with security. If member states so chose, such an association of states could be loose, involving merely close cooperation and/or Schengen-type open-border arrangements. Or it could go all the way to full fiscal and political union.

Belgium is an interesting case for possible change. It could perhaps aspire to join the northern core group of countries – if they would have it. But Germany might well resist, not least given Belgium's high debt levels. In that event, Belgium might conceivably try to form a close association with France, or even to join it. More likely, though, Belgium would break up, as it has threatened to do for years, into two independent small states, or with the southern, French-speaking part combining with France, and perhaps the northern, Flemish-speaking part joining the Netherlands, or remaining independent. After all, Belgium is a completely artificial country, formed in 1830 at the behest of the British in order to prevent the land, particularly the estuary of the Scheldt and the port of Antwerp, falling into the hands of France. No such considerations would apply today.

Greece and Ireland are outliers. Both could remain solo, integrated into the new European Free Trade Area and whatever other forms of Europe-wide cooperation emerged, but not seeking close association with other member states. In the case of Ireland, however, it would have the option of forging some form of close association with the UK, although this would be fraught with difficulties for obvious historical reasons.

If Europe did coalesce into various groupings, serious questions would be raised over the former Communist countries of central and eastern Europe. Some of them might seek close allegiance with the German-led bloc, if such an entity emerges. Some might form a loose association among themselves and/or some might seek some association with the UK. On the other hand, assuming open trade links within Europe and some sort of pan-European cooperation over matters such as the environment and defence, about which I have more to say below, most or all of these states might prefer to stay on their own.

EU defence and security

If the EU broke up, millions of people around Europe, but particularly people in the former eastern bloc countries, would be seriously concerned about defence. In many people's eyes, defence against a belligerent Russia is becoming a key reason for the EU's continued existence. Without the EU, the former members of the eastern bloc would be worried about falling back into the Russian sphere of influence – or worse.

This is deeply ironic, because European defence policy has been particularly weak. Indeed, several EU members seem notably reluctant to spend the amounts of money on defence needed to make the EU a credible military force against Russia – and it is precisely this that has prompted President Trump's unhelpful remarks about NATO, made in early 2017, suggesting that the alliance was now no longer relevant.

With the exception of France and the UK, members of the EU adopt a generally unenthusiastic stance with regard to defence issues. Unilateralism and pacifism tend to be strong. If the UK had to rely on other European countries for its defence, then heaven help it. And if they had to rely on themselves for their own defence then heaven help them!

Nevertheless, in practice, although NATO has its problems, for the foreseeable future, the defence of Europe will depend on it – which means primarily the US and the two European nation states with strong military capacity and a history of being prepared to use it, namely the UK and France.

This is of key relevance to the former members of the Soviet bloc. All EU members that were formerly members of the Soviet bloc are already members of NATO, and if the EU did dissolve, NATO would take on increased importance as a bulwark against a resurgent Russia. In fact, the membership of the EU and NATO is largely overlapping. Of NATO's 28 members, only 6 do not belong to the EU: Albania, Canada, Iceland, Norway, Turkey and the US; and of the EU's 28 members, only 6 do not belong to NATO: Austria, Cyprus, Finland, Ireland, Malta and Sweden.

Brexit's implications for defence

It is sometimes argued that European security will be imperilled by the UK's departure from the EU. This view is somewhat incongruous. It is the UK's membership of NATO that gives it protection and binds it to protecting other European countries. That will continue even after it leaves the EU. Indeed, the UK has just committed troops, tanks and planes to the 'front line' in Estonia, Poland and Romania. Moreover, as mentioned in Prime Minister Theresa May's Lancaster House speech in January 2017, it is likely that the UK will seek to maintain a very close defence and security relationship with its former EU partners.

Mind you, in her Brexit letter to the EU sent in March 2017, Theresa May hinted at the possible use of the UK's military and security prowess as a bargaining chip. This raises the alarming possibility that if the UK and the EU fail to reach an agreement, then the UK would in some sense downgrade its commitment to the defence of Europe. This would tend to undermine the strength of NATO. Combined with Donald Trump's unhelpful attitude, it could be enough to finish NATO off. In practice, though, the UK's commitment to NATO is likely to endure long after leaving the EU.

Of course, to some people the UK might seem of diminished importance once it has left the EU, such that these considerations no longer count for much. But the UK will remain a key global player. Ironically, before it voted to leave the EU, if there were an immediate threat to its permanent membership of the UN Security Council it came from the EU which, as mentioned earlier, has been keen to replace its seat – along with France's – with a seat for itself. Outside the EU, there is no comparable threat to its continuing UN Security Council membership.

Meanwhile, in intelligence and counterterrorism the UK continues to punch well above its weight. It is a member of the so-called 'Five Eyes' group of countries that share intelligence: the United States, the UK, Canada, Australia and New Zealand. There are no prizes for noticing the key feature that all these countries have in common.

Strikingly, after the Brexit vote, France and Germany stepped up their own efforts to establish a European defence capability. This too, in time, could weaken NATO and even lead to its demise. In the short term, though, European defence capability could be built up alongside, and within, NATO. In any case, it remains to be seen whether members of the EU will be willing to spend the money necessary to build up an effective defence capability.

Ironically, the logic of the developing global situation, including America's apparent wish to disengage from Europe, is that it makes sense for the Europeans to develop a common defence capability even if that excludes the

Americans (and Canadians). As the world's largest economic area, Europe should be able to afford to defend itself, as well as playing a security role on the world stage. Although a monetary, fiscal and political union does not fit in with the essential nature of Europe and its circumstances, a shared role in the realm of defence makes sense. The problem, as so often, is political. Up until now, with the EU bent on supplanting nation states, every move towards a common European defence capability met with resistance in London. But once things have settled down after the UK leaves the EU, things will not necessarily stay this way.

Initially, of course, the UK will be keen to keep the Americans involved and NATO together. But if NATO were to fracture – and this is largely under the Americans' control – then the UK might want to take part in a pan-European defence pact. This could be true whether the EU survives or breaks up. The key thing to realize is that countries do not have to share a common currency or plunge into a political union in order to take part in mutual defence. After all, NATO itself provides pooled defence without requiring, or trying to form, a political union between its members. That deluded objective was pursued only by its European members (plus some non-NATO European countries).

In sum, if the EU breaks up then NATO will take on increased importance. There is no reason to suppose that, with or without some European defence association, it will be incapable of fulfilling its role. Similarly, despite the pessimistic warnings of some erstwhile Remainers, there is no reason why, post-Brexit, the UK should not continue its membership of several European agencies such as Europol and Euratom. Many such institutions already have non-EU partners.

The EU and European war

Some of the EU's keenest support has come from people who believe that it has prevented another European war. As I argued in Chapter 1, this is far from being an open and shut case. NATO and the fear of nuclear weapons probably deserve more of the credit. Nevertheless, the view lingers on.

Could it be imagined that without the EU a war could break out between western European countries? I find this unthinkable. The critical factor is not alliances or treaties but the mindset of European people. In particular, Germany is a completely different country from the one that three times in seventy years went to war with France. Throughout western Europe, the culture is much less militaristic and also less nationalistic. People may retain enough sense of national difference and national pride not to want to submerge their identity in a greater Luxembourg, but that does not at all mean that they would be prepared to take up arms against fellow Europeans.

Mind you, if a war in the west of Europe remains unlikely, the same is not necessarily true in the eastern part of Europe. In March 2017, speaking after US President Trump appeared to welcome the prospect of Brexit leading to more countries leaving the EU, Jean-Claude Juncker, the President of the European Commission, uttered the words quoted at the beginning of this chapter: 'Do not say that, do not invite others to leave, because if the European Union collapses, you will have a new war in the western Balkans.'

This was a reference to the fact that in 1991, at the end of the Cold War, after the break-up of the former Yugoslavia, there was a brutal ethnic war between Croats, Serbs and Bosnian Muslims. It is telling that it was not the EU that ended that war but NATO. If war were to break out again, with or without the EU, it would surely again fall to NATO to impose a peace.

Solving the Turkish problem

NATO's future and the future of the Balkans brings us neatly on to the position facing one of NATO's key members – Turkey. One clear benefit from the end of the EU as we know it would be the chance to integrate into its replacement, whatever it is, three countries currently outside it. The first two, Norway and Switzerland, represent only small gains, but the third, Turkey, is potentially highly significant.

As it is, by insisting on forging ahead to ever closer union, and now perhaps including fiscal and political union, the leaders of the EU have effectively excluded Turkey from their plans. The electorates of Europe are never going to stomach having Turkey as a full and equal member of the EU; their leaders have known this and have therefore been forced to drag their feet on the question of Turkish membership. This has already alienated Turkey and risks pushing the country further eastward in outlook, perhaps even to the point of it becoming an Islamic state. Under its assertive President, Recep Tayyip Erdoğan, now even more powerful after winning a referendum on 16 April 2017, substantially increasing the powers of the presidency, Turkey has been moving away from the western ambit. Erdoğan has even sought to establish much closer relations with President Vladimir Putin of Russia.

Yet, for powerful strategic reasons, it is important to have Turkey anchored in the West. The EU may well have blown the chances of this – with disastrous consequences. But for a post-Erdoğan Turkey, and a post EU-Europe, the litmus test for the desirable form of European association of the future is that it must be one in which Turkey can play a full and equal part. As currently constituted, the EU manifestly fails this test. My suggestion of something like EFTA plus cooperation on the environment and defence (within NATO) but without free movement of people, monetary, fiscal and political union, not to mention the pursuit of 'ever closer union' and all the other integrationist mantras, passes this test.

The importance of the World Trade Organization (WTO)

As matters stand at the moment, the defence against European countries encountering trade discrimination by other countries, whether singly or as part of a beefed-up EFTA bloc, is the series of trade agreements fostered and supervised by the World Trade Organization (WTO). This was established in 1995 as the successor to the General Agreement on Tariffs and Trade (GATT), set up immediately after the war to bring down tariffs and other trade barriers. GATT and the WTO have opened up trade through a series of multilateral agreements negotiated in rounds. Until recently, the latest completed round, the eighth, was the so-called Uruguay Round, which was concluded in 1994. Seven years later, in 2001, the ninth instalment, the Doha round (named after Doha, the capital of Qatar in the Persian Gulf), commenced. However, progress was extremely slow, causing disillusionment with the WTO and a distinct move towards bilateralism across the world.

It has become fashionable to argue that the era of globalization is coming to an end and that the world is about to enter a new era of protectionism. But this view, at least in its crude form, does not do justice to the WTO. Through the WTO, all major countries are locked into legally binding commitments not to raise tariffs. It is only possible to abandon these commitments if they compensate other WTO members. Despite these achievements, the WTO has become rather sleepy. The adoption by the US in recent years of a bilateral approach to trade – taken even further by President Trump – has undermined the relevance of the WTO. This is a pity. Once it is out of the EU, the UK is in a unique position to galvanize the WTO and shake it out of its torpor.

Let us be clear, though, that the WTO has been, and still is, a second-best arrangement. Its role has been to help bring about reductions in tariff barriers in a world where countries believed in tit-for-tat. But the enshrinement of the principle of reciprocity is definitely not the best arrangement. In a better world, countries would unilaterally give up trade restrictions, following the path laid down by New Zealand, Singapore and Hong Kong. If perhaps America embraced unilateral free trade (UFT) there is a good chance that the rest of the world would do the same. And if that were to happen we would not need the WTO.

Shut out from the world's trade blocs

Of course, America might not just reject the WTO but, far from embracing UFT, it could turn isolationist and protectionist. If America did become protectionist, and the outside world put up barriers, for the countries of Europe, whether still adhering to some sort of union or not, the world could seem very uncomfortable.

More generally and more worryingly, on a superficial inspection the world seems to be moving in the direction of domination by several large trading blocs, with the EU, NAFTA, ASEAN and MERCOSUR being the leading ones at present. Interestingly, in none of these trading blocs nor, to the best of my knowledge anywhere else, have countries opted to abandon or pool national sovereignty. It is only in the EU that national sovereignty is supposedly past its sell-by date. (In fact, looking at the last few decades, national sovereignty has been extremely popular. In 1946 the membership of the United Nations was 51 countries; today it is 192.)

Over and above these trading blocs, as mentioned above, there is the possibility of a 12-nation Pacific Rim trade pact, entitled the Trans-Pacific Partnership (TPP), originally set to include China, Japan and the United States. Mind you, President Trump has recently withdrawn the US from this grouping and its future, without the US, now lies in doubt.

Meanwhile, Russia has been pursuing a plan to develop a Eurasian Economic Union to link former members of the Soviet Union, over and above Belarus and Kazakhstan, which already have a Customs Union with Russia. So it is possible that the world will fall into a new era of protectionism and that we will come to see the post-war world of progressively freer trade as the result of the particular position of the US in the world economy and the international polity of states.

While we should regard this as a plausible worst-case scenario, it is, in my view, not very likely. Even if it were in a more isolationist mood, the US would not want to turn its back entirely on Europe and would want to conclude trading agreements with European partners, either collectively or individually.

Moreover, even though much of the world has formed into blocs, these are not protectionist in the shape of putting up barriers to trade with other countries, nor do NAFTA, ASEAN or MERCOSUR prevent their members from making Free Trade Agreements with other countries. Unless something went very wrong with the world, there is no reason to believe that the members of these groups would be resistant to making trade agreements with outside countries.

Europe and the world

In Chapter 1, I pointed out how anxiety about the rising East was one of the primary factors behind the push for European integration. The prevailing fear is that in a world inevitably dominated by China, unless they are united in the European Union, the countries of Europe will be eclipsed by Asia. In that telling phrase, none of the economies, not even Europe's big three – Germany, France and the UK – will have a seat at 'the top table'. That word 'inevitably' again. You would think that knowledge of recent world history would have caused European elites to be more circumspect about deploying the I-word. We should all have learned that the future may be quite different from what we imagine.

For a start, China's sustainable growth rate is slowing. China specialists at my firm, Capital Economics, believe that unless she manages to undertake a programme of radical reform, as China's working-age population contracts, her growth rate could slow to about 2%. This is tremendously important. At that rate, China would never overtake the US to become top dog. A more likely candidate for the top slot would be India, but probably much later.

Of course, the Chinese authorities may manage to introduce a programme of radical reform so that the slowing of the Chinese growth rate is more moderate. But whatever they do, there will be a definite slowing, just as there was for Japan, Taiwan and Korea after their initial bursts of rapid, catch-up, growth.

The most likely scenario for the next few decades is that three countries – the United States, China and India – become of roughly equal economic weight and no single one achieves hegemony. (The US, of course, will continue to have a much higher GDP per capita and will doubtless retain its technological lead.) In this scenario many smaller – though still large – countries would be significant. Among the newcomers, Mexico, Brazil, Indonesia and Nigeria may be especially important. Among the older powers, surprise, surprise, the usual suspects will still be on the scene – Japan, Germany, France and the UK. It is simply lazy thinking to assume that, unless they unite into a political union, the countries of Europe will soon count for nothing on the world stage.

In my view, it is nonsensical to believe that unless European countries are able to influence the global architecture they will somehow be at a grave disadvantage. It is typical of the bureaucratic thinking that has dominated the EU for so long that it is somehow taken for granted that the things that determine prosperity emerge from the fountain pens of politicians and officials.

It is remarkable that many people still believe this when there are so many examples of small countries that have had next to no influence on the world stage doing extremely well. My favourite example is Singapore but Switzerland is another case. These countries have not worried about not having a vote over decisions on the global architecture. They have simply stuck to their knitting. They have just got on with the business of good government in the national interest. If, after the EU's demise, the countries of Europe could bring themselves to do the same then they too could enjoy a surge of prosperity.

The vision thing

It is now time to draw the threads of this book together and to reach a conclusion.

Why is the EU in such an intense existential crisis? The leaders of the EU have suffered from a fundamental failure of vision. Like generals who have a habit of trying to fight the last war, they are fixated on the idea of a tight economic and political association with countries that are geographically close together. It is interesting to note that this fits with the continental experience up to the First World War of large swathes of territory being united in a contiguous empire. Taking into account what has happened to the world over the recent decades, though, this can be seen to be completely out of kilter with modern reality.

It also stands in complete contrast to the seaborne political and economic associations of the past, which were spread over vast distances. Britain, France, Spain, Portugal and the Netherlands all ruled huge empires across the seven seas. In the seventeenth century, and even still in the nineteenth and early twentieth centuries, communication between the far-flung parts of these empires was difficult – but it could be done. Of course, the form of political association that sustained these groupings was not something we would find acceptable today; namely, empire. Nevertheless, at the time it was an association that worked.

Britain forged and managed its widely dispersed empire, the largest the world has ever seen, and made its living (and endured much of its dying) around the world in an age when distance really counted. It is extraordinary that in the age of the internet the UK should have believed that it must do the economic and political equivalent of marrying its next-door neighbour. If ever there was a time when matters of language, culture, shared history, law and fellow feeling should trump geography, surely this is it. What modern communications have done is to transform the possibilities of association. Instant communication across the world means that groupings are not restricted to members who are geographically close. This is clearly recognized in the world of economics and is, after all, what globalization is all about.

In the world of politics, globalization seems to have made scarcely any impact. Yet there is no good reason now why political, and other close, associations cannot flourish across large distances. In saying this I am not rejecting the importance of distance altogether. When it comes to environmental and security issues, for instance, it is with countries that are geographically close that one has most in common. But just as households that are neighbours may form neighbourhood watch groups to enhance their security without putting their financial or social affairs together, so the countries of Europe could cooperate on security and environmental matters without forming a monetary, fiscal and political union.

The European policy establishment has been in the grip of three serious economic and political delusions: top-table syndrome, sizeism and proximity fetishism. Yet the development of the world economy over the last 20 years, and especially the advance of so many of the emerging markets, stands out against these pretensions to economic wisdom. The EU pulls off a remarkable feat: it is both too small and too large at the same time. It is too large to make a successful political entity and yet too small to be a self-contained, or even self-centred, economic bloc. In economic affairs, the only entity that it makes sense to belong to is the world. Of that, all the countries in the EU are already members.

Intellectual consensus

Given the obvious failings and dangers of the integrationist project, it is a puzzle why so many intellectuals – particularly among the European elites, but also inside the American establishment – have not recognized the EU project for what it is. (Of course some have. Under President Trump, the US seems to have become notably eurosceptic.) The reason is surely that they see what they want to see. And where they do acknowledge problems, they apply liberal doses of hope for improvement.

Such a systematic tendency towards widespread delusion has a distinguished pedigree. Early in the twentieth century, countless European intellectuals, including George Bernard Shaw, H. G. Wells, Heinrich Mann and Simone de Beauvoir, were taken in by Communism and gave enthusiastic support to the Soviet Union.

In the 1920s, delegations of admirers visited the Soviet Union and were impressed with what they saw. It hardly seems to have occurred to them that they were being shown 'Potemkin villages', that is to say, industrial, agricultural and other scenes specifically constructed for their delectation and approval. (The expression refers to Count Grigory Potemkin, Catherine the Great's 'favourite', who was charged with developing the Russian Empire's new territories but showed off to visitors only specially prepared sites, while most of the rest of the country languished in a much more basic, less developed form. I experienced a similar phenomenon when visiting China in the early 1980s – although not with the same effects on my view of the country.)

The essential question is why so many clever and sophisticated people were so easily taken in. The answer is because they were dissatisfied with what they saw in capitalist society and wanted to believe that there was something better. And, as regards Russia, they were well aware of the defects of the Tsarist system that had preceded Communism.

During and after the Second World War, alignment with the Soviet Union became even more attractive to many intellectuals since the Soviets stood so bravely against Fascism and had contributed so much to its defeat. This supposedly contrasted with the lily-livered behaviour of the western democracies in appeasing Hitler prior to the war. This was, to say the least, a rose-tinted view, since it brushed over the fact that Stalin had acceded to the Nazi–Soviet Pact and that the countries that first declared war and fought against Hitler were Britain and France! Still, why let the facts get in the way of a convenient myth?

I am not suggesting that the European Union, or the idea of closer European integration, is to be compared with the evils of Communism. Rather, my point is that it is plainly possible for many intelligent and well-meaning people to be thoroughly misled about the great issue of the day, especially when that issue is tinged with matters of high moral purpose.

Nor is the pulling power of such ideas necessarily restricted to the intellectual elite. They can easily come to form a beguiling consensus view that sucks everyone, or nearly everyone, in. People can be led to believe what they want to believe, because it gives a comfortable view of the world and its future. Such intellectual bromides are like a drug – and the addiction is very difficult to shake off.

For the last few decades, the intellectual consensus across Europe, including the UK, has been overwhelmingly in favour of the EU. Supposedly, it has been seen as the bringer of peace, prosperity and security. Accordingly, the UK's vote in 2016 to leave the EU and the assorted threats to the EU's survival have been met with dismay among European intellectuals in both the UK and the wider EU. Still, several thousand intellectuals *can* all be wrong. After all, as I pointed out above, this wouldn't be the first time.

Interestingly, once it had recovered from its difficult birth, and withstood the onslaught of Hitler's armies during the Second World War, the Soviet Union seemed to be set for something like eternal life. Yet, once you peered beneath the facade, it was visibly crumbling. In the end, its collapse was total and rapid. Could something similar happen to the EU? The Soviet Union came into being as a result of the revolution of 1917, although its existence was not formalized until 1922. It collapsed in 1991. If the EU followed the same timetable it would last until 2031, or perhaps only 2026. In fact, I suspect that it may not last that long.

Politics and economics

What has gone wrong with the EU is about more than economics: it is about democracy and the quality of governance. But, as I have argued in this book, economic consequences follow from bad governance. On the basis of experience so far and of the diverse nature of the countries that would need to be forced into some sort of fiscal and political union in order to save the euro, it is surely right to expect the worst from the EU. It has already given us Esperanto money (the euro) and it may be about to give us Esperanto government (political union).

Admittedly, the euro is not the sum total of the EU's problems. Equally, the EU is not the source of everything that has gone wrong in Europe. In that regard, extreme eurosceptics overstate their case. But European leaders have been focused on utterly the wrong things. Their dreams have been about building unity when they should have been about creating excellence, even if that means diversity, which it has throughout most of European history.

Knowing little or nothing of economics, these European elites have acted almost precisely against the interests of Europe, being obsessed with treaties, agreements and restrictions in pursuit of commonality. They little understood that the prosperity of nations is built on the seemingly humdrum actions of ordinary people in factories, shops or service businesses, large and small – if only they are able to pursue their business interests relatively unrestricted by bureaucratic encumbrance.

Meanwhile, in following the integrationist agenda and their social model, Europe's national governments have been pursuing a chimera. These governments are big, but that does not make them effective. On the contrary, they are hopelessly ineffective at doing what governments have traditionally been there to do: defend citizens against internal and external danger. Whether it is immigration or defence, the modern European state is a pathetic failure – big, dithery, expensive, but incompetent. That is the critique from the right. Meanwhile, from the left now comes the complaint that the state is failing in its role as provider of 'social security', under the onslaught of globalization and market pressures. Both critiques have cogency. But without the EU hanging over them as a mixture of shield, excuse and threat, even European national governments might start to wake up to what needs to be done.

The decline of Europe is the result of the interaction of economics and politics. Economic prosperity has allowed indulgence in self-destructive habits. Degenerate politics have perpetuated the sources of decline, as the politicians have dished out various opiates to the people. The incessant draw of 'ever closer union' has been a massive diversion from the objective of creating European success. In the less successful members of the European Union, opposition to the policies of the European elites is tempered by knowledge of the weakness of their own institutions and their own dodgy recent history. They have tolerated for too long the combination of arrogance, incompetence and corruption that wafts out of Brussels.

But this is beginning to change. Across Europe the people are stirring. Will the elites respond? If not, we are going to be faced with something very ugly. The combination of economic stagnation – or, in extreme scenarios, collapse – lack of faith in political institutions, xenophobia and racism could be deadly.

One hope to emerge from this book is that by fundamentally reforming its workings and its nature, the EU will be able to contribute to future European success. But if it cannot achieve this, then the hope must be that the EU dissolves, leaving the nation states of Europe, whether singly or as part of some new association, to bring increased European prosperity and enhanced European influence in the world.

The trouble with Europe

This book has identified four main sources of trouble with Europe. Interestingly, each has found new endorsement in the events that have occurred since the first edition was published in 2014.

First comes the Union's fundamentally undemocratic nature. The European Commission is unelected. The European Parliament is a much weaker body than equivalent national parliaments. Meanwhile, the European Court of Justice is above challenge. European integration is a project of the European elites imposed on the people below.

Second, partly because of its institutional structure, the EU makes some appallingly bad decisions. Bad decision-making emerges from a peculiar cocktail of characteristics: a dreamlike quality, emanating from the origins of the EU and its ultimate ambition to become a fully fledged state; horse-trading between the individual member states; an over-powerful bureaucracy, disdainful of national differences, with little knowledge of markets and even less respect for them; weak parliamentary supervision; with the Parliament having next to zero connection with the European electorate.

Third, because of its bad decisions, from the macro disaster of the eurozone to the myriad micro interferences that inhibit business, the EU is a gigantic zone of economic failure. Despite the manifest advantages of its European heritage, the EU is underperforming, not just the emerging markets but also the older economies of the world. Meanwhile, its labour markets are a disgrace, condemning millions of people, particularly the young, to lives of misery.

Fourth, the EU does not know what it is and what it is there for. Its current ambition seems to be to get bigger and bigger. Its negotiations with Ukraine over some form of associate membership played a key role in prompting President Putin's annexation of Crimea and the destabilization of eastern Ukraine. The EU needs to lower its sights and, if it is to survive, to work well for the people who are already citizens. If it cannot do that, then it deserves to break up. On balance, I reckon that this is the more likely prospect.

The EU's number is up

As we all know, the UK did not play a role in how the EU began. But I reckon that it is set to play a major role in how it ends. This would be fitting. Speaking as a proud British citizen, and without any sense of false modesty, the people of the UK have made a marvellous contribution to the world. But it is not evenly spread. Our contribution to popular music is outstanding – but our contribution to unpopular, i.e. classical, music is not in the same league. Wonderful though our classical composers are, you could not say that their music bears comparison with the greatest from Germany (and Austria). In painting we cannot match the Italians, the Spanish or the French, or perhaps the Dutch. Our literature is wonderful, but so is the literature of so many European countries. Of course, our native cuisine is unique – but not quite in the way we might hope.

A leading candidate for our greatest contribution to the world is science and the advance of knowledge. And here we have indeed been outstanding. Even so, I suspect that the area where the UK has made the greatest contribution is not in this exalted sphere but rather at the other end of the spectrum, in the messy business of democratic government. Parliament and the common law are the foundations of freedom and democracy – and not just in the United Kingdom.

More recently, it is striking that the continuing British genius (or is it the abiding tendency of Perfidious Albion?) somehow enabled us to avoid the two greatest errors of the EU's ascendancy – the euro and the Schengen passport-free zone. Still, these victories are only minor. The EU hurtles towards a ghastly end – economically, politically and socially. Being outside the euro and having voted to leave the Union, the British will be able to avoid the worst of the coming crisis, but they will be unable to avoid entirely the fallout from the gathering disaster across the Channel.

Yet there is hope. Although there will be many painful wrenchings ahead, the UK's departure from the EU may set off a series of consequences that will save, not just the UK, but Europe as a whole. In keeping with what the British are best at, they will soon be in pole position to help construct a new Europe from the wreckage of the old.

Postscript: History Moves On

In 2012, the year of the euro's existential crisis, I visited Schönbrunn Palace, which lies on the outskirts of Vienna. It is a sort of Mitteleuropean Hampton Court, only grander. From one of its magnificent rooms, next to the desk from which the Habsburg emperors administered their huge territories, you look out onto a majestic park and, in the other direction, down a straight avenue leading to central Vienna.

The place oozes power and prestige. Indeed, for centuries the Habsburg Empire was one of the Great Powers of Europe. On the eve of its dissolution at the end of the First World War, who could have thought that Vienna would shrink back to be only the capital of tiny Austria – all musical heritage and Sachertorte? Yet that is what has happened, with only the wonderful buildings, like Schönbrunn, to remind us of past grandeur.

In some not too distant future, I wonder if tourists will also visit the EU buildings in Brussels and muse on lost power (if not be overcome by the wonder of the marvellous architecture), with the city now shrunken back from being the de facto capital of Europe to what it was not so long before – the crossroads of cultures and the home of wonderful moules-frites.

Glossary

Aggregate demand The overall level of demand for goods and services in the economy.

Article 50 A clause of the Lisbon Treaty, signed in 2007, governing the procedures under which a member country can leave the EU. The UK Prime Minister, Theresa May, triggered Article 50 in a letter to Donald Tusk, President of the European Council, on the 28 March 2017.

ASEAN Association of Southeast Asian Nations. Established in 1967, its membership consists of Brunei, Cambodia, Indonesia, Lao PDR, Malaysia, Myanmar, Philippines, Singapore, Thailand and Vietnam. This is a free trade area and not a customs union.

Authorised Economic Operators (AEOs) This designation allows traders to register all documentation concerning border trade electronically in advance.

Basel 3 A global regulatory framework applying to banks' capital adequacy, stress-testing and market-liquidity risk.

CAP Common Agricultural Policy. This serves to raise the income of European farmers, but thereby keeps the price of agricultural produce artificially high.

Clearing House An institution that facilitates financial trades by guaranteeing each counterparty's liabilities and effecting settlement.

Common External Tariff (CET) The tariff rates set by the EU, which must be imposed by all EU members on imports from outside the EU. These tariff rates differ considerably from one type of good to another.

Common Fisheries Policy (CFP) Governs the numbers and types of fish that can be caught, and by whom, in the waters of EU members.

Common Market The colloquial name for the EEC, which was established by the Treaty of Rome in 1957.

Competitiveness The position of one country's general price and wage level compared to others when translated at the current market exchange rate. If that price level is high relative to others, the country is said to be uncompetitive.

Customs union A grouping of countries that impose common restrictions on imports from outside the union, but operate free trade, or nearly free trade, between members.

Deflation A period when the general level of prices falls; the opposite of inflation.

Devaluation or depreciation The process of one currency's value falling compared to others. This is a way in which a country can restore its competitiveness without having to undergo falling prices.

ECB European Central Bank. Based in Frankfurt, this is the central bank for the whole eurozone.

ECHR This acronym is used to refer to both the European Court of Human Rights, not to be confused with the ECJ, and the European Convention on Human Rights.

ECJ European Court of Justice. Established in 1952 and located in Luxembourg, it dispenses judgments that have legal force throughout the EU.

Economies of scale The tendency for average unit costs to fall as the volume of output rises.

ECSC European Coal and Steel Community. Established in 1951, this was a forerunner of the EEC.

EEC European Economic Community. Established by the Treaty of Rome in 1957, this later became the European Community (EC) and then the European Union (EU).

EFSF European Financial Stability Facility, a fund for extending financial support to troubled members of the eurozone.

EFTA European Free Trade Association, formed in 1960. This was a sort of rival to the EEC, but when Britain left it in 1972 it lost more members and faded in significance. It still exists, with Iceland, Liechtenstein, Norway and Switzerland as members, and it could become the kernel of some new European trade grouping if the EU were to disintegrate.

EMU European Monetary Union, the system in which the countries of the eurozone have a single currency.

ERM Exchange Rate Mechanism, a forerunner of the euro.

ESM European Support Mechanism, a fund for extending financial support to troubled members of the eurozone.

EU European Union, the present name for the association that first began life as the EEC with the Treaty of Rome in 1957.

European Commission The de facto government of the EU.

European Economic Area (EEA) This consists of Norway, Iceland, Liechtenstein and the members of the EU. It gives the three non-EU members certain rights and privileges and imposes certain obligations similar to membership of the EU but these stop short of full membership.

European Social Charter Established in 1961, this provides guidelines on working conditions and intervention in the labour market in favour of certain specified groups.

Eurozone The group of countries using the euro as their currency.

Exclusive Economic Zone (EEZ) Waters designated as under national control before the CFP supplemented earlier arrangements.

Financial Transactions Tax (FTT) Sometimes known as the Tobin Tax after one of its early proponents, the American economist James Tobin. There has been a proposal to levy a tax on all financial transactions within the EU.

Foreign Direct Investment (FDI) The investment by companies in plant, machinery, buildings or other business assets in another country.

Free trade The practice of buying and selling goods and services across countries without the imposition of tariffs, quotas or other restrictions.

Free Trade Agreements (FTAs) Signed between countries guaranteeing tariff and interference free trade between them.

GATT General Agreement on Tariffs and Trade, set up in 1947 to negotiate and implement multilateral agreements on the liberalization of trade. It was succeeded in 1995 by the World Trade Organization (WTO).

GDP Gross Domestic Product, the most commonly used measure of national output, or income.

Gold Standard The system of tying currencies to a specified amount of gold into which these currencies would be exchangeable. This had its heyday in the nineteenth century under British leadership, although Britain left it twice, in 1914 and again, having returned to it in 1925, in 1931. The Gold Standard effectively broke down during the late 1930s.

Inflation A process in which prices in general rise; the opposite of deflation.

Internal devaluation The process of falling prices through which a country can restore its competitiveness without changing its exchange rate.

Keynesian Relates to John Maynard Keynes, or Lord Keynes as he later became. He is generally regarded as the greatest economist of the twentieth century and one of the greatest of all time. The adjective 'Keynesian' is often deployed to refer to a policy of boosting aggregate demand, sometimes by running government budget deficits.

Lisbon Agenda A programme of objectives to reinvigorate European economic performance. Announced in 2000, it is generally regarded as a flop.

MEP Member of the European Parliament.

Mercosur Mercado Común del Sur (Common Market of the South) is an economic integration project established in 1991. Its membership comprises founding members Argentina, Brazil, Paraguay and Uruguay and associate members Venezuela, Chile and Bolivia.

Mutual Recognition Agreements (MRAs) Agreements between countries to accept conformity with certain quality and safety standards.

NAFTA North American Free Trade Association. Established in 1994 between the US, Canada and Mexico, this is a free trade grouping and not a customs union.

NATO North Atlantic Treaty Organization. This commits member countries, which include most of western Europe and the US, to mutual defence.

NTBs Non-tariff barriers on trade.

OECD Organisation for Economic Co-operation and Development.

OMTs Outright Monetary Transactions, the policy of the ECB standing ready to purchase the bonds of troubled members of the eurozone, potentially without limit. The policy was announced in July 2012, but by the end of 2013 it had not yet been implemented.

Open Europe A British-based think tank.

Optimum Currency Area The extent of a group of countries or regions that, according to certain theoretical criteria, can best operate with a single currency rather than each country or area having its own currency.

'Passporting' The arrangement under which banks and other financial businesses can provide financial services throughout the European Union from a single base within the Union.

Productivity The amount of output produced in a given time per unit of inputs. Productivity is often measured in relation to the input of labour, when it means the level of output produced per capita.

Review of Competences A major research initiative announced by the British government in July 2012, consisting of a range of reports on a wide variety of subjects. The last seven reports in the series were published in December 2014.

Rest of the World (ROW) The world outside the EU.

Rotterdam/Antwerp effect The tendency of some British exports to countries outside the EU to be routed through the ports of Rotterdam and Antwerp, thereby inflating the figures for the percentage of British exports that go to the EU.

Rules of Origin A complex set of EU rules governing the liability of goods exports from Norway and other partner countries of the EU to tariffs, depending upon what proportion of the value of the goods exported originates in the partner country.

Schengen The agreement signed in 1995 that allows travel without passport control in various European countries.

Single Market A system that combines both free trade between members and the common imposition of agreed standards and regulations across all member countries. The European Single Market was established in 1992.

Stability and Growth Pact An agreement put in place in 1997 in order to restrain the government budget deficits of members of the eurozone.

Subsidiarity The principle that within the EU decisions should be taken as close to the citizen as possible.

Target 2 Balances The claims on or obligations of one central bank or other central banks within the eurozone under the clearing system known as Target 2. The German Bundesbank has substantial claims on other central banks.

Tariff A tax on imports levied by the importing country.

Tit-for-tat Granting other countries access to your market only in exchange for reciprocal concessions from those countries.

Trans-Pacific Partnership (TPP) This was originally set to include China, Japan and the US in a trade pact. US President Donald Trump has withdrawn the US from the planned arrangements.

Treaty of Rome Signed in 1957, this established the European Economic Community (EEC), which evolved into the European Union.

TTIP Transatlantic Trade and Investment Partnership. This is still under negotiation between the EU and the US, but if successful it would establish a north Atlantic free trade area.

Unilateral Free Trade (UFT) The declaration of free trade by a country without an agreement by other countries to give reciprocity.

World Customs Organization (WCO) Inter alia, this administers the system of AEOs.

WTD Working Time Directive, which, among other things, lays down maximum daily and weekly working time restrictions.

WTO World Trade Organization, established in 1995 as the successor organization to GATT.

Selected Bibliography

Acemoglu, D., & Robinson, J. (2012) *Why Nations Fail: The Origins of Power, Prosperity and Poverty*, London: Profile.

Alesina, A., & Spolaore, E. (1997) On the number and size of nations, *Quarterly Journal of Economics*, 112(4): 1027–56.

Alesina, A., & Spolaore, E. (2003) *The Size of Nations*, Cambridge, MA: MIT Press.

Alesina, A., Angeloni, I., & Schuknecht, L. (2001) What Does the European Union Do? NBER Working Paper 8647, Cambridge, MA: National Bureau of Economic Research.

Bannerman, D.C. (2013) *Time to Jump: A Positive Vision of an Independent Britain Outside the EU in an EEA Lite Agreement*, Epsom: Bretwalda Books.

Barro, R.J. (1991) Small is beautiful, *Asian Wall Street Journal*, October 11.

Becker, G.S. (2005) Response on small is beautiful, Becker-Posner blog, 22 April, http://www.becker-posner-blog.com/2005/04/response-on-small-is-beautiful-becker.html, viewed on 11 September 2013.

Becker, G.S. (2005) Why small has become beautiful, Becker-Posner blog, 17 April, http://www.becker-posner-blog.com/2005/04/why-small-has-become-beautiful-becker.html, viewed on 11 September 2013.

Becker, G.S., & Mulligan, C.B. (2003) Deadweight costs and the size of the government, *Journal of Law and Economics*, 46(2): 293–340.

Booker, C. (2001) *Britain and Europe: The Culture of Deceit*, London: The Bruges Group.

Booker, C., & North, R. (2003) *The Great Deception: The Secret History of the European Union*, London: Continuum.

Booth, S., & Howarth, C. (2012) *Trading Places: Is EU Membership Still the Best Option for UK Trade?* London: Open Europe.

Buchan, D. (2012) *Outsiders on the Inside: Swiss and Norwegian Lessons for the UK*, London: Centre for European Reform.

Burrage, M. (2014) *Where's the Insider Advantage?* London: Civitas.

Burrage, M. (2016) *Myth and Paradox: How the Trade Benefits of EU Membership Have Been Mis-Sold*, London: Civitas.

Burrage, M. (2017) *It's Quite OK to Walk Away: A Review of the UK's Brexit Options with the Help of Seven International Databases*, London: Civitas.

Cameron, D. (2013) EU speech at Bloomberg, https://www.gov.uk/government/speeches/eu-speech-at-bloomberg, visited 31 January 2014.

CBI (2013) *Our Global Future: The Business Vision for a Reformed EU*, London: Confederation of British Industry.

Charter, D. (2012) *Au Revoir, Europe: What if Britain left the EU?* London: Biteback Publishing.

Chevènement, J.P. (2013) *1914–2014: L'Europe sortie de l'histoire?* Paris: Fayard.

Congdon, T. (2004) *Will the EU's Constitution Rescue Its Currency?* London: The Bruges Group.

Congdon, T. (2009) *The City of London under Threat: The EU and Its Attack on Britain's Most Successful Industry*, London: The Bruges Group.

Congdon, T. (2012) *How Much Does the European Union Cost Britain?* Newton Abbot: UKIP.

Connolly, B. (2012) *The Rotten Heart of Europe*, London: Faber and Faber.

Dixon, H. (2014) *The In/Out Question*, London: Scampstonian.

Dustmann, C., & Frattini, T. (2014) The fiscal effects of immmigration to the UK, *Economic Journal*, 124(580): F593–F643.

Eichengreen, B., & Boltho, A. (2008) *The Economic Impact of European Integration*, London: Centre for Economic Policy Research.

Erickson, J. (2004) Size Matters, review of *The Size of Nations* by A. Alesina & E. Spolaore, *SAIS Review of International Affairs*, 24(2).

Fresh Start Project (2013) *Manifesto for Change: A New Vision for the UK in Europe*, London: Fresh Start Project, http://www.eufreshstart.org/downloads/manifestoforchange.pdf, visited 31 January 2014.

Gamble, A. (2003) *Between Europe and America: The Future of British Politics*, Basingstoke: Palgrave Macmillan.

George, S. (2008) *An Awkward Partner: Britain in the European Community*, 3rd edn, Oxford: Oxford University Press.

Giannakouris, K. (2008) *Ageing Characterises the Demographic Perspectives of the European Societies*, Luxembourg: Eurostat European Communities.

Giddens, A. (2014) *Turbulent and Mighty Continent: What Future for Europe?* Cambridge: Polity Press.

Grant, C. (2008) *Why Is Britain Eurosceptic?* London: Centre for European Reform.

Grant, C. (2013) *How to Build a Modern European Union*, London: Centre for European Reform.

Green, D. (2013) *What Have We Done?* London: Civitas.

Green, D. (2014) *The Demise of the Free State*, London: Civitas.

Hannan, D. (2012) Switzerland is a more attractive model than Norway, but Britain could do better than either, *Daily Telegraph*, 15 December.

Harari, D., & Thompson, G. (2013) *The Economic Impact of EU Membership on the UK*, London: House of Commons Library.

Heisbourg, F. (2013) *La fin du rêve européen*, Paris: Stock.

Hewish, T., & Styles, J. (2012) *Common-trade, Common-growth, Common-wealth*, Cheltenham: The Hampden Trust.

Hindley, B., & Howe, M. (2001) *Better Off Out? The Benefits or Costs of EU Membership*, London: Institute of Economic Affairs.

HM Government (2013) *Review of the Balance of Competences between the United Kingdom and the European Union: The Single Market*, July.

HM Treasury (2005) *The Economic Effects of EU Membership for the UK*, https://www.gov.uk/government/uploads/system/uploads/attachment_data/file/220965/foi_eumembership_presentation.pdf, visited 31 January 2014.

Howell, D. (2014) *Old Links and New Ties: Power and Persuasion in an Age of Networks*, London: I.B. Tauris.

Johnson, J. (2012) *Britain Must Defend the Single Market*, London: Centre for European Reform.

King, A., & Crewe, I. (2013) *The Blunders of Our Governments*, London: Oneworld Publications.

Kremer, M., & Parkes, R. (2010) *The British Question: What Explains the EU's New Angloscepticism?* Berlin: Stiftung Wissenschaft und Politik, Berlin.

Lea, R. (n.d.) *Britain's Contributions to the EU: How to Save £5bn, Minimum*, London: The TaxPayers Alliance.

Liddle, R. (2014) *The Europe Dilemma: Britain and the Drama of EU Integraton* (Policy Network), London: I.B. Tauris.

Lindsell, J. (2014) *Softening the Blow: Who Gains from the EU and How They Can Survive Brexit*, London: Civitas.

Llewellyn, J., & Westaway, P. (2011) *Europe will work – But it needs to strengthen its governance, fix its banks, and reform its structural policies*, Nomura Global Economics, March.

Mansfield, I. (2014) *A Blueprint for Britain: Openness not Isolation*, London: IEA.

Marsh, D. (2011) *The Euro: The Battle for the New Global Currency*, New Haven, CT: Yale University Press.

Marsh, D. (2013) *Europe's Deadlock: How the Euro Crisis Could Be Solved – and Why It Won't Happen*, New Haven, CT: Yale University Press.

Milne, I. (2004) *A Cost too Far? An Analysis of the Net Economic Costs and Benefits for the UK of EU Membership*, London: Civitas.

Milne, I. (2007) *Lost Illusions: British Foreign Policy*, London: The Bruges Group.

Milne, I. (2011) *Time to Say No: Alternatives to EU Membership*, London: Civitas.

Milne, I. (2013) The British car market and industry, *Civitas Review*, 10(1).

Minford, P. (1992) *The Cost of Europe*, Manchester: Manchester University Press.

Minford, P. (1999) So what NAFTA then? *Daily Telegraph*, 19 July, www.euro-know.org/europages/telegraph/dt990719.html, viewed on 12 November 2013.

Minford, P. (2006) Measuring the economic costs and benefits of the EU, *Open Economics Review*, 17.

Minford, P., Mahambre, V., & Nowell, E. (2005) *Should Britain Leave the EU? An Economic Analysis of a Troubled Relationship*, Cheltenham: Edward Elgar Publishing.

North, D. (1991) Institutions, *Journal of Economic Perspectives*, 5(1): 97–112.

North, D.C., Wallis, J.J., & Weingast, B.R. (2013) *Violence and Social Orders: A Conceptual Framework for Interpreting Recorded Human History*, New York: Cambridge University Press.

Oliver, T. (2013) *Europe without Britain: Assessing the Impact of the European Union of a British Withdrawal*, Berlin: Stiftung Wissenschaft und Politik.

Olson, M. (1974) *The Logic of Collective Action: Public Goods and the Theory of Groups*, Cambridge, MA: Harvard University Press.

Olson, M. (1984) *The Rise and Decline of Nations: Economic Growth, Stagflation and Social Rigidities*, New Haven, CT: Yale University Press.

Pain, N., & Young, G. (2004) *The Macroeconomic Impact of UK Withdrawal from the EU*, London: National Institute of Economic and Social Research.

Peet, J., & La Guardia, A. (2014) *Unhappy Union: How the Euro Crisis – and Europe – Can Be Fixed*, London: Profile.

Persson, M. (2013) Hey Berlin, this is what an EU without Britain would look like, *Daily Telegraph*, 7 June.

Portes, J. (2013) Commentary: The economic implications for the UK of leaving the European Union, *National Institute Economic Review*, 226.

Posner, R.A. (2005) The size of countries, Becker-Posner blog, 17 April, http://www.becker-posner-blog.com/2005/04/the-size-of-countriesposners-comment.html, viewed on 11 September 2013.

Siedentop, L. (2001) *Democracy in Europe*, New York: Columbia University Press.

Smallwood, C. (2010) *Why the Euro-zone Needs to Break Up*, London: Capital Economics.

Smith, A. (2011) *The Theory of Moral Sentiments*, Seattle, WA: Gutenberg Publishers. (Reprint of 1759 London edition.)

Van Middelaar, J. (2013) *The Passage to Europe: How a Continent Became a Union*, New Haven, CT: Yale University Press.

Vaubel, R. (1995) *The Centralisation of Western Europe: The Common Market, Political Integration and Democracy*, London: Institute of Economic Affairs.

Vaubel, R. (2009) *The European Institutions as an Interest Group: Dynamics of Ever-Closer Union*, London: Institute of Economic Affairs.

Notes

1. Sources: Worldology; Hitler Historical Museum; History Place; Jean-Jacques Arzalier (2000) The campaign of May–June 1940, the losses? in C. Levisse-Touzé (ed.) *La Campagne de 1940*, Paris: Editions Tallandier; and John Ellis (1993) *World War 2: A Statistical Survey*, New York: Facts on File.
2. Charles Moore (2013) *Margaret Thatcher: The Authorised Biography, Vol. One: Not for Turning*, London: Allen Lane.
3. Douglass North (1991) Institutions, *Journal of Economic Perspectives*, 5(1): 97–112.
4. Charles Grant (2013) *How to Build a Modern European Union*, London: Centre for European Reform.
5. I am grateful to Christopher Smallwood for emphasizing this.
6. For a brief guide to the evolution of the English constitution and the gradual rise of parliament, see David Green (2013) *What Have We Done?* London: Civitas.
7. See Anthony King and Ivor Crewe (2013) *The Blunders of Our Governments*, London: Oneworld Publications.
8. World Trade Organization, *EU Trade Policy Review*.
9. R. Allen, M. Gaiorek and A. Smith (1996) Trade Creation and Trade Diversion Summary, Single Market Review Series, Subseries IV: Impact on Trade and Investment, Luxembourg: European Commission; S. Booth and C. Howarth (2012) *Trading Places: Is EU Membership Still the Best Option for UK Trade?* London: Open Europe; A.M. El Agraa (2011) *The European Union Economics and Policies*, 9th edn, Cambridge: Cambridge University Press; European Commission (2011) *External and Intra-EU Trade: A Statistical Yearbook*, Luxembourg: EuroStat; Y. Kandogan (2005) Trade creation and diversion effects of Europe's regional liberalization agreements, Working Paper No. 746, Ann Arbor, MI: William Davidson Institute.
10. Open Europe Briefing Note, Another 50 Examples of EU Waste, 10 November 2010.
11. According to a report in *The Guardian* on 18 September 2013.
12. See R.J. Barro (1991) Small is beautiful, *Asian Wall Street Journal*, October 11; A. Alesina and E. Spolaore (2003) *The Size of Nations*, Cambridge, MA: MIT Press; J. Erickson (2004) Size matters, review of *The Size of Nations* by A. Alesina & E. Spolaore, *SAIS Review of International Affairs*, 24(2); G.S. Becker (2005) Response on small is beautiful, Becker-Posner

blog, 22 April and Why small has become beautiful, Becker-Posner blog, 17 April; A. Alesina, I. Angeloni and L. Schuknecht (2001) What Does the European Union Do? NBER Working Paper 8647, Cambridge, MA: National Bureau of Economic Research.

13. David Gilmour (2012) *The Pursuit of Italy: A History of a Land, Its Regions and Their Peoples*, London: Penguin.

14. Yanis Varoufakis (2017) *Adults in the Room* (London: Bodley Head).

15. HM Treasury (2016a) 'The Long-term economic impact of EU membership and the alternatives', https://www.gov.uk/government/publications/hm-treasury-analysis; and HM Treasury (2016b), 'The immediate economic impact of leaving the UK', https://www.gov.uk/government/publications/hm-treasury-analysis.

16. See Patrick Minford (2016) *The Treasury Report on Brexit: A critique* (London: Economists for Brexit); and David Blake (2016), *Management without Theory: On the extraordinary abuse of economic models in the EU referendum debate* (London: Cass Business School).

17. Quoted by Chris Giles in *Financial Times*, 17 April, 2017.

18. See Richard North (2016) *Flexcit: A plan for leaving the European Union*; Richard Whitman (2016), *The EEA: A safe harbour in the Brexit storm* (Chatham House); Adam Smith Institute (2016), *The case for the (interim) EEA option*. On these and other issues see also Andrew Tyrie (2016), *Giving Meaning to Brexit* (London: Open Europe).

19. Burrage (2017) *It's Quite OK to Walk Away: A Review of the UK's Brexit Options with the Help of Seven International Databases* (London: Civitas).

20. I am grateful to Martin Howe QC for this point.

21. See House of Commons (2017), *The UK's Contribution to the EU Budget*, CBP 7886.

22. Bruegel (2017) *Divorce Settlement or Leaving the Club? A Breakdown of the Brexit Bill*.

23. Quoted in J. A. Hobson (1919) *Richard Cobden: The Internationalist Man* (New York: Holt).

24. Patrick Minford (2016) *Trading Places: Consumers v Producers in the New Brexit Economy* (London: Politeia).

25. A significant proportion of UK exports are initially routed through Antwerp and Rotterdam, and are therefore counted as exports to the EU even though their ultimate destination is outside the EU.

26. Michael Burrage (2017), op. cit.
27. I am grateful to Dan Lewis, chief executive of the Economic Policy Centre, for pointing out these examples in an article in *City A. M.*, 18 October 2016.
28. See Raoul Ruparel (2016) 'Post Brexit, Leaving the customs union is a no-brainer', London: Open Europe.
29. See Minford (2017), op.cit.
30. Sir Robert Peel, when announcing the repeal of the Corn Laws in the House of Commons in 1846.
31. For an analysis of UFT both recently and in the nineteenth century see Jagdish Bhagwati (ed.), *Going Alone: The Case for Relaxed Reciprocity in Freeing Trade* (Cambridge, Mass: MIT Press, 2002).
32. Michael Burrage (2017), op. cit.
33. John Maynard Keynes (1931) *Essays in Persuasion* (London: MacMillan).
34. Society of Motor Manufacturers and Traders (SMMT) (2017), *Motor Industry Facts 2017* (London: SMMT).
35. See Roger Bootle and John Mills (2016) *The Real Sterling Crisis* (London: Civitas).
36. Ueli Maurer, Swiss Finance Minister, quoted in *Financial Times*, 26 March 2017.
37. See Economists for Free Trade (2017), Launch Document, www.economistsforfreetrade.com
38. Sir Lockwood Smith (2017) *The Future of UK Trade Policy*, delivered at the Marshall Wace Asset Management Post-Brexit Conference, 26 April 2017, http://www.ubiqus.co.uk
39. Sean Rickard (2017) *Ploughing the Wrong Furrow* (London: IEA).
40. Royal Society (2016) *GM Plants: Questions and Answers* (London: Royal Society).
41. Richard Wellings (ed.) (2017) *Sea Change: How Markets and Property Rights Could Transform the Fishing Industry* (London: IEA).
42. On the issue of passporting rights and other matters concerning the City and Brexit see the Financial Services Briefing by the Legatum Institute's Special Trade Commission, published by the Legatum Institute, London, in October 2016.
43. Oliver Wyman (2016), available at http://www.oliverwyman.com.
44. Quoted in *Financial Times*, 11 April 2017.
45. François Hollande, President of the Republic of France, quoted in *Financial Times*, 29 June 2016.

46. For a discussion of the stifling impact of EU regulation on the City, see Tim Congdon (2014) *The City of London in Retreat* (London: Bruges Group).

47. John Bolton, 'Free of the EU Herd, Britain Can Become a Global Force Alongside America', *Sunday Times*, 2 April 2017.

48. David Howell (2013) *Old Links and New Ties: Power and Persuasion in an Age of Networks* (London: I. B. Tauris).

49. UK Government (2017) *Legislating for the United Kingdom's Withdrawal from the European Union*, London: HMSO.

50. HM Treasury (2016), op.cit.

51. European Commission (2017) *White Paper on the Future of Europe* (European Commission, COM 2025).

52. For a relatively sanguine view on the effects of immigration on UK wages and the public finances see Stephen Nickell and Jumana Saleheen (2015), 'The Impact of Immigration on Occupational Wages: Evidence from Britain', Bank of England Staff Working Paper No. 574; and Christian Dustmann and Tommaso Frattini (2014), 'The Fiscal Effects of Immigration to the UK', *Economic Journal*.

53. Paul Ashton, Neil MacKinnon and Patrick Minford (2017) *The Economics of Unskilled Immigration* (London: Economists for Free Trade).

54. These views were expressed at a dinner attended by David Goodhart and reported in his book (2017), *The Road to Somewhere* (London: Hurst & Company).

55. A number of prominent supporters of the EU have put forward ideas for Europe to consist of at least two (and possibly more) rings of association. The inner circle, which would be close to the present EU minus the UK, would have deep fiscal and political integration. The outer circle would have much less integration. In time, countries such as Turkey and Ukraine, which one could not readily imagine joining the EU, could be part of this outer circle. See, for instance, Jean Pisani-Ferry et al. (2016), *Europe After Brexit: A Proposal for a Continental Partnership* (Brussels: Bruegel).

56. Reported in *Financial Times*, 24 March 2017.

Index

About the Author

One of Britain's best-known economists, Roger Bootle is Chairman of Capital Economics, Europe's largest macro-economic consultancy, which he founded. Roger appears frequently on television and radio and is also a regular columnist for the *Daily Telegraph*. In 2012, he won the Wolfson Prize and was named Economics Commentator of the Year. He is the author of three other widely acclaimed books: *The Trouble with Markets, Money for Nothing* and *The Death of Inflation*.